4-Gen Leadership

4-Gen Leadership

Thriving in a Multi-Generational Workplace

Mark White and Sami Scarpitti

BEP

BUSINESS EXPERT PRESS

Leader in applied, concise business books

4-Gen Leadership: Thriving in a Multi-Generational Workplace

Copyright © Business Expert Press, LLC, 2025

Cover design by nskvsky

Interior design by Exeter Premedia Services Private Ltd., Chennai, India

First published in 2024 by
Business Expert Press, LLC
222 East 46th Street, New York, NY 10017
www.businessexpertpress.com

ISBN-13: 978-1-63742-736-1 (paperback)
ISBN-13: 978-1-63742-737-8 (e-book)

Business Expert Press Collaborative Intelligence Collection

First edition: 2024

10 9 8 7 6 5 4 3 2 1

Description

4-Gen Leadership: Thriving in a Multi-Generational Workplace **is a practical guide for those aspiring to be multi-generational leaders in today's evolving business landscape.** Four-gen leadership is the philosophy, and actions leaders can take to help all generations (baby boomers, Gen X, millennials, and Gen Z) be accepted, honored, and united into one effective, harmonious team. The authors have created a resource that leaders across every industry at all levels of leadership will find useful. This book helps established and emerging leaders understand the generations in their workforce and how to bridge the new generation gaps in their organizations.

Each chapter contains reflective questions to help the readers apply the book's concepts to their work environment: a section titled *Voices from the Generations*, which shares insightful views from one of the many successful leaders interviewed for the project; a Real-World Connection segment, which is a scenario in which the readers see how a hypothetical problem might be solved by using a multi-gen leadership lens; and finally, an activity worksheet that points readers toward the next steps they can take to strengthen their multi-gen leadership skills and the culture.

Contents

Introduction

My quest to understand the generations and the new types of generation gaps in the workforce began in 2019. I was leading a workshop for elementary school teachers in which I was helping them to understand how today's students, Gen Zers and Gen Alphas, have different interests from many teachers, especially the teachers who were boomers and Gen Xers. I separated the teachers into four groups by generation (baby boomers, Gen Xers, millennials, and Gen Zers). I wanted them to see how rapidly the world had changed and how different the growth experiences were for each generation, so I asked, "What technology changed your life when you were growing up?"

The answers ranged widely from boomers watching three black and white TV channels to Gen Zers surfing the internet on their iPhones. Then I asked, "Which mindset do we have in our schools? Is it a mindset that accommodates the learning needs of Gen Zers and Gen Alphas, or do we still design lessons as if we are teaching boomers?" We had a great discussion. Then, without prior planning, I asked the question that led to one of the great epiphanies of my career: "Gen Z teachers, if you could redesign this workshop or other professional development session to better fit your learning needs, what would you tell the trainer to do?"

Around 50 teachers were in the room, but only three of them were Gen Zers. I had put them on the spot. The other teachers all turned to them, curious about what the youngest teachers with the least amount of experience would say to me, their seasoned trainer with decades of experience, about what I should be doing differently. The first two teachers smiled and didn't want to answer, but the third teacher, a young 20-something, bravely said, "I wish they would just tell us what they want done and then leave us alone to figure it out."

This brought a lot of hoots and laughter from the other teachers, who turned to me, wondering what I would do. I, too, laughed, and I thanked her for her honesty, but deep inside I felt that young teacher had plunged a Gen Z knife into my baby boomer heart.

Because she was entirely right.

In too many trainings today, the facilitators are still using traditional presentation methods and don't understand that as the generations have evolved, their training and learning needs have also evolved. The Gen Zer's words hit me like a professional thunderbolt. I knew right then, standing in front of those Gen Z teachers, that I, too, had to change. "Of course," I thought. "She makes sense. Gen Zers are 'The Figure It Out' generation. They don't read directions when they open new apps get new devices or log into new video games or social media channels. They just 'figure it out.'" I also realized baby boomers and Gen Xers (including people like me in the older generations who often plan and lead training sessions) want something different than the millennials and Gen Zers: we want explicit instructions on what to do along with a clear picture of how our finished product should look. We like to wait for orders; we don't like to just be left on our own to go "figure it out."

By the end of that day, I still couldn't get the Gen Zer's words out of my head. That generational epiphany led to yet another epiphany: Understanding the five generations in schools (the four generations in the staff and our youngest students, the Gen Alphas) and how to bridge the new generation gaps between the five generations would be the topic of my next book. Two years later I released *5-Gen Leadership: Leading 5 Generations of Schools in the 2020's* through Corwin Press.

As educator leaders around the country read the book, they told me of the many "A-ha" moments the book provided and how the generation gaps they were encountering suddenly made sense. When I spoke about the book at conferences, they would tell me that same thing after the session, or they would see me in a foyer the next day and say, "I heard your presentation yesterday, and I can't get those generations out of my head. It all makes sense now."

Strategies for Business Leaders

I began to read some articles about generation gaps in businesses, and I noticed the generational characteristics I had detailed in the book in various news stories about boomers trying to adjust to technology, Gen

Xers taking on management roles in the most generationally diverse work environment we have ever had, millennials bringing their different philosophies into the workplace, and Gen Zers struggling to find their place in a business environment often led by generations who don't understand what motivates or resonates with Gen Zers.

I realized the ideas in my book for education leaders could translate into a similar book for business leaders and emerging leaders.

However, I had spent most of my career as an educator. I had over three decades of experience as a teacher, principal, and school superintendent, but I needed insight into the terminology, philosophies, and practices used in modern businesses. In 2021, I had a conversation with Sami Scarpitti, with whom I had worked several years prior in a small start-up. We discussed the generational ideas in my education leadership book, and I learned that she, too, had a great interest and passion in delving more deeply into the generations. Sami has spent her entire career thus far in the corporate world, working in sales and marketing for several professional development organizations. She too saw the writing on the wall, that today's training programs were missing the mark and did not solve the real-world issues that businesses face. It lacked the connection of skill-building for individuals with the dynamics of 4 generations in the workforce and how creating powerful teams needs to start with understanding the complexity of the current workforce and the distinct characteristics of the 4 generations. Together we began to make presentations, lead trainings and workshops, interview people across all generations, roles, and industries, and write about our research and observations.

This book is the culmination of those efforts. Sami and I present this book to business leaders to help them understand the generations in their workforce and how to bridge the new generation gaps found in their organizations. We write it as a cross-generational team: I am a male baby boomer, and Sami is a female millennial. Together, we bring our own generational characteristics, experiences, and perspectives into this discussion.

However, we want to stress a point we make repeatedly in the book: as we write about the generations and their characteristics, *we are not trying to say all the people in that generation have those characteristics.* We are basing the generational generalities on multiple sources that include:

- The ideas presented in various trusted online sites and articles about the generations
- The conclusions of numerous polls and surveys released by reputable national and international survey groups
- The ideas shared by the many individuals from multiple generations and varied fields who we interviewed for this book
- Our observations about the generations as we interacted with them online and in person
- Our informal polling in training sessions found hundreds of individuals who said they possessed many, usually the majority, of their generation's characteristics

With that stated, we will be the first to say everyone is an individual. Each person has his or her own, unique traits. This includes both me and Sami. As a boomer, I have many boomer characteristics; yet, I also have ways in which I am like a millennial. Sami, as a millennial, says she has many millennial characteristics; yet, she says she has a few traits that are more often attributed to Gen Xers or boomers. So, if someone says to us, "But those traits don't fit me!" we will readily accept that statement. These generational characteristics occur in individuals because of their growth experiences and life experiences which often form the lens through which individuals see the world. These traits are experiential, not biological. Yet, we've learned enough through our research to feel comfortable saying "Boomers often act this way...and Gen Zers often act this way."

When Sami and I first envisioned this book, we wanted to create a practical, easy-to-read resource that business leaders across every industry at all levels of leadership could use. This book can be read by individual readers or as part of a professional development book club. To make the book more digestible for busy readers, each chapter begins with four summary points of what will be covered in that chapter. The passages are written in short chunks with headers that help the readers to process the content. Reflective questions are placed throughout each chapter for the reader to apply concepts they are learning to their work environment.

Each chapter has a section titled *Voices from the Generations*, which shares insightful content from one of the many interviews we led. We then close the chapter with a real-world connection segment, which is a scenario in which the readers see how a hypothetical problem might be solved by using a multi-gen lens. Finally, each chapter has an activity worksheet which is a series of questions after the chapter that points the readers toward the next steps they can take to strengthen their multi-gen leadership traits and the multi-gen culture of their team or organization.

Of course, readers don't have to be leading a team to gain generational insight from this book. Team members at all levels, including individual contributors, can read this content and think of how it applies to them and their teams. A key point about leadership and growing emerging leaders in today's rapidly changing workplace is this: people don't always have to have formal leadership titles to lead. Individuals at all levels can affect positive change through initiative, determination, and just as importantly, knowledge.

The Book's Organization

The book is written in 11 chapters. The first two chapters, *From Boomer to Gen Z* and *Different Generations, Parenting and Perspectives*, serve as introductions to the generations, the new types of generation gaps, and just as importantly, what shaped the generations. When leaders have a firm grasp of how generational characteristics formed (like the power of the internet and different ways the generations have been raised), they gain great insight into why they and the members of their multi-gen teams react in certain ways in various situations.

The third chapter, *The Multi-gen Foundation: Culture, Communication, and Coaching*, provides a plan for leaders to lay the building blocks of an effective multi-gen workforce. Organizational success begins with creating a positive culture. Communication and the types of generational coaching used will be a huge part of that culture and set the stage for success. These three areas are all intertwined and show up today as one of the most important parts of any company's measured growth strategy: employee performance reviews. It's imperative that leaders understand how to communicate, coach, and grow their employees of different generations through feedback in job evaluations and performance reviews. It is important to connect feedback to individualized career-growth plans because that can make or break a culture.

Chapters 4 and 5, *Recruiting the Four Generations* and *Retaining the Four Generations,* provide a generational view of two of the increasingly difficult business tasks today: how to recruit and retain highly skilled team members. A key to success in these areas today is to ask, "What are the different generations looking for in a company and their leadership, and how do they need to be productive, fulfilled, and grow as professionals?"

Chapter 6 covers a new term, but not necessarily a new concept, *Quiet Quitting: Generational Selfishness or Survival,* Another new term, *loud quitting,* is also described along with strategies of how to leverage a 4-gen lens to take steps to understand the core issues of workplace discontent and to find solutions.

No book about the various generations and their disparate views would be complete without a look at how they all view diversity, equity, and inclusivity (DEI) initiatives, which is the focus of Chapter 7: *DEI and the Generations.* Employees bring a wide range of emotions into DEI efforts, and some of these emotions are shaped by their generations.

Much has been said and written about our youngest employees, the Gen Zers. No generation has ever entered the workforce with so much to offer—and perhaps so much to overcome. Chapter 8: *Welcoming Gen Z to the Workplace* provides insights into how Gen Zers view the world, their work, and what leaders can do to help them thrive in a professional environment that is different than what they have experienced in life so far.

Chapter 9: *Personal Brands for Each Generation* tackles one of the newest challenges for professionals today: creating, developing, and evolving their personal brands. For millennials and Gen Zers, personal branding is a natural extension of who they are, but for baby boomers and older Gen Xers, who tend to downplay individual recognition in favor of being part of a team, the idea of standing out through branding requires a significant mind shift. Yet, research shows when everyone embraces their brands, the organization is more productive.

Chapter 10: *Professional Development for Four Distracted Generations* is filled with techniques 4-gen leaders can leverage to engage the various generations. The internet has done more than just change the way millennials and Gen Zers process information; it's also affected how boomers and Gen Xers like to learn, which means adult education needs to be redesigned to meet the common needs of the generations while also differentiating for their different learning styles.

Finally, Chapter 11: *Generations of the Future* peeks into the decades ahead to see how generations might be affected by AI and other technology advances, climate change, education transformation, environmental sustainability, and other forces that will shape them. The world, and business landscapes, will continue to change rapidly. Leaders of the future will have to learn how to harness the power of the evolving generations to stay ahead of the challenges that will come at even faster rates.

With Thanks to All Who Helped Us

We'd like to thank Scott Isenberg and the other team members at the Business Expert Press for quickly spotting the potential of this book and helping us through the acquisition, writing, and publication process. We appreciate Scott using his decades of business acumen to steer us toward the finish line in a kind, efficient manner.

Also, we'd like to thank the many people we formally interviewed for this book. We also would like to share an appreciation for the thousands of people with whom we've conversed, trained, and mentored throughout this process and in the years leading up to this project. The different generations and the generation gaps were frequent topics, and these individuals often broached these topics; they recognized that generational dynamics were shifting in their teams and wanted help.

We'd also like to give a special thanks to Shane Boroff for all his support. He too recognized this is an area in which many businesses are looking for education on multi-generational workforces and solutions to help build succession plans for their organizations. We are grateful for the many business connections he has made for us and grateful for the continued support as we accept engagements around the globe.

Throughout this book, Sami and I mention the need for leaders to develop their multi-gen leadership skills. We hope you find this book useful as you navigate the constantly shifting generational landscape and transition into a 4-gen leader.

Mark White
February 2024
St. Petersburg, Florida

CHAPTER 1

From Boomer to Gen Z

Key Points of This Chapter

1. Four distinct generations are now in our workforce, and they exist at every level of most organizations.
2. Generation gaps are more pronounced today because the rapid growth of technology has resulted in different growth experiences for each generation.
3. Leaders must understand the generations to effectively adapt and lead them.
4. Leaders must use new tactics to blend the four generations into one cohesive workforce.

"OK, Boomer…"

In November of 2019, this phrase became a generational battle cry when 25-year-old Chloe Swarbrick, a member of the New Zealand Parliament, addressed her fellow parliament members about the dangers of climate change or, more precisely, about their lack of action in preventing it. "In the year 2050, I will be 56 years old. Yet, right now, the average age of this 52nd Parliament is 49 years old," she said, hoping to spur her more senior colleagues into action. As Swarbrick spoke, an older parliament member sitting in the audience began to heckle her. Without pausing, Swarbrick deftly, calmly interjected, "OK, Boomer," into the middle of a sentence and continued her speech, silencing the heckler—and becoming a viral sensation.[1] Within hours, her response was being shown on news stations around the world. Today, it's been viewed millions of times on YouTube.

While Swarbrick didn't invent "OK, Boomer," she became its heroic face for millennials and Gen Zers everywhere who have grown increasingly frustrated with the societal and political structures put into place by baby boomers. What was accepted in the past will not be readily accepted by today's younger generations, and Swarbrick's "OK, Boomer" moment summed up the angst of young people around the world as they interact with older family members, politicians, and business executives.

Of course, generational discord is not just a feeling of the younger generations.

Many baby boomers (referred to simply as boomers from this point forward) and Gen X business leaders today are wringing their hands and asking, "What's up with these millennial and Gen Z workers? They're different than previous generations!" And they're right. Millennials and Gen Zers *are* different.

Figure 1.1 Note the generation birth years and technology that helped shape them

Another viral story involving generational conflict occurred in April of 2022—this one spotlighting the frustration of older leaders as they work with millennials and Gen Zers—when a Dollar Store manager in Indiana posted a handwritten note that said, "I apologize for us closing again. My two new cashiers quit because I said their boyfriends couldn't stand here for their entire shift." Then he added, "Don't hire Gen Z's. They don't know what work actually means. Now hiring. Baby boomers only, thanks." The note was considered age-discriminatory—and the manager was fired by the company, which disavowed the note and its contents[2].

This story epitomizes a growing problem in the workforce: different generations are bringing different views, habits, and biases into their jobs. If the store manager understood more about his Gen Z employees, could he have found a solution without firing them (and not getting himself fired in the process)? And if the Gen Z employees understood him, could they have done more to accommodate his wishes and kept their jobs?

It's always been hard to lead businesses, and the challenges of the rapidly shifting, post-COVID-19 environment with the Great Resignation and Great Reshuffling (discussed with a generational view in Chapter 4) are daunting, but executives must recognize their missions have become more complicated because of this new generational disruption. To adapt, they must add two new terms to their vocabulary: *generational acknowledgment* and *4-gen leadership*.

- **Generational acknowledgment** is the understanding that leadership must be approached differently today because of the four disparate generations in the workforce.
- **4-gen leadership** is the philosophy adapted and actions generated by the leader so that all four generations are accepted, honored, and united into one effective, harmonious team.

Effective business leaders have always known their businesses from A to Z; now they must also know their workers from B to Z—from boomer to Gen Z.

> **Have you noticed any generational conflicts in your organization?**

Understanding the Four Generations

Exactly who are these four generations of team members today, and how are they similar and different? Before diving into the perilous process of generational stereotyping, a few quick points need to be made about members of all generations.

- Members of all generations are all unique individuals, and it's possible some of them don't fit many of their generational stereotypes.
- Some people might feel the generational characteristics don't fit them at all—and they could be right.
- Some people see themselves as a mixture of some or all the generations.

Blanket assumptions should *never* be made that *all* people of a certain age have certain characteristics, but enough research and anecdotal evidence are present to propose that business leaders should at least consider generational characteristics to understand their colleagues. In other words, birth years matter. When leaders recognize each employee's formative decades, then the leaders are more likely to help them bridge the generation gaps and understand each other.

Managers should also understand generational diversity is a positive attribute for organizations today. One study in 2022 found:

> ...89 percent of respondents considered generation diversity in the workplace as a positive element of work and 87 percent viewed the opportunity to learn from each other as a good thing for their experience. This is indeed one of the main benefits of all kinds of diversity in the workplace—age-related and otherwise—multiple perspectives enhance learning and also improve outcomes. With the complexity of work today, no one viewpoint is ever complete, and being able to check in with others who see things differently shapes better solutions[3].

Before looking at the four generations that comprise 99 percent of today's business world, let's briefly examine two generations that preceded them, the Greatest Generation (birth years 1901–1927) and the Silent Generation (birth years 1928–1945). The majority of the members of the Greatest Generation and the Silent Generation are retired. Yet, these generations raised the baby boomers and helped shape much of the traditions and norms of the modern workplace.

The Greatest Generation was given its name by journalist and author Tom Brokaw in his book of the same name, in which he asserts this generation, because of its accomplishments in the face of great adversity, was the greatest generation to ever live. As adults, they led the way in creating technological advances like the radio and telephone while enduring the Great Depression. Members of the Greatest Generation were the civilian and military leaders of World War II[4]. Members of the Greatest Generation were known for being personally responsible, humble, and imbued with a strong work ethic. They were also seen as being frugal and committed to marriages, jobs, and causes. They valued honesty and trustworthiness and were committed to sacrificing for the common good[5]. These traits were passed to the next generation, the Silent Generation.

The Silent Generation members were given their name because they were silent during some of the most volatile times in American history. As children, they grew up in the Great Depression and became the young sailors and soldiers of World War II. As adults, they stoically endured the threat of nuclear war in the late 1940s and the volatility of McCarthyism in the 1950s. Through it all, they maintained the attitude that they would work as a team, accept the good with the bad of America, and carve out a better life for their families. They are known as a group that would rather work within the system than change it. Because of this trait, they are also called Traditionalists[6].

In 2024, the youngest worker of the Silent Generation will be 79 years old. Members of this organization are known for their patience, desire to be part of a team, loyalty, and respect for tradition[7]. They passed these characteristics on to their children. In teams, boomers and Gen Xers will adjust easily to Silent Generation members, while millennials and Gen Zers will have the most to learn about them.

To see the vast range of characteristics of the American workforce, compare the Silent Generation with Gen Z. For example, the Silent Generation members will be more patient when working toward goals, while Gen Zers will be more inclined to want to see immediate results. Silent Generation members will want to slow down and accomplish the mission as a team, while Gen Zers (who can work well as a team) will be more inclined to push ahead as individuals if they see the need to do so. Silent Generation members will be more inclined to blindly accept the reasoning of management, while Gen Zers will want to ask questions and seek more understanding of management's intent. Silent Generation members will respect the tradition and status quo of a company and its operations, while Gen Zers will advocate for change and constantly seek new and more effective ways of working.

However, the Silent Generation members and Gen Zers have common bonds. They grew up in frightening times, during the Red Scare of the 1950s and the aftermath of 9/11 in the 2000s. They tend to be thrifty because the Silent Generation members endured the Great Depression, and Gen Zers have a strong desire not to accumulate debt like the millennials. Also, family is important to both groups; Silent Generation members often needed the family for survival, and Gen Zers grew up as central, participatory members of their families[8].

In teams, Silent Generation members need to be respected, listened to, plugged in, and patiently upskilled. They will be technologically challenged. They tend not to react as well to change as other generations, so managers should be careful in how they are approached about new systems or upgrades. However, Silent Generation members will respect authority and want to please authority figures. They will work hard and be committed to success[9].

The boomers (birth years: 1945–1964) were raised to be loyal, committed, and to have a sense of duty to society and their country. Their parents also taught them that you need to pay your dues to get ahead; success comes to those who work hard and play the game right. However, not all boomers followed the traditional script: many of the Hippies of the 1960s and 1970s were boomers who refused to buy into the lifestyles of their parents and refused to embrace the concept of chasing the American Dream. Boomers grew up in an age when households had one phone that hung on a wall; they still believed in the power of phone calls and face-to-face communication. They grew up using paper and had to make late transitions to digital products. However, 90 percent of boomers have Facebook pages, mainly to stay in touch with younger family members and lifelong friends—and to proudly post pictures of their grandkids[10].

In businesses today, boomers have become the seasoned professionals of their organizations. Sometimes they see themselves as the sages, the wise ones, the employees who remember work before it became so tech-oriented. Over the last three decades, they've seen their jobs become busier and more complex. For hundreds of years, the oldest workers were the most revered workers, but boomers have seen this idea be greatly diminished as technology and new types of skills have overtaken them and their vocations. Boomers fall into one of two categories: those who have adapted to the current best practices in the workforce and those who spend their days pining for a forgone era and are dragged reluctantly through each iteration of change.

While some boomers are working longer than earlier generations, many have reached retirement age and are rapidly fading out of the workforce. As boomers retire today, the other generations climb the corporate ladder to fill their roles, and Gen Zers fill the gap in open positions. This creates an interesting paradigm where some boomers are being supervised by millennial and Gen Z managers, which is creating new types of tensions for both the boomers and the young leaders.

The Gen Xers (birth years: 1965–1980), are the latchkey, MTV generation who first began to reap the benefits of advancing technology and digital devices. In the 1980s and 1990s, they saw entertainment become more personal and mobile. Instead of having only three TV channels from which to choose, they suddenly had hundreds of cable channels. Instead of listening to music selected by disc jockeys on transistor radios, they could choose their own music and carry it with them on a Sony Walkman. Their cynicism comes from seismic events that shook their world: growing divorce rates among their boomer parents, the outbreak of the AIDS epidemic, and the first rise and fall of technology companies in the dot.com boomers. While the boomers were more blindly loyal to companies and their professions, the Gen Xers became the first generation to question the balance between work and personal leisure. Today, they can still resist change if it affects their personal lives. They are thought of as the *Forgotten Generation*, the smaller generation wedged between the massive post-World War II boomers and the technology savvy millennials. It should be remembered, however, that Gen Xers are more likely to embrace new technology than boomers[11].

In our offices today, Gen Xers are in their 40s and 50s. Like the boomers, they, too, have become the formal and informal leaders of the workforce. But while the boomers have reached retirement age, the Gen Xers still have years to go before they can retire, and they sometimes feel trapped between their simpler past and the years of increasingly complex change they must endure before they, too, can step away from their jobs. Some of them are still raising kids (or grandkids), and some of them are taking care of their elderly parents (many of them older boomers), which is adding a new financial and emotional burden to Gen Xers that is cutting into their leisure time. By 2028, Gen Xers will outnumber the boomers[12]. They are the last pre-Internet generation of leaders. After the Gen Xers retire, all future leaders will have grown up with the Internet.

The millennials (birth years: 1981–1994, also known as Gen Y) have seen their world shaped by two extremes: the violence of Columbine and 9/11 and the promise and challenges of the emerging digital world. They grew up as the Internet entered society on a broad scale, and it gave them an outlook dramatically different from any previous predecessors. They are the first set of digital natives, the first generation to avidly embrace the use of new types of devices, and the first to use social media on a broad scale and to use it to stay connected. Millennials embrace Uber and other services they can share with society; for them, it's not about ownership but instead, it's about access. They also believe in wellness. They exercise more, eat smarter, drink less alcohol than previous generations, and they might like to keep track of their progress in these areas on their iPhone apps. Millennials are viewed, correctly or incorrectly, as the sheltered kids who always got trophies whether they won or lost their childhood soccer games. They became the helicopter parents of Gen Z[13].

Some have referred to millennials as the *Lost Generation* because the early millennials entered the workforce during the recession that began in 2008 and the last of the millennials entered the workforce during the COVID-19 lockdowns of 2020 when a staggering 52 percent of people under the age of 45 were laid off, put on leave, or had their hours reduced, compared with 26 percent of people over the age of 45. They have had fewer opportunities to find high-paying jobs while carrying record amounts of college debt they will be paying off for decades. Today, they are the largest generational segment of the American workforce They make up most of America's bartenders, half the restaurant employees, and a large share of its retail employees. Because of their financial insecurities, they've been less likely to buy houses. They have also waited longer to get married and have children[14].

Today, millennials are in every level of the organization, from entry-level positions to management roles and some own their startups. After the COVID-19 shutdowns of 2020, many millennials took stock of their lifestyles—especially how their jobs affected them emotionally—and changed their lives. They were not content to settle for traditional pursuits of paychecks and mortgages. They wanted to live a more purpose-driven existence.

The Gen Zers (birth years: 1995–2010) are the latest generation to enter the workforce. They can be characterized as the most technologically savvy, socially challenged, stressed, diverse, and distracted group ever led. Their mindset has been formed since their birth by the Internet, social media, Starbucks, and artificial intelligence (AI) in a post-9/11 world. America has been at war for most of their entire lives. The COVID-19 pandemic shutdowns had a significant negative impact on their mental health, social skills, and education. Most of them got their first smartphones when they were 10.3 years old. The Girl Scouts of America recently redesigned their uniforms; the number one request from the girls was a pocket for their iPhones. They tend to be more independent than millennials, and they value their devices more than any previous generation, even more so than millennials, but they prefer to work with millennial managers because they have more in common with them than with boomers and Gen Xers. Gen Zers tend to be more fiscally conservative than millennials because they've seen how millennials are burdened with college debt[15].

Gen Z also is shaping up to be the most free-thinking, original, purpose-driven generation. One study found that 41 percent of them want to be entrepreneurs, and half of them believe they can change the world[16]. Gen Zers have also seen other young people start their own online companies, become wealthy e-gamers, and create original content to launch their influencer status on social media. They are also seeing that a significant number of today's college graduates can't find the jobs they want. Their role models include David Hogg and Emma Gonzalez, survivors of the Parkland High School shootings who are antigun activists, and Greta Thunberg, who is perhaps the world's most famous environmental activist. These young activists became famous as high-school students, and they have inspired Gen Zers around the world to follow in their footsteps by following their passions and chasing their dreams. Some Gen Zers have become depressed when they feel they can't be as successful as their peers they know locally or their heroes they see on the Internet.

In the workforce, Gen Zers need coaching from their leaders and the freedom to work with peers and to be creative and unique. They tend to be more driven than millennials, and their drug abuse, smoking, drinking, and teen pregnancies are lower than in previous generations[17].

> **What generation are you and what characteristics do you align with best?**

Recognizing the Digital Generation Gaps

Generation gaps aren't new. They've occurred throughout history. But, the rate of change used to be slower; technology was advancing at a slower pace. Then it sped up in the 1960s when, according to Moore's Law, processing speeds began to double every 18 to 24 months. This explosion of knowledge explains the amazing technological innovations we've seen since the 1970s[18]. Each decade brought amazing new advances and new devices, new mobility, new individualism, and new, broader windows on the world for young people growing up in each successive decade. The rise of the Internet society deepened the generation gaps and accelerated the changes seen in each generation. The result was a new type of generation gap, a *digital generation gap*, between all four generations.

Many experiences shape people in their youth, such as gender and gender identity, socio-economic status, religion and spiritual beliefs, ethnicity, sexual orientation, and geographic location. Technology has been the tool that allows young people to view their world; thus, it has played a critical role in how people develop their mindsets during their formative years.

Here's another way of viewing how technology has shaped adults. Consider what the world looked like when generations were growing up:

- Boomers grew up being exposed to the world on three highly regulated TV networks. They were restricted in seeing only what network executives chose to share with them via news programs a few times each day during local and national news programs.

- Gen Xers grew up with more options with the advent of cable TV and 24/7 news channels. While they were still seeing only what mass media executives chose to air, Gen Xers were able to access it when they wanted, and they began to see variations in how it was presented.

- Millennials grew up viewing world events 24/7 in real time on new Internet streams—and they began to interact with people around the world in real time. They began to see videos and opinions posted by their peers, not just the mass media executives.

- Gen Zers never experienced a world without a digital-first mindset. They grew up with even more streams and more ways to interact. More importantly, they began to create and curate Internet content, sometimes with other Gen Zers in other parts of the world. They moved from being consumers to being creators.

These four groups now bring their differing experiences, views, and ideas of their place in a global society, and what they want to achieve in their lives into their workplace, but here's an essential point: these different views can mesh effectively into one effective team if the leaders become 4-gen leaders who understand their workers and help them understand each other.

The Internet Generation Gap

A simple way to begin the evolution into 4-gen leadership is to place the four different generations in two groups with the boomers and Gen Xers in one group and the millennials and Gen Zers in the other group. Why? The Internet began to reshape society at the end of Gen X's childhood and at the beginning of the millennials' childhood. This means the boomers and Gen Xers grew up *without* the Internet, and the millennials and Gen Zers grew up *with* the Internet. The millennials and Gen Zers have known the Internet with its devices, cloud computing, apps, and icons for their entire lives. The boomers and Gen Xers, on the other hand, have spent the past two decades watching this new technology emerge and playing catch-up with the technological changes reshaping their lives and their workplaces.

Think of this gap as the Internet generation gap, but this gap between the older and younger workers is deeper—it's a generational valley, and it's at the crux of generational leadership. So much of business acumen today revolves around the ability of business executives of all generations to understand how technological advancements have shaped their workers who grew up on different sides of this valley.

This Internet generation gap has had another significant impact on the two generations on either side of it, and this impact is related to hyper-change, which occurs when changes arrive in faster and faster rates because of technology innovations, which lead to dramatic changes in lifestyles, societal norms, and business strategy. In looking at the bottom of Figure 1.2, one can see the arc representing the rate of change that began in the 1970s has increased dramatically into the current 2020s. This arc (not drawn to an exact scale) is based on Moore's Law.

Boomers and Gen Xers grew up in an era when the rate of change was slower, and they've had to adjust to hyper-change, but for Millennials and Gen Zers, hyper-change is all they've ever known. Boomers and Gen Xers keep having to adjust to the constant stream of new devices and software iterations, often reluctantly, while millennials and Gen Zers welcome them as a daily part of life.

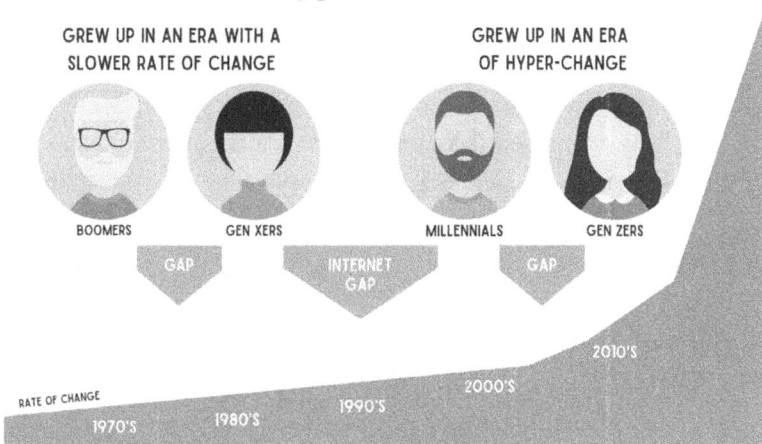

GREW UP IN AN ERA WITH A SLOWER RATE OF CHANGE

GREW UP IN AN ERA OF HYPER-CHANGE

BOOMERS   GEN XERS   MILLENNIALS   GEN ZERS

GAP   INTERNET GAP   GAP

2010'S

2000'S

RATE OF CHANGE

1990'S

1980'S

1970'S

Figure 1.2 The internet generation gap and the rate of change has helped shape generations

Another way of understanding the significance of this Internet gap on generations is to consider the advent of the global economy, which came into sharper focus in the 1990s as the Internet became stronger and businesses of the world became more interconnected. The boomers and Gen Xers grew up in a slower-paced, less-complicated business world, but for the millennials (many of whom grew up in the 1990s) and Gen Zers, a globally linked, rapidly evolving business landscape is all they've known. Important reminder: A person's age, and the side of the Internet generation gap on which the person grew up, does not *always* define how that person will view a job, use technology, or transform with the times. While age and growth experiences are factors to consider, some individuals will have philosophies and skillsets that cross generational boundaries. This, too, is something a 4-gen leader must know.

Developing a Multi-Generational Lens

To bridge the new generation gaps, 4-gen leaders need to view workplace issues through the eyes of all the generations they are leading. They need to develop a *multi-generational lens*.

- A **multi-generational lens** is a lens used by leaders at all levels of the organization to view their actions and policies through the eyes of different generations.

This lens is needed because today's leaders must guide their organizations through complicated, new personnel issues that didn't exist at the beginning of the 21st century—and because the different generations they lead could react differently when encountering these new personnel issues.

The use of this lens to view multiple types of generation gaps will be discussed throughout this book, but let's start with one example: wellness. An important new area of concern for leaders (and employees) in a post-COVID-19 world is the overall wellness (which includes mental, physical, and emotional health) of their employees and what can be done in the workplace to assist them[19]. But, consider how the different generations view wellness. In the past, when organizations were dominated by boomers and Gen Xers, mental and emotional health was often not acknowledged, and it was rarely discussed in the workplace. Individuals who confronted their mental and emotional health issues and spoke publicly about them were often considered weak and a vulnerability for the company. Today, while many boomers and Gen Xers today still don't want to acknowledge they might need help, more of them are starting to publicly confront their wellness challenges. Millennials and Gen Zers, on the other hand, tend to be much more in touch with their overall health and are more likely to seek assistance and publicly discuss their issues. They want to work for companies that acknowledge their stress and help them manage it.

This is where the multi-generational lens, as shown in Figure 1.3, is needed.

Figure 1.3 A multi-gen lens is needed by all leaders today to help build successful teams

If a boomer leader refuses to acknowledge wellness issues and sees little need to help his or her employees, then the employees who need assistance will feel ignored and isolated. Also, mental and emotional health initiatives are significant factors considered by millennials and Gen Zers when they interview with companies, which means the failure of the boomer leader to understand the younger job seekers could result in a smaller pool of applicants[20].

It's not just boomer leaders who need to understand the different generations. If a millennial leader, for example, implements an extensive wellness initiative without using a multi-generational lens, the millennial could face a different problem: the failure to understand the boomers' reticence to discuss wellness issues. This initiative, while well intentioned, will be less likely to be successful with the older employees because they won't buy into the program.

When the leaders of all generations view the other generations through a multi-generational lens they can dialogue, plan, anticipate problems, and often keep the problems from occurring. The boomer leader would see millennials and Gen Z employees wanting, and in some cases, demanding mental and emotional health assistance in the workplace. In turn, the millennial leader would see that boomers and Gen Xers need more assistance in acknowledging their needs, so theleader could have more dialogue with them and help them confront their needs.

An old saying is that we tend to see the world from our own bell tower—a multi-generational lens helps us see the world from other bell towers, in this case, the different bell towers of other generations.

What must you do to develop your own multi-generational lens?

New Issues, New Generational Challenges

Wellness is just one of the new areas 4-gen leaders must address. Other areas that spark generational responses (areas discussed in later chapters) include:

- **Diversity, equity, and inclusion (DEI):** Ensuring all generations understand and connect how their leaders value diversity, promote equity, and systemize inclusion.
- **Innovation pioneer mindset:** Establishing a culture of entrepreneurial thinking by tapping into the experiences of boomers and Gen Xers while incorporating the free thinking of millennials and Gen Zers who have grown up in an era of constant, accelerating disruptions.
- **Remote/hybrid work environment:** Rethinking the use of office space and working remotely from home and other locations and what it means to the different generations.

- **Recruiting and retention**: Establishing a new protocol to ensure the four generations are attracted to the company, and then look at ways to retain the employees after they are onboarded.
- **Parenting impact**: Realizing how each generation has raised kids differently, and how it affects them as adult employees.
- **Learning methods**: Focusing on the importance of upskilling and reskilling in a reshuffled workplace and the best methods for training each generation.
- **The ascendance of millennials and Gen Z**: Realizing within the next decade an increasing number of millennials and Gen Zers will move into leadership roles, and they will be tasked with leading companies in a world becoming increasingly dominated by technology and AI.

More than ever, 4-gen leaders must recognize how different generational strengths, weaknesses, and initiatives help shape organizational culture (discussed in depth in Chapter 3). An organization's customs, traditions, rituals, behavioral norms, symbols, and general way of doing things are the visible manifestations of its culture. A goal must be for all leaders, and all generations to understand each other—4-gen leaders must bridge the new generation gaps.

Do You Have a 4-Gen Leadership Team?

Leadership teams are found at all levels of an organization from the C-Suite to regional offices. Each leadership team must begin its journey to 4-gen leadership by taking three initial steps previously mentioned:

- It must acknowledge that different generations are in the organization.
- It must commit to being a new type of team—a 4-gen leadership team—that bases its actions on its knowledge of the generations it is leading.
- It must view all actions and initiatives through a multi-generational lens.

Each team should examine its generational composition to see which generations are represented, but just as importantly, which generations are *not* represented. This is the beginning of 4-gen leadership. A leadership team missing generations does not have to add permanent members of the generations to the team just because they are different, but the team needs to know it has a blind spot in its lens. It will have to find a way to consult formally or informally with the missing generations and consider their views.

While there are many variations in leadership teams, here are five common types broken down by generation representation.

1. **Leadership teams made up of one generation.** In some organizations, the C-Suites or leadership teams are occupied exclusively by boomers or Gen Xers. In some startups, the leaders are exclusively millennials or Gen Zers. A team made exclusively of one generation will have the most adaptions to make as it creates a multi-generational lens to incorporate the views of the three other generations not serving on the team.

2. **Leadership teams made up of both boomers and Gen Xers.** This would be a team made up of a mix of the oldest two generations, and while it has two of the four generations present in the organization, it would need to be sure to understand the two younger generations.

3. **Leadership teams made up mainly of boomers and Gen Xers with a few millennials.** This team is becoming more common as more millennials move into leadership positions. The handful of millennials on the team would have to be heard, and while some of their views would overlap with Gen Zers, their perspective would be missing.

4. **Leadership teams with a balance of boomers, Gen Xers, and millennials.** This team would possess the views of the three generations that form the majority of today's workforce. If millennials have equal representation, they can play an active role in forming the multi-generational lens. All three groups

would have to find a way to include the views of their Gen Z colleagues.

5. **Leadership teams with a balance of boomers, Gen Xer, millennials, and Gen Zers.** When forming a multi-generational lens, this leadership team comprising the four generations is the most effective—and it is the rarest because most Gen Zers have not yet moved into leadership positions.

Of course, effective leadership is not just generational; it's also representative of different genders, lifestyles, and ethnicities found in the organization. Leadership teams made up of individuals of the same sex, ethnicity, and sexual preference would be strengthened with more diversity in their membership. A truly desirable leadership team represents all generations and all types of individuals.

Voices From the Generations

A product of 4-gen leadership is the creation of cultures that promote friendships, mentorships, and profound conversations among team members from different generations. Caitlin Ziegert McCombs, a millennial, is a successful development specialist at a major American research university, and she shared how the advice given to her by a boomer has affected her career. "I got this great advice from a woman I met when I was studying abroad…She said, 'Caitlin, when you think about your career it should be in the center of four different things: what you're good at, what you love, what will pay you well, and what will help other people or change the world.'"[21] Caitlin is living this philosophy. Like other millennials, she wants to have a strong sense of purpose in her job, which is accomplished as she works to establish funding that helps students receive a high-quality education at their university. She is dedicating to improving her part of the world. But note her advice came from an older team member. Boomers also care about their impact, and this one helped shape Caitlin's outlook on life. It's important for 4-gen leaders to recognize how the generations are different and similar—and to create opportunities for deep dialogue and impact between them.

Your Real-World Connection

What are some ways generation gaps occur within teams? One gap could be around how different generations approach decision making and take the initiative to surface a problem as they encounter challenges.

Consider this scenario: A team of four employees is made up of a boomer, a Gen Xer, a millennial, and a Gen Zer. This team is assigned a project by the company; however, halfway through the project, they encounter a problem and are unsure of how to proceed.

- The boomer, being deferential to management, would want to await directions from a higher authority on next steps.
- The Gen Xer, being less blindly loyal to management than the boomers, would be less inclined to await instructions from a higher authority; however, the Gen Xer would consult with all team members to begin to try to find a solution.
- The millennial, being more of an independent problem solver, would want to push ahead and resolve the issue without waiting for guidance, perhaps using technology to expedite the resolution.
- The Gen Zer would side with the millennial and would expect to play an equally important role in deciding the outcome, regardless of the fact the Gen Zer has less experience than the others.

Depending upon the type of problem, it's possible that each member of the team could be correct.

- The boomer could be correct, in that there are times when guidance from a higher authority is needed.
- The Gen Xer could be correct, in that there are times to wait for guidance, but there are other times when the team can work together to resolve the issue.
- The millennial could be correct, in that there are times when the team can immediately move forward in seeking a resolution, and the digital component should be immediately considered.

- The Gen Zer could be correct, in that sometimes a fresh approach from the youngest team member could be what is needed to find a solution.

If the team members exhibit their generational characteristics without considering the generational views of the other team members (which is one reason teams become dysfunctional in today's workplace), the team could become deadlocked.

- The boomer, who might have the most seniority, could obstinately refuse to move forward until clearance is given from a superior, even if the other three team members are eager to begin work.
- The Gen Xer, unable to find a consensus in the team, could begin to work independently.
- The millennial, seeing no reason to wait for guidance, could become discouraged that they are not doing the job assigned to them.
- The Gen Zer could feel the boomers and the rest of the team are not responding to his or her entreaties and could become despondent or disillusioned.

To resolve the deadlock, a 4-gen leader intervening in this situation would first realize generational views are contributing to this problem. The leader would meet with the team and point out that they are all bringing different generational outlooks (and perhaps different backgrounds and different personalities) into the team, which can bring about both positive and negative results. In this case, the generational views are slowing their progress in achieving their assigned task.

The 4-gen leader would then guide them into the next steps of their project and point out what the right approach would have been (awaiting next steps or resolutely moving forward, depending upon the situation). However, the 4-gen leader would need to ask some reflective questions.

- Had the company done enough training around generational views to allow the different generations of team members to understand and spot these issues without having to bring the 4-gen leader into the process to break the deadlock?
- The team members had become deadlocked. Was this generation, or did the culture in the company not do enough to foster creative problem-solving?
- Did the Gen Z employee feel undervalued? Did the 4-gen leader need to do more to ensure the culture was inclusive of all employees regardless of age or experience?
- Were there any other issues creating the team conflict, such as personality traits, previous conflicts, or preconceived ideas team members had about each other?

The philosophy of 4-gen leadership should be a new, permanent pillar of leadership. Four generations will be in the workforce throughout the 2020s and into the 2030s, which means the current generation gaps will be present and popping up around new types of workplace issues as the landscape and technology continue to evolve. In the 2030s, as boomers retire a new generation will be entering the workforce: Gen Alpha. After Gen Alpha will come Gen Beta.

This generational leadership philosophy is here to stay.

NEXT STEPS

4-GEN *leadership*

HELPING ALL YOUR GENERATIONS THRIVE IN THEIR TEAMS!

What is the composition of generations on your team and the organization's leadership team, and what adjustments may need to be considered for future succession planning?

What are the generational gaps affecting your organizational culture and how can you leverage a multi-gen lens to support creating new solutions that embrace diverse generational views?

What steps can you take to develop your own generational awareness and build skills around the 4-gen leadership philosophy?

Figure 1.4 Chapter 1 next steps worksheet

CHAPTER 2

Different Generations, Parenting and Perspectives

Key Points of This Chapter

1. Each generation was raised with different parenting styles.
2. These parenting styles affect how generations view their careers, other generations, and the world today.
3. Four-gen leaders must understand these different parenting styles to understand some of the generation gaps in their teams.
4. To be effective coaches, four-gen leaders must educate their teams about how being raised in different parenting styles sometimes leads to misunderstanding and different ways of viewing roles and responsibilities.

One thing most managers agree upon is that Gen Zers are entering the workforce with different attitudes and expectations than previous generations. Some Gen Zers, and their managers, are having a challenging time adjusting to each other's expectations.

A boomer executive from a Fortune 500 company in Orlando recently mused on the differences he's seeing in how the generations approach their jobs, and the executive was especially concerned about the company's youngest workers, the Gen Zers. "These young workers today," he said with an exasperated tone, "I just don't understand them! Sometimes, they just don't want to do what they're asked to do!"[1]

In a conversation with one of the authors, a millennial elementary principal in South Texas recounted how she asked a Gen Z education aide to temporarily go into another classroom to assist in that classroom, but the Gen Zer protested that she was hired to do one specific job in her current classroom and didn't want to go into the other classroom. The principal reminded the aide that all employees in schools must often step into various classrooms to do different jobs and the job descriptions for most jobs in schools include the phrase "and other duties as assigned." This is a standard, long-standing practice in schools. The aide still protested, even to the point that the aide called the district office in an attempt to get the principal's decision overturned. The aide's appeal was rejected. However, the principal was amazed that the Gen Zer would take the extraordinary step, one the principal had never experienced, of going up the chain of command to overrule her, especially for such a minor task.[2]

This is not to say Gen Zers, or members of any generation, are wrong to question or protest a management decision if they see an illegal or immoral aspect to it, but many managers feel Gen Zers are more likely to challenge them over routine decisions more often than previous generations.[3] A post by a manager in the United Kingdom in 2022 went viral and sparked a contentious debate when he wrote, "I manage people from the late teens to early 60's. The younger group are by far the hardest workers,"[4] and one manager interviewed for this book went as far as to say young workers seem to revel in "sticking it to The Man," meaning they enjoy antagonizing their managers more than previous generations.[5]

Some people, however, take a different view and say Gen Zers are misunderstood because they see things differently. One adolescent psychologist interviewed about Gen Z in a post online defended the generation, saying there are "a lot of misconceptions about Gen Z employees, and this is causing companies to lose cash and calm due to conflicts, retention issues, and turnover."[6] Another commentator has written that Gen Zers, "often labeled 'Strawberries' or 'Snowflakes' because of their (supposed) lack of resilience and inability to deal with hardship" are "actually a generation of activists, conscious consumers, and future goal-based leaders."[7] Another blogger noted on Yahoo Finance that the challenges of working with Gen Zer often mask the complex reality that they are "incredibly ambitious. They're just not interested in climbing your corporate ladder."[8]

So why are these misunderstandings occurring, and why are Gen Zers bringing such a different perspective into their roles at work? In Chapter 1, it was pointed out the two major factors to shape generational views of the world: the availability (or unavailability) of the Internet when the generations were growing up and the rate of change the generations experienced because of technological advances during their childhood and formative years. However, a third key force has played a key role in how generations view the world, authority, and their jobs: the parenting style used to raise each generation.

What forms of technology did you use during your formative years and during the years when you entered the workforce?

If today's managers are going to transform into four-gen leaders, they need to understand the huge differences in parenting for the generations, ranging from how the boomers were raised in the 1950s to how Gen Zers were raised in the 2000s. This will go a long way in helping leaders relate to their team members, and if the team members understand the differences in how they were all raised, it will help them understand each other and why they act or react in certain ways.

Raising the Boomers

To understand how boomers were raised, let's remember the attributes of their parents, the members of the Greatest Generation and the Silent Generation. The Greatest Generation rallied from the depths of the Great Depression to help win World War II, and the Silent Generation silently endured the challenges of post–World War II America as it fought a war in Korea, went through McCarthyism, and witnessed the awakening Civil Rights Movement. They believed that if you worked hard, paid your dues, and were loyal, then you would move up in the world. They felt if everyone worked within the system, then those who worked the hardest could move the furthest within the system, which was a significant part of the American Dream.[9]

A mantra uttered to boomers by their parents was, "Children should be seen and not heard," as a way of reminding the kids their opinions were of secondary importance to the parents, and they were to not question parental authority. This phrase was first used in the 15th century and its original form said *young women* should be seen and not heard.[10] At some point, *children* was substituted for *women*. Regardless of when this switch was made, it is notable that generations from the 1400s (and earlier) to the 1960s (when the last of the boomers were being raised) were brought up in families dominated by the parents, most often the males. The emphasis in parenting was on obedience to authority, not individuality. This obedience was to extend to the institutions that maintained order in society and their lives. They were taught not to stick out, and not to do anything that might upset the established norms. Today's boomers are known for the respect they still have for society's institutions, including the courts, schools, and government. This philosophy also extends into the workplace as they show respect for organizations, traditional ways of doing things in the workplace, and their managers. Some of them might even be so averse to change that they are considered closed-minded.[11]

However, four-gen leaders should remember about a third of the boomers openly rejected the Silent Generation's views,[12] opting instead to be hippies and to join the Counter Culture, an alternative approach to life that "manifested itself in a variety of activities, lifestyles, and artistic expressions, including recreational drug use, communal living, political protests, casual sex, and folk and rock music."[13] If these boomers are in the workforce today, they might conform just enough to survive in the system as they question its authority and the status quo.

Raising Gen Xers

To understand how parenting impacted Gen Xers in the workplace, let's remember they were raised by the Silent Generation and the boomers. Their mothers joined the workforce in greater numbers than previous generations, which led to Gen X being called *the latchkey generation*, meaning they were the first generation to return home after school to empty homes.[14] This led to a heightened state of independence and individualism, which could still be seen today as they performed their tasks at work.

While Gen X is often referred to as *The Forgotten Generation* because it is wedged between the massive boomer and millennial generations,[15] the Gen Xers can also be viewed as the gateway generation for future generations: They were more ethnically diverse, the first to see how advancing technology could become a central part of their lives, and they were the first to advocate for a greater balance between personal lives and professional careers. If Gen Xers are exhibiting more cynicism in their jobs than their peers, it could be because of what they experienced as they were growing up: the tension of the cold war, the fear of nuclear war in the 1970s and 1980s, higher divorce rates among their parents, and the first dot.com booms and busts. Gen Xers also experienced the first wave of the post-civil rights years and were raised by their boomer parents with a more tolerant view of diversity, which means they have led the way in opening doors for under-represented groups[16] in the workplace. Gen Xers were the first free thinkers, and they began to dismantle the idea of exhibiting blind obedience to society and their jobs. In doing so, they broke out of the mold that had been casting children for hundreds of years.

Their boomer parents were the first generation to have wide access to universities, and they passed this option to their Gen X kids; the result was a higher education level among Gen Xers than the boomers.[17] Their level of education has benefited them in their climb up the corporate ladder. Gen Xers now hold many leadership positions globally. The average age of incoming CEOs in 2023 was 54, meaning they are Gen Xers.[18] The generation raised to be more independent, to be more cynical, and to ask more questions than their predecessors is now firmly in charge.

Raising Millennials

Understanding the change in parenting that arrived with millennials, who were raised by boomer and Gen X parents, is of particular importance for four-gen leaders. The parenting trends that began with the Gen X years became a parenting tidal wave for millennials—they were raised with a deeper sense of individualism and allowed to have a more expansive use of technology in everyday life (coinciding with the growth of the Internet) and were encouraged to take a broader, global view,[19] which are traits they often exhibit in the workplace as they solve problems with fresh ideas and adapt to new technology.

Gen X parents were the first to adopt the *helicopter*[20] parenting style in which some Gen X parents constantly hovered over their millennial kids and became much more involved in their social and educational growth.[21] The millennials were perceived to be *trophy kids*, meaning previous generations only received trophies, ribbons, and other prizes when they won events, whereas millennials began to receive awards, for better or worse, for not only winning the events but often just for participating, which has led to a perception in some boomers and Gen Xers that millennials were coddled more than previous generations.[22] However, the millennials counter it's unfair to criticize them for this trophy philosophy because it was the decision of the boomer and Gen X parents to hand out the trophies.[23] In the workplace, these perceptions can cause tension within teams, especially between boomers and millennials if the boomers perceive the millennials as being soft or not falling into line with the boomers.[24]

Millennials surpassed the Gen Xers in education levels. By the 2020s, "4 in 10 millennials had earned a bachelor's degree or higher."[25] To effectively lead millennials, four-gen leaders need to remember the traits of the millennial childhood and provide them with the latest technology, allow for a work/life balance, collaborate with them, listen to them, help them to keep growing, and be authentic.[26]

Raising Gen Z

The Gen Zers in the workforce were raised by Gen X and millennial parents. Gen Zers have grown up seeing other Gen Z heroes they follow online or in the news, many of whom are making an impact in areas such as fighting climate change, promoting reforestation, pushing for LGBTQ rights, promoting gun reform, advocating for women's safety, and encouraging social justice.[27] Many Gen Zers want to make their own impact and this includes in the workplace.

While millennial parents often work outside the home, they still manage to spend as much time with their Gen Z kids as the boomers and Gen Xer parents spent with them. Multitasking allows today's parents, even if holding full-time jobs, to give even *more* time to their Gen Z kids than the Silent Generation gave boomers in the 1950s.[28] A critical point four-gen leaders need to know about Gen Zers is they were raised in a much more participatory model than previous generations. One recent study found:

- Millennial parents feel closer to their children than they think their boomer and Gen X parents were to them.
- Millennial parents are more afraid of disobeying their boomer and Gen X parents than their Gen Z and Gen Alpha kids are afraid of disobeying their millennial parents.
- Millennial parents consider their Gen Z and Gen Alpha kids to be some of their best friends.
- Seventy-one percent of millennial parents seek the opinions of their Gen Z and Gen Alpha kids when making most purchases—and this number is higher for millennial parents outside the United States.[29]

In other words, today's youngest members of the workforce have been raised in families where the parents are closer to their kids than in previous generations, the kids have less fear of disobeying their parents, parents and kids are best friends, and kids have more say in family decisions than in the past. If workplace leaders fail to include Gen Zers in decision making, or if the Gen Zers feel they are being left out or ignored, they will begin to feel disenfranchised and will be more likely to seek work elsewhere (topics to be covered more thoroughly in Chapter 5).

> **Are any parenting styles influencing or affecting the decision making of any team members in your organization?**

The Impact of Parenting Models on Today's Workforce

When four-gen leaders understand the generational parenting models, as shown in Figure 2.1, they can understand why team members react as they do in certain situations—it could be partly because of the thinking model they developed as kids. To summarize what has happened in parenting through the generations, consider this chart, which roughly shows the shift in parent and child authority from the boomers to Gen Z.

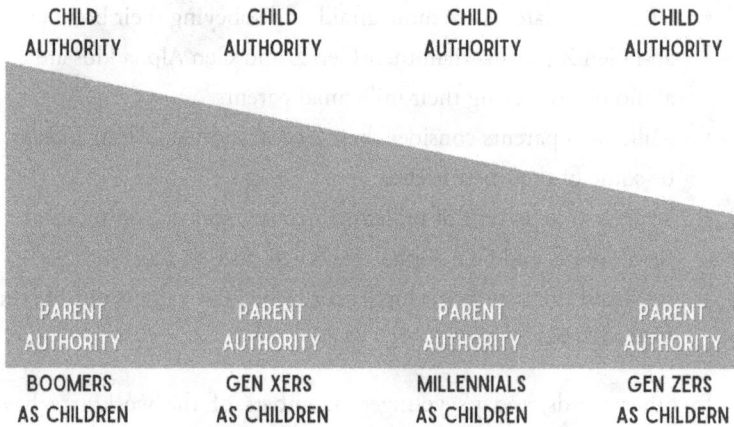

Figure 2.1 Authority

Another way of viewing the shift for this chart is to replace *authority* with *individualism, technology usage, social activism, the need for work/life balance, questioning the status quo,* and *seeking passion and meaning in work and life.* All these areas have increased in importance with the passing of the generations.

> **Were you raised in a parenting model where your parents were dominant authority figures or more like partners?**

Now let's look again at the managerial frustrations about working with Gen Zers documented in the opening of this chapter, but this time, let's see them through a multi-gen lens to see how some of the issues could be connected to parenting styles.

- The Fortune 500 executive, a boomer who expressed frustrations about Gen Zers not wanting to do what they were told to do, would need to understand that Gen Zers were raised as partners with their parents and were not used to functioning in an environment in which they constantly commanded to do something, especially if they don't understand why they are being required to do it. This concept ran counter to the parenting model in which boomer was raised. The boomer would have been taught to work hard, sacrifice, and obey directions given by authority.

- The elementary principal, an older millennial who expressed frustration that the Gen Zer teaching aide who didn't want to take on a new part of her job in a different classroom, would need to recognize that the Gen Zers' partnership model usually involves transactional deal-making with their parents, which means the Gen Zer aide took the job with the district with certain explicit expectations, and when those expectations were changed without her consent, she felt she was being unfairly treated. The millennial principal, who was closer in age to Gen X than Gen Z, would have been less sympathetic than a young millennial or Gen Z manager due to the circumstances of their upbringing and closer parenting styles.

An important note to remember, though, as stated earlier is that not all members of a generation will react in ways that align with their generation. Personalities, experiences, and individual talents also shape a person. However, the generational characteristics are worth noting. Parenting models used to raise team members could result in the team members having differing views and expectations.

Parenting impacts the generational topics covered in this book:

- Recruiting in ways that appeal to different generations
- Retaining employees with coaching and team member involvement
- Stressing diversity, equity, and inclusion (DEI) to include all voices
- Helping Gen Zers adapt to the workplace
- Assisting all generations as they create personal brands
- Reimagining training to appeal to the different needs in the generations
- Moving forward into a future in which millennials, Gen Zers, and Gen Alphas dominate the workplace

Voices From the Generations

Jessica James, who is a mix of an older millennial and a younger Gen Xer, owns her own successful consulting business. She's raised two Gen Zer children. As a child, she and her Gen X siblings were raised by a boomer mom and a silent generation dad. She says, "The traditional middle-class values of family, faith, and hard work were engrained in everything we did."

Early in James's career, she was motivated to earn several college degrees and shift from an administrative role into a career for which she was more passionate and would provide more for her growing family. "As young parents," she says, "we were always the youngest parents in the room, and we worked really hard to be able to provide for our kids and give them the best life possible. Gratefully, we had a lot of help from our families to help us with kids." As a parent of Gen Zers, she says, "I like how the world is changing. It has a lot of positive aspects to it." She thinks today's Gen Zers have more options than she did at their age. "They have more of a voice and are definitely more vocal. They can stand up for what they believe in a different way than I could," she says.

James recognizes the image of youth that is portrayed through social media to young kids is that "you're supposed to be perfect, lead a perfect life, and pretend everything is perfect. It's a challenge that takes a toll on a kid's mental health." She says it's important to remind kids that "we are human, and everything is not always great—and that's okay!"

While school, education, and allowing kids to find activities are important, she stresses she let her kids take "mental health days when they needed it in high school, and it had a positive impact on their well-being. At the end of the day, they were still kids and sometimes needed that break." Another positive shift in society, especially as a parent that she is happy about, is "this concept that you must go to college directly after high school isn't a priority for all kids anymore. They have the option to find their own niche and pursue something that they are excited about instead."

While talking about a parenting style, she says, "There is a time in life when you make all the decisions, and you lead your children because they are so young and still learning, but as they've gotten older I do believe in having more of a parent–child partnership. It makes the things we do as a family much more enjoyable when we all have a say and get to do something we love together."[30]

Your Real-World Connection

Consider this scenario: A boomer team member has been employed by a company for over two decades, and this team member has almost 40 years of experience working in this field. The newest member of the team is a Gen Zer, who has one year of experience. The two individuals are assigned a project on which they must work together to meet the project's goals, budget, and deadlines.

- The boomer, who has decades of experience, immediately wants to take the lead to guide the project to its completion.
- The Gen Zer offers alternative views and insists on playing the role of co-leader.
- The boomer feels insulted that the Gen Zer is not deferring to the boomer's experience.
- The Gen Zer is insulted that the boomer is not treating the Gen Zer as an equal.

A four-gen leader would resolve this conflict by helping the two team members realize that parts of their reactions are based partly on the different ways they were raised.

- The boomer was raised to accept the views of authority, and authority was usually based on position and age. The boomer would feel he or she has been working in the field and at the company for decades, and this would give the boomer a natural right to lead in this project since the other team member is much younger and new to the field and the company.

- The Gen Zer was raised in a participatory, permissive parenting style, which means the Gen Zer was constantly consulted in decision making, regardless of his or her knowledge or experience with the topic. The Gen Zer was not raised with the same willingness to automatically accept the views of others, simply because of age. In questioning the views of the boomer and wanting to be a co-leader, the Gen Zer is not being disrespectful but is doing what he or she has always done: participate, offer his or her views, and want to be heard and honored.

The next step for the four-gen leader would be to remind each team member of the expertise he or she brings to the project.

- The boomer would be assured his or her vast experience was highly valued and a reason he or she was asked to work on this project. The boomer would, however, be reminded that working on multi-generational projects means all team members must understand each other, and that the Gen Z team member is also valued and has been brought into the company to offer fresh ideas as an active member of the team.

- The Gen Zer would be assured that he or she is a highly valued young employee, and that the views of the boomer should be respected because of their experience and expertise; however, this does not mean that the Gen Zer would always have to agree with the boomer. The Gen Zer should be reminded that he or she was hired to bring fresh views into the company and to help the company stay relevant in today's rapidly evolving world.

An important part of resolving the preceding scenario and bridging the generation gaps would be for the four-gen leader to understand how the generations like to communicate—and how these styles and modes evolved as each generation was growing up. Multi-gen communication will be covered in depth in Chapter 3.

NEXT STEPS

4-GEN *leadership*

HELPING ALL YOUR GENERATIONS THRIVE IN THEIR TEAMS!

How does the way you were raised affect your decision making as a leader and do you need to adjust your perspective to understand other generations?

Do you see any parenting styles influencing the behavior or decision making of your team members?

Boomers?

Gen Xers?

Millennials?

Gen Zers?

Moving forward, what will you do differently as you work with Gen Zers who might have been raised with more of a partnership/participatory parenting style?

Figure 2.2 Chapter 2 next steps worksheet

CHAPTER 3

The Multi-Gen Foundation

Culture, Communication and Coaching

Key Points of This Chapter

1. Culture, communication, and coaching are three intertwined subjects that form a multi-gen foundation for the organization.
2. Being an authentic leader is crucial when communicating, coaching, and creating a unique multi-gen culture.
3. There is a clear difference between managing and coaching employees.
4. Generations respond differently to performance reviews, and generational characteristics should be considered when providing feedback.

While leaders today must understand the generations and what shaped them, a significant step in developing an effective, inclusive team is to also understand three critical, intertwined subjects that form a multi-gen foundation: organizational culture, cross-generational communication, and multi-gen coaching. Think of them as the Critical Three Cs. These three elements are not new; leaders have been working for decades to form a strong culture, strengthen communication, and coach employees to greater productivity. However, the evolution of the four disparate generations has created a need for 4-gen leaders to see that these areas are now tightly linked—one area impacts the others—and are of high priority for success today.

Creating a Vibrant Multi-Gen Culture

To fully understand the multi-gen workplace culture needed today, let's look back at how workplace culture has evolved in the past 75 years. After World War II, office cultures were factory-like. Work was meant to be coldly efficient with managers, usually white males, in charge of the workspace and employees working busily to produce products, memos, or reports. Offices were often large, open spaces filled with rows and rows of identical desks crammed tightly together so that everyone was visible and could supervised.[1] The employees were seen as interchangeable, independent parts. Skill levels were lower; if one worker left, he or she could be quickly replaced by another one. This was the world of the Greatest Generation, the Silent Generation, and the early boomers.

Through the decades, the leaders began to see the benefits of adding more inclusive human elements to work environments, partly because the leaders began to realize content employees were more productive but also to help retain employees in an economy becoming increasingly more skills-oriented. The workplace culture began to evolve as organizations added more women, people of color, diversity in thought and lifestyles, work–life balance, and social-emotional wellness and support. The workplace transitioned from a hierarchal model in which the leader made all the decisions to one in which teams could play a vital role in both day-to-day operations and long-term strategic planning.[2] Then, technology began to make work more efficient and faster, and it has allowed the hybrid workplace to evolve, which has created a new element in forming a positive workplace culture.[3]

Organizational leadership is now transitioning into another iteration, one that includes all the humanistic, inclusive attributes of the previous model but also includes the element of multi-gen awareness, a realization that leaders must blend the generations while effectively leading and coaching individuals in different generations. It's no longer enough to just have a positive culture; now the culture must be multi-generationally harmonious and productive to draw on the strengths of all individuals in an increasingly competitive and shifting business landscape.

Highly skilled workers are in high demand today, and this includes employees of all generations. A positive workplace culture helps with retention. One study found the higher an employee rates the culture, the lower the chances the employee leaves the company.[4] Culture can also increase engagement; a Gallup survey found that "teams with high engagement show 21 percent more significant profitability in comparison to disengaged teams,"[5] which means culture is one of the most important drivers for success and sustainability.

Another new requirement has entered the workplace cultures with the entrance of the younger millennials and the Gen Zers: the necessity for leaders to be sensitive and responsive to the requests and needs of these generations. This concept requires a paradigm shift for leaders. For centuries, the leaders were the rulers of the office. Seventy-five years ago, the Greatest Generation and the Silent Generation would have never consented to share authority with the employees. The leaders were in charge and issued edicts. However, effective 4-gen leaders will remember that the younger workers were raised in more of a partnership parenting model; they grew up being listened to and acting in many ways as partners with their parents. As one study from Deloitte about Gen Zers in the workplace put it, Gen Zers "want to be seen for who they authentically are, heard, supported, and given the space and opportunity to thrive as they develop their personal and professional selves."[6] A good rule for 4-gen leaders is to also apply this concept to younger millennials. If millennials and Gen Zers enter a workplace culture that doesn't give them freedom to express themselves and prevents them from being partners with their leaders, they will feel their leaders are insensitive and not open to understanding who they are or how they see the world.

At the end of each calendar year, Merriam-Webster, the international publisher of dictionaries, chooses a Word of the Year.[7] The firm announced that its Word of the Year in 2023 was *authentic*. People around the world reported that in an age of misinformation found in social media posts and AI-generated responses, they were looking for authentic sources and authentic information. There had been a dramatic increase in 2023 in the number of times *authentic* had been used in online searches.[8] However, another reason this word was so important in 2023 is that *authentic* is a crucial part of multi-gen leadership. All generations want to see authenticity in their leaders, but for the leaders to effectively coach their employees today, especially the millennials and Gen Zers who demand this trait in their managers, they must be viewed as being honest, purpose-driven, and acting in the best interest of all workers.[9] Authenticity will grow in importance: by 2030, millennials and Gen Zers will make up around two-thirds of the American workforce.[10] Four-gen leaders need to add *authenticity* to their list of most important, visible leadership traits.

Different Generations and Different Modes of Communication

Communication is the second critical component of a multi-gen foundation. Effective communication "boosts employee morale, engagement, productivity, and satisfaction .... Ultimately, effective workplace communication helps drive better results for individuals, teams, and organizations."[11]

Unfortunately, communication has always been one of the major generation gaps. For centuries, when older and younger people disagreed on ideas, they had trouble discussing them.[12] These disconnects still exist, but they've been compounded by the different modes the generations prefer to use when they communicate present, and absorb information. Think of how communication has changed since the 1970s. When our senior workers, the boomers, were growing up, they used face-to-face communication, rotary phones mounted on the wall to call each other, and letters and postcards sent through the U.S. mail. If we look to the other end of today's communication spectrum, we'll see our Gen Zers are texting, using video calls on Face Time and WhatsApp, and sending emojis to express their thoughts and feelings.

So, not only do the different generations see the world differently, but they also prefer diverse ways of sharing and discussing what they see. In the past, parents and their children sometimes communicated past each other—today, it might be happening in the workplace. Four-gen leaders need to know the communication modes of each generation so that they can communicate with their team and help the team members in different generations communicate with each other.

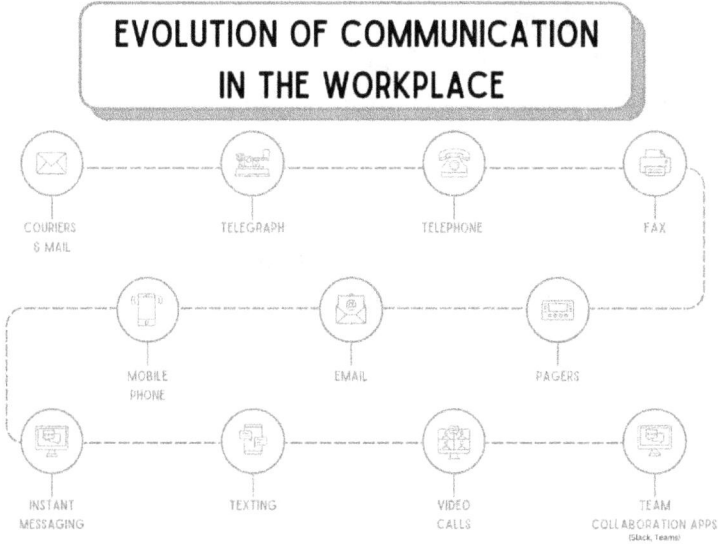

Figure 3.1 Workplace communication has evolved more quickly as technology has become more powerful

Communication by Generation

Boomers grew up in a time when there were not as many communication options. They prefer face-to-face communication, especially when making decisions and setting disagreements. They have, however, adapted to e-mail. They still like paper copies, perhaps more so than other generations. They tend to write longer, content-rich documents, often to the chagrin of the other generations. Their main social media platform is Facebook. They are not as adept at using Instagram or X, and only some of them might be on LinkedIn.[13]

Gen Xers grew up with e-mail, and it is perhaps their favorite way to communicate. Unlike boomers, Gen Xers tend to use technology to manage their lifestyles, such as paying bills online, shopping, and completing education courses. They care more about their personal time than boomers, so they want the communication to be efficient and to the point.[14]

Millennials grew up in a Web-based environment where information could be found online. Social media platforms began to arrive during their formative years, so they tend to adjust quickly to new ways to communicate. Because they grew up surfing the Web, they tend to want their information given to them in shorter, more precise chunks. They are the first generation to be mobile-friendly, meaning they are comfortable getting their information and responding on multiple devices.[15] Skimming and scanning became a common trait for this generation.

Gen Zers are the first true digital natives in that they grew up with cell phones; however, one study recently pointed out 44 percent of Gen Zers believed their formal education had only given them basic computing skills, and 37 percent of them felt their schooling had not given them the technical skills they needed for their careers.[16] Gen Zers like face-to-face communication with colleagues. Forty percent of Gen Zers want daily interaction with their managers. They sometimes struggle with wording and writing style in professional communication, especially online,[17] and they tend not to like making phone calls; 60 percent of Gen Zers report they dread making phone calls and would rather book appointments and make orders through the Internet.[18] Another key point about Gen Zers is that many of them don't like e-mail. For Gen Zers who feel stressed, e-mail is a reminder of deadlines and new tasks. Some think of e-mail as the *eternal chore.*[19] Instead of using e-mail, Gen Zers prefer to share ideas and information through Google Docs.[20]

When leaders and team members don't understand the communication styles preferred by their teammates, they might make several mistakes that make communication less efficient or possibly even contentious. For example, what if a boomer sends a Gen Zer an e-mail filled with long paragraphs when the Gen Zer just wants bulleted points? The boomer won't understand the communication style is wrong for that generation. The Gen Zer would prefer shorter, more precise messages and wouldn't want to be forced to read formal writing conventions such as thesis sentences, transitions, and reiterations. What if the Gen Zer then responds to the boomer with text messages sent to the boomer's phone and uses too much slang? The boomer could think the Gen Zer is being unprofessional and might even feel insulted that the Gen Zer didn't take the time to send a more formal note or continue to use the platform that the discussion was initiated. What if they both decide to continue the discussion, but the boomer wants to have a phone conversation, not realizing Gen Zers are not comfortable with that mode of communication?

> **Do the communication styles between the generations affect your organization's culture and productivity?**

Four-gen leaders will take communication preferences into account when they interact with the different generations, and 4-gen leaders will help all team members understand the preferences of their teammates.

Tips to foster cross-generation communication would be to:

1. Ask team members how they like to communicate.
2. Decide what can be covered online versus what should be covered in person, in meetings, and in one-on-one conversations.[21]
3. Have open discussions with the entire team about their communication styles so that they can do more to understand each other and avoid misunderstandings.
4. Mix the generations on important projects to keep team members from only mingling with their generation (with whom they are most comfortable as they communicate) so that they can hone their cross-generational communication skills.
5. Use a multi-channel approach to distribute information.
6. Adjust the tone of the message based on the generation to which the communication is going.

From Managing to Leading to Coaching

The third critical part of the multi-gen foundation is coaching, which in an earlier format began to be incorporated into developing business leaders in the 1970s and 1980s. Its two main features at that time were focused on tasks and processes, including one-on-one conversations and an emphasis on leadership performance.[22] Coaching in that era didn't involve developing the rank-and-file employees but instead focused on finding ways to help the executives be more productive to increase profits. The individuals being developed were traditional leaders who could act alone and dominate the workspace.

Since that era, think of how the idea of management has changed. The business world has transitioned from using hierarchal decision makers to seeking out and promoting team-oriented, inclusive leaders. As mentioned in Chapter 2, management is out, and leadership is *in* when developing today's employees. Consider some of the most important exemplars sought in today's leaders: *delegation, integrity, empathy, self-awareness, gratitude, courage, respect, communication*, and *learning agility.*[23] While 4-gen leaders must excel in these areas, they must also be adept at understanding how these characteristics can be used to understand and guide the generations in their teams. This generational awareness has created the need for another transition—from the old style of management (in which senior white males issued edicts) to the current style of leadership (in which leaders of different genders, races, cultures, and backgrounds bring a more humanistic view to their roles) to the need to move to 4-gen leadership (in which diverse leaders use these humanistic views but also understand how each generation needs to be developed and coached). One-on-one traditional coaching is still effective for individuals in which they meet periodically with experts to assist them with professional and life goals, but 4-gen leaders must be able to develop all individuals and teams they lead daily. Today, every employee has a voice, and every employee must be, to a certain extent, individually coached.

> **How can you adjust your coaching style to fit the needs of each generation?**

Performance Reviews: Opportunities for Growth or Disaster

Effective 4-gen leaders understand how the critical three Cs (culture, communication, and coaching) come together in an area that has always been a traditional stressor for all generations but has now become an even greater stressor and plays an even larger role in affecting an organization's culture and ultimately, the organization's success: annual evaluations or performance reviews.

All generations want feedback on their work, and they want it delivered in a fair, professional manner. But times, and the generations of team members, have changed. It used to be that a manager could schedule a yearly conference with each employee and sit down for an hour and discuss that employee's progress and future goals—and it wasn't always a discussion but more of a one-sided lecture with the manager telling the employee what needed to be done. Those days are gone forever; even today's boomers, the generation most familiar and most comfortable with the old way of having performance reviews, want to have a two-way conversation with their managers about their work. Another change in "the performance review process has been the shift toward continuous feedback. Rather than conducting evaluations only once or twice per year, many companies now provide employees with regular feedback on their performance, allowing for more timely and actionable information."[24]

Today's 4-gen leaders must be in constant communication with the employees they are supervising and have a variety of communication and coaching options available to match the needs of the four generations.

Boomer Performance Reviews

Boomers like straightforward and honest feedback, and they like to see data and specific examples cited in their reviews. They grew up talking in person and will want to talk in person to their managers. The world is changing rapidly, especially its technology, and boomers often feel left behind. Even though they tend to be extremely loyal to the company and its mission, senior employees have never felt so vulnerable. It used to be that senior employees were the most revered team members because of their vast experience; however, the acceleration in disruptions means some of their experience acquired through prior decades is no longer relevant. All generations of employees are learning new ways of doing things, so the playing field has been somewhat leveled, and if the job has a new digital element, the boomer's world has been turned upside down. It is important for leaders to acknowledge the boomers' seniority when leading performance reviews. For them, the playing field has become unleveled. It's essential for managers to acknowledge their accomplishments and remind them they are still valuable members of the team.[25]

If a boomer's attitude is deteriorating, check the age of the boomer's manager. Is it a young Gen Xer? A millennial? A Gen Zer? That could be part of the problem. Forty-six percent, or almost half, of boomers think millennials feel entitled and lack a solid work ethic,[26] which contributes to the overall challenge of a younger employee managing and older peer. Or, does the boomer's team consist of many millennials and Gen Zers? If the boomer is part of this 46 percent who don't appreciate millennial workers, it could be hindering the boomer's quality of work. The manager could tactfully broach the subject—and then provide training to educate and assist the boomer so the younger employees can be understood and appreciated by the boomer.

Boomers often prefer their feedback in traditional ways, as in the standard yearly performance review. They like to sit down annually in a private place and discuss their progress with their manager. Boomers prefer stability and predictability. A lack of stability or lack of predictability is upsetting to most boomers. To assist them, managers should adhere to an established performance review system and schedule and be sure to keep the boomers informed if the system or schedule is changed.

Gen Xer Performance Reviews

When evaluating Gen Xers, 4-gen leaders should remember they view themselves as independent workers who tend to view their superiors as their equals. Gen Xers want to be shown respect. When coaching Gen Xers, managers are encouraged to speak to them as equals, not subordinates. Gen Xers like to function in teams, and they tend to be less judgmental of other generations; they want to bring out the best in others. A strategy to help them be better is to remind them of their role in the team and what they can do to improve their performance and that of the team.[27] They also tend to view all team members as equally important.[28]

Gen Xers were also the first to advocate for more balance in their jobs and personal lives. Gen Xers will sacrifice for the team, but managers setting goals with them need to remember Gen Xer's enthusiasm for the job, as in time spent in the office, will be tempered by a desire not to be consumed by the job.[29]

Another important element to remember about Gen Xers tended to have their kids later in life, which means now almost half of them have senior parents and are either raising children or have adult children still living at home.[30] If they have become more stressed, distracted, or absent, it could be because they are tending to elderly parents.

Millennial Performance Reviews

A recent survey conducted by a human resource company revealed some startling data about how millennials view their job evaluations.

- 62 percent of them feel blindsided by their performance reviews.
- 74 percent feel in the dark about how their managers view their work before their performance reviews.
- Over 50 percent said that they lacked confidence in their evaluator to properly assess their work.

- Almost 50 percent of them said that their evaluations made them feel like they couldn't do anything right.
- 25 percent have called in sick because of the stress caused by performance reviews.
- 15 percent have cried because of their performance reviews.
- 28 percent have looked for a new job because of their performance reviews.
- 35 percent have complained to coworkers about what was in their performance reviews.[31]

In summary, these data show performance reviews can dramatically and negatively affect a significant number of millennials. What's to be done when millennials feel their managers don't understand what they do and don't trust them to give accurate feedback? Change the approach. Here are tips for approaching Millennial evaluations.

First, millennials require constant feedback, not just the year-end evaluation. They want to have a relationship and be assured of where they stand with their managers. If 62 percent of the millennials feel blindsided by their reviews and 74 percent don't know how they are viewed by their managers, it could be the managers are not communicating frequently enough. The evaluation process should be thought of as a continuing conversation that naturally leads into a formal observation, not a separate task to be performed periodically.

Millennials want to be coached and not just given mandates. What does effective coaching look like? Besides being given constant feedback, the employees must be in a culture that allows them to comfortably respond to their managers. Managers must be open to new ideas offered by the millennials, and the manager must find ways to build confidence in the employees in their ability to do their jobs—and confidence in the evaluation system. Most significantly, and one of the most difficult parts of coaching to achieve, is for the manager to build a relationship so the millennial will take risks and occasionally fail.[32] Growth and confidence come when employees try new things, fail, learn, and then overcome the obstacles to find success.

A critical part of establishing goals is that clearly set goals must be reinforced with effective training and skill building to help the employees achieve their goals established in the performance reviews. One survey found 94 percent of employees across multiple generations exiting a workplace would have remained if the employer had established a better system of training. The same tenets of coaching must be used when implementing training: the millennials, and other generations, must have input and faith in the system and the people implementing the training (covered in Chapter 10).

Gen Zer Performance Reviews

Gen Zers typically seek constant feedback and praise in their jobs, even more so than the millennials and other generations. Managers should make efforts to be in continuous communication that provides feedback. Sixty percent of Gen Zers want weekly check-ins, and 40 percent want daily check-ins.[33] Many managers don't have the time to provide weekly or daily check-ins; perhaps they can find team leaders or mentors to assist with the frequent check-ins.

Gen Zers want to be heard, and they want to know their purpose and be reminded of the company's mission and their part in achieving it. However, when they interact in person with their managers, they want fast conversations. Sixty-seven percent of Gen Zers say they want their check-ins to be five minutes or less. They feel long check-in conversations distract them from their work,[34] which means managers of Gen Zers must balance being in contact without taking up too much of their time. Imagine the frustration of the Gen Zers if they feel their boomer or Gen X managers are out of touch with the Gen Zers, don't value their input, and are not authentic.

Managers should leverage their 4-gen lens and understand Gen Zers have been raised as a vital part of the family unit as individuals who were included in most decision making and were freer to voice their opinions than previous generations. These same traits carry over into the workplace, which means Gen Zers are more inclined to challenge their supervisors.[35] If they question a decision or process (or part of the findings in their performance reviews), it shouldn't necessarily be viewed as disrespectful—it's just the way Gen Zers have always interacted with authority and want clear answers.

When evaluating Gen Zers, managers need to establish relationships, be transparent, and if needed, assist them in transitioning into the professional culture.

Where can you improve the performance review process for all generations?

Voices From the Generations

Connor Inglis is a 31-year-old millennial who has a sales role at a cyber-security firm. He says one of the biggest problems he sees with the different generations is too many people don't understand themselves. He also thinks flexibility is key. "You just have to understand everyone's difference and be willing to change," he says.

While he lives in a high-tech world, he feels fortunate to have grown up in the low-tech world of the early 2000s. "I used to call friends on phones they had at home," he says, "and I played computer games that ran off of floppy disks." He says living through the shift into a digital world has given him insight into how technology has affected people in different generations.

One of the biggest generational gaps he's spotted is in communication.

He knows a Gen Zer who would "die if he called her on the phone" and would much rather text than speak in person. Yet, he knows boomers who are on the other side of the gap "who would rather have a 15 minute conversation than send 50 different texts." Inglis works with an older coworker who still uses pen and paper to take notes, and Inglis realizes that works best for the coworker, so he works to bridge the communication gap. "Pen and paper don't help me, but it helps him be successful, so we meet once a month to debrief."

He's also noticed that "boomers are routine driven." He knows some retired boomers who like to do some of the same tasks at the same time every day. "For years they worked and had guardrails," Inglis says, "but now those guardrails are gone, so they've established new routines." The boomers have in a sense established new guardrails and new comfort zones. They like to know what is happening and when, which is the opposite, according to Inglis, of how millennials like to function. "We don't have routines … millennials like to be outside their comfort zone."

However, Inglis says, "Sometimes millennials change too quickly and fail." He cites several steps for success, including "being tactical while also seeing the big picture." Inglis has a passion for his work and finding solutions for his customers. He says he's not a salesperson; yet, it's clear he's allowed his passion for his work to shape his career, and this allows him to naturally sell his services. Like many other millennials, Inglis is seeking *fulfillment.*

Like other millennials, Inglis wants feedback. He is constantly asking, "How am I doing? What are things I can be better at? This continuous loop of feedback is essential." For Inglis, it's all about *removing barriers.* Inglis has noticed how the generations have different approaches to work. "Loyalty is a thing of the past," he says. "That's gone with millennials. We're not going to sacrifice," for a company.

The type of commitment of the older and younger generations is different. It's "living to work versus working to live," he says. The older generations are focused on the company and the job, but the younger generations are focused on living. "I want to travel … I want to have my time…" Inglis says. At the end of each year, Inglis and his wife ask some deeply reflective questions that show their priorities: "Did we volunteer enough this year? Did we travel enough?"

Inglis has another trait of millennial team members: he expects transparency from leadership. "Transparency is one of the most important things" he says. "The more open leadership can be, the farther they'll get with us." He says it's frustrating when leaders don't let them *see the big picture.* Millennials and Gen Zers don't want to be just a small piece of the corporate machinery quietly working away on a task they don't see as relevant. They need to know how it all fits together and how their task is helping the team be successful.

When asked if any leadership books have influenced him, Inglis cites two books. Both are powerful works written decades apart. The first is *The Go Giver* written by Bob Burg and John David Mann in 2007.[36] The book stresses the importance of putting the interests of other people before your own, which is a central theme of millennials. However, the other book goes way back in time, all the way to 1936 during the era of the Silent Generation: Dale Carnegie's classic leadership book *How to Win Friends and Influence People*,[37] which recommends we prioritize listening, be genuinely interested, and use other self-effacing techniques to build relationships—which are also techniques and traits highly valued by millennials. Inglis's interest in Carnegie's words shows that some leadership traits are eternal and transcend all generations.

Inglis is optimistic about the multi-gen workforces of today and the future. He sees a workforce coming in which Gen Xers, millennials, and Gen Zers all work well together. Inglis has this advice to be successful in a multi-gen workforce today and in the years ahead: "We need to take advice from younger people... Be a good person. Don't be a jerk... Be optimistic. People will continue to work better together. They'll ask, 'Where is their role in the common good?'"[38]

Your Real-World Connection

Consider this scenario: A millennial manager must conduct a performance review for a boomer employee. The millennial manager has been working for the company for two years, and the boomer employee has been working for the company for close to three decades. The boomer is doing an acceptable job, but there are areas in which the boomer can improve. What should the millennial manager do to ensure the boomer feels the review is fair, accurate, and supportive?

Before the formal performance review meeting, the millennial manager:

- Is aware the boomer might not be open to receiving feedback from a millennial.
- Increases the one-on-one interactions with the boomer to provide informal feedback and strengthen the relationship.
  - Makes a point of praising the boomer for the boomer's accomplishments, expertise, and experience.

- o Dignifies the boomer by asking for their ideas for how the boomer can improve, how the manager can improve, and how the company can improve.
- o Ask the boomer if the boomer needs any support in any area, especially with the adoption of new technology.
- Schedule the formal performance review meeting with the boomer through a face-to-face conversation or a phone call.
- Gathers data about the boomer's performance to help the boomer understand and accept the review's findings.

In the formal performance review meeting, the millennial manager:

- Clearly and directly lays out the positive aspects of the review and areas for improvement.
- Gives the boomer some autonomy in next steps, both in continuing the progress cited in the review and in improving in other areas.
- Works with the boomer to establish clear, measurable goals.
- Helps the boomer to understand what progress in meeting the defined objectives will look like by establishing objectives and timelines.
- Discusses a clear schedule for providing the boomer support and feedback in the future.
- Assures the boomer that the boomer is a highly valued member of the team.

After the formal performance review meeting, the millennial manager:

- Conducts regular, scheduled check-ins with the boomer.
- Tries not to make any changes in goals or expectations without including the boomer in the discussion.
- Continues to be clear and direct when praising and critiquing the boomer.

In summary, when dealing with boomers, the millennial manager is aware of how the review might be received and takes proactive steps to alleviate tension and gain their trust. The millennial manager knows boomers like clear, direct feedback, so the millennial manager carefully and concisely tells them in the formal performance review meeting where the boomers are excelling and what needs to be done to improve. Boomers like to be in control, so they are given some autonomy over the improvement plan and are given a clear picture of what is expected, how progress will be measured, and the timeline in which the progress is to be accomplished. After the meeting, the millennial manager continues to check with them regularly. Boomers like structure, so the millennial manager is careful not to adjust any parts of the boomers' individual goals without consulting with them. Throughout the entire process, the boomers are clearly shown how they can be successful and that they are still an integral part of the organization.

NEXT STEPS

4-GEN leadership

HELPING ALL YOUR GENERATIONS
THRIVE IN THEIR TEAMS!

What are the potential challenges that may arise when fostering a multi-
generational culture, and how you might handle these challenges as a 4-gen
leader?

What are some ways you can improve communication between the different
generations in your team, and how will you implement these improvements?

How can you implement a new performance review program that caters to the
unique needs of each generation?

Figure 3.2 Chapter 3 next steps worksheet

CHAPTER 4

Recruiting the Four Generations

Key Points of This Chapter

1. All generations are seeking competitive pay and benefits.
2. Millennials and Gen Zers are seeking additional qualities that emphasize personal growth, wellness, and corporate responsibility.
3. Four-gen leaders should adjust their interview process to fit the needs of each generation.
4. Four-gen leaders need to reflect on their hiring practices to ensure generational biases are not affecting their decisions.

As the world shut down in 2020 because of the COVID-19 pandemic, a significant number of employees around the world, especially Gen Zers and millennials, who grew up seeing rapid changes and adjusting to new ways of doing things, took stock of their lives and decided they wanted to do something else with their careers, and in many cases, with their lives. They decided to change jobs, explore different fields, and chase their passions.[1] This period of corporate history in which tens of millions of Americans changed their career paths has been branded the Great Resignation or the Great Reshuffling.[2] Individuals began resigning from jobs to take new jobs or to reinvent themselves by going into different fields or different roles within the same company—which led to a reshuffling of their lives. Companies adjusted their operations and reinvented themselves to hold onto their employees. This wasn't just a white-collar phenomenon: workers at all levels were part of this transition. Blue-collar and white-collar job fields were equally affected.[3]

In the aftermath of the COVID-19 shutdown and the ensuing Great Resignation and Great Reshuffling, employers struggled to find workers. Generous government stimulus checks allowed workers to stay home, and some of them feared returning to work in environments where they could be more susceptible to catching the virus. A major cause of the labor shortage was that a lot of workers just didn't want to work in the old system anymore. They no longer accepted the corporate culture that demanded long hours, unfulfilling work, and stressful interactions with management.[4] As a McKinsey & Company article stated:

> What we are seeing is a fundamental mismatch between companies' demand for talent and the number of workers willing to supply it. Employers continue to rely on traditional levers to attract and retain people, including compensation, titles, and advancement opportunities. Those factors are important, particularly for a large reservoir of workers we call "traditionalists." However, the COVID-19 pandemic has led more and more people to reevaluate what they want from a job—and from life—which is creating a large pool of active and potential workers who are shunning the traditionalist path.[5]

Some have said the Great Resignation ended in July of 2023 when the jobless rate fell to 2.3 percent, which was the prepandemic rate of February 2020.[6] However, the negative feelings among employees about work and corporate culture have lingered. Some hiring managers are now saying that reinventing company culture (as covered in Chapter 3) is the most important goal of the company, and work/life balance has become the most sought-after trait for employees, even more important than pay and traditional benefits.[7] Companies are being forced to examine their operations, their job titles, and their expectations—and they are looking more closely at the steps they take to effectively recruit talent.

The Old Way of Recruiting Versus the New Way of Recruiting

Before the opening of the new generation gaps, employers could use one interview style and process to hire their new team members. Today, hiring managers need to know the different generations and tailor their approaches to fit the generational wants and needs. When leaders view recruiting issues through a multi-generational lens, the recruiting issues become clearer. It's not just the type of jobs or the change in the culture that matters—reinvention today is also about bridging the new generation gaps to know how to recruit and hire the four generations in the workforce.

When boomers and Gen Xers first entered the job market, managers used the methods that had been in place for decades. A job opening would be posted on a piece of paper on some sort of communal job board, or it might be posted in the jobs section of the newspaper. (For younger readers, it might come as a surprise that people found jobs by reading a hard copy of a newspaper and looking in a special section titled *Jobs!*). The applicant would call the employer, make an appointment, and go into the office for an interview where a manager, often a white, middle-aged male, would describe the job and ask the applicant some questions about the applicant's background knowledge, education, and goals. Then the applicant would ask a few questions, and that would be the extent of the interview.

Times have changed, and generations have changed. Of course, it's still acceptable to ask all generations about their background knowledge, education, and goals. This is still the expectation for many boomer candidates, but candidates of other generations are bringing these expectations and new ones to the hiring process. For over a century, the hiring process has been about finding what the applicant can bring to the company, but the needs of Gen X, millennials, and Gen Zers have turned that concept upside down. In today's hyper-competitive, employee-centered job market, finding what the applicant can bring to the organization is only half the objective. The other half of the objective is for the candidate to learn what the organization can do for the applicant. The hiring managers need to start with *you*, as in letting the applicant know all the things the organization can do for *you*.

> **When interviewing applicants, how do you stress that the organization is dedicated to their personal and professional growth?**

Putting the *You* in Job Postings

The most popular way to find a new job today is through online job boards. According to one recent study, 41 percent of new employees found their jobs through an online job board, around 25 percent found their jobs through networking, and 14 percent found their jobs through social media. The job boards are more popular with women: 44 percent of the women found their jobs through job boards and 33 percent of the men found their jobs through job boards. Sixty-one percent of the applicants thought automatic job alerts were helpful.[8]

But when applicants see job postings, what are they reading? In the 20th century, a job posting might have looked like this:

> *Wanted: Salesman with experience and good work ethic. Hours: 9:00 to 5:00 with an hour for lunch. Call this number to arrange an interview …*

Companies today would have adjusted this job description. First, there might be a paragraph or two about the company's mission and the positive attributes the company is seeking in its employees.

> *Our mission is to bring our knowledge and great customer service to all our customers. Our products are designed to last and enhance the lives of all who buy them. We take pride in our store's appearance and work to give our customers our very best each day. Our team recognizes that keeping small businesses alive and well takes people who value this mission. We are small, yet we have a big dream.*

*Those who lead with passion, ambition, and a love of learning are
those who we want to join our team.*

Note that the company says it values "passion, ambition, and love of
learning," which would fit especially well with the goals of millennials
and Gen Zers.

After the company description would come the bulleted job
requirements. The word *man* in the 20th-century job description, as
in salesman, would be replaced with a gender-neutral term like *associate*,
as in *sales associate*. The goal focuses on a more diverse and inclusive
workforce.

The posting might say "We are looking for someone who has these
talents" and then list:

- *Friendly and engaging*
- *Can prioritize multiple tasks in a fast-paced environment*
- *Verbal communication skills; handles phone calls and face-to-face
  interactions effectively and professionally*
- *The ability to work a flexible schedule based on store needs
  (weekends, nights, holidays)*
- *Detail oriented*
- *Solution seeker*
- *Team player*

While many of these points for a sales associate are timeless (being
a solution seeker, detail-oriented, and flexible), an important addition
is being a *team player*. Employers are recognizing the importance of
inclusion and collaboration, and employees of all generations are putting
more emphasis on the need for professional development.

Consider this transition that has occurred in recruiting: job
descriptions have moved from describing the job in male-centric terms
to describing both the company's mission and the job with more
inclusive language. Companies have gone from being coldly neutral
to being warmer and more inviting. Today, companies want applicants
to know who they are and the values for which they stand. However,
it's time for the next transition in recruiting to occur: companies must

still describe their mission and values, but they must view their job postings through a multi-gen lens. They must also focus on what the organization and the job can do to help the applicant grow and develop personally and professionally. They must lean more heavily into the *You* when recruiting.

Here's an example from Apple, one of the global innovators in redefining job titles, roles, the workplace, and the workspace, and it's a company that values what young employees bring to its workforce.

> *Do you love music? Photography? Fitness? Games? Video? Whatever your passion, bring it. Because sharing what you love through Apple products sparks others to pursue their own passions. And that's why we're continuously reinventing the retail experience: to open up all kinds of potential for our customers—and you...Whether you work up front or backstage, every day you'll have the chance to make a big difference—for your customers, your team, and yourself.[9]*

Note the fun parts of this description: music, fitness, games, and video, helping others pursue passions, reinventing the system, helping *you* reinvent yourself, and making a big difference. Apple has realized something most businesses don't yet comprehend employees, especially Gen Z and millennial employees, need to feel that they matter, that they are developing individuals and not just *cogs* in the corporate machine. As 4-gen leaders create productive teams they need to make sure all team members feel as important as the customer. It's a good philosophy for all.

So, what does Apple do to attract management candidates? Here's one description Apple has used on its website to attract leaders.

> *As an Apple leader, you'll do more than manage employees. You'll help build diverse, highly collaborative teams that deliver the amazing customer experiences people expect from Apple. You'll lead through inspiration, using our culture of open, honest feedback to actively develop each team member's talent and skills. You'll also build relationships with the local community and its businesses, creating an atmosphere where all are welcome.[10]*

This job description uses the pronoun *You*, as in "You'll help build …" and "You'll lead…" Apple is putting the *you* in its sought-after leadership traits.

For decades, professionals have been taught not to use *you* in their writing and to write in the third person, which eliminates *I* and *you*. It feels coldly professional and impersonal—which is the opposite of what most of the generations are seeking today. They want to see the soul of the organization; they want to hear *you*. We live in a less formal world now, which is the crux of switching leadership styles from managing to coaching: a struggle has begun between the professional and personal sides of our identity. The professional side tends to be clinical; the personal side tends to be passionate. It used to be clear what was expected of us as professionals of all ages, but those expectations have blurred with the mixing of the generations in our workforce.

This shift to a less formal leadership and writing style will benefit most employees. The torch has been passed from the formal boomers to the less formal Gen Xers, millennials, and Gen Zers, who will make up almost 80 percent of the American workforce by 2030.[11] This torch should also light the way when recruiting.

> **How can you make your job postings more 4-gen friendly and attract more candidates?**

Essential Interview Topics for Each Generation

While job descriptions have transformed into more positive, humanistic versions, the next step for hiring managers is to bring generational components into the recruiting process, which means they need to understand how to approach each generation.

However, there's some good news for hiring managers as they begin to add more layers to their interview process: a common trait of all generations is that they are still seeking some of the same job qualities sought by previous generations. They all want:

- A safe and pleasant work environment and culture

- Competitive pay
- Health care and wellness benefits
- Retirement plans
- Overall stability in the company and the position

These topics are the building blocks of hiring, but 4-gen leaders need to know the other qualities the generations seek so they can tailor their questions and techniques to the generation of the person being interviewed.

IMPORTANT NOTE: Besides knowing the generations, effective hiring managers also understand and are sensitive to the biases some applicants have faced in their careers based on their gender, skin color, ethnicity, sexual preference, and background. A true 4-gen leader has a well-rounded understanding of how employees have been shaped by a wide range of both positive and negative experiences. They also remember that not all members of a generation fit that generation's characteristics.

Recruiting Boomers

Boomers are the most traditional of the generations when it comes to interviewing. They care about the essential interview topics listed previously, and they will want to know who's in charge, especially of their performance reviews. They will also want to know what kind of feedback they'll get and how often, but boomers tend to be the most independent of the generations and don't need as much feedback as other generations. However, they will want to hear clear expectations of their goals. Hiring managers should mention ways boomers can be recognized for their work, which like other generations, is important to them.[12]

One of the first points to consider when interviewing boomers is they feel they are facing a type of generational discrimination—they feel they are the victims of ageism. They feel some of their younger coworkers, and the corporate leadership, are biased against them because of their age. One study found that 45 percent of boomers feel they have been unfairly stereotyped by today's employers, and many unemployed boomers feel they have been discriminated against because of their age.[13]

Ageism shows up in the attitudes of some managers when hiring boomers. The employers sometimes feel the boomers:

- Are too stuck in their ways and don't want to use modern technology
- Will drive up the cost of the company's health care
- Have negative attitudes
- Don't get along with millennial and Gen Z employees[14]

One study by USA TODAY/LinkedIn found millennials and Gen Zers think boomers should retire so that they can move up the corporate ladder. According to the study, 41 percent of millennials said they're having trouble advancing in their careers because the boomers are waiting longer to retire.[15] They feel these boomers are *bottlenecking* their access to better jobs.[16]

Boomers are bringing a new type of emotional concern into their interviews: a fear of being obsolete. The workplace has become an unstable environment fraught with new obstacles, and boomers need to be reassured they will be valued and given assistance as they are onboarded and settle into their new positions. It should be stressed they will be coached through any new software programs. They need to be told they bring value, are vital for the company, and are being recruited because of the qualities they bring to their positions: experience, leadership, dedication, and credibility. Plus, boomers need to be reminded they provide a highly valued element of diversity in a workforce trending toward millennials and Gen Z.[17] They have been lifelong learners, and they like the idea of being trained in new areas and interacting with different people from different generations. Boomers are well into middle age, so interviewers also should stress the benefits of the company's health care program and wellness initiatives.[18]

Also consider that while boomers might be working longer into their careers, it doesn't mean they all want 40-hour-per-week jobs. Many of them want to work two or three days each week, and many of them like the option of working remotely. One study in 2023 found 40 percent of boomers wanted options in where they work, and they are the least likely to want to work in a shared office.[19] They like the idea of being trained in new areas and interacting with different people from different generations.

Recruiting Gen X

The Gen Xers, wedged between the massive boomer and millennial generations, are in their 40s and 50s and still comprise a significant part of the workforce. They like to stay with organizations for at least five years, and 40 percent of them want to stay with a company for at least seven years.[20]

When recruiting Gen Xers, recruiting managers should remember they are more tech-savvy than boomers, and while they didn't grow up with the Internet like the millennials and Gen Zers, they began their careers as the Internet began to reshape the job market, which means they've spent most of their careers learning and using digital tools.[21] However, the first Gen Xers were in their late 20s when this transition began, which means there could be more of a digital divide between older and younger Gen Xers. One study found that 91 percent of boomers and Gen Xers surveyed felt overwhelmed by new technology, and 26 percent felt overwhelmed several times each week.[22]

Gen Xers were the first generation to request more life balance, meaning they are dedicated to putting in long hours but might not be as willing as the boomers to be consumed by their job. Hiring managers need to also be sensitive to the fact that more Gen Xers are taking care of aging parents—while also raising their kids—which means Gen Xers might be pulled away from the job to tend to different generations in their families.[23]

Hiring managers should remember Gen Xers are strong team players with decades of experience, and this makes them excellent candidates to evolve into mentors for millennials and Gen Zers. They are still saving for retirement, so they are seeking good retirement plans and financial benefits. Some of them are still, after decades of work, paying off student debt, so any sort of loan relief would be beneficial.[24] Salary levels are especially important for this generation because of the financial obligations of a multi-generational home, including helping to pay off the loans of their college-aged children.

Gen Xer's have been in the workforce long enough to know what they are seeking in a job and their career path. While they are not all in leadership positions, they still could be seeking entry into a supervisory role and would like training and assistance in their development. They tend to hear about job openings from colleagues, by looking at the company website, or by searching online platforms like LinkedIn and Indeed. When recruited, they prefer to be contacted via e-mail or by telephone.[25]

Recruiting Millennials

Millennials care a great deal about the quality of people with whom they work, which means hiring managers should stress the core values of the company and its employees.[26] When interviewing millennial applicants, it would help to have the applicant meet the members of the team so they can get to know each other and see if the applicant and team are good mutual fits.

Millennial applicants will want to hear about corporate social responsibility (CSR) or environmental/societal/governance (ESG) initiatives. It's a key part of attracting them to a company: up to 85 percent of millennials think making a positive impact on the world is more important than their professional recognition. Some data indicate women care more about CSR initiatives than men. Millennials want to identify strongly with the organization's brand, so hopefully CSR and ESG are a strong component of the company's mission and image.[27]

Growing as individuals and professionals is important to millennials. Hiring managers should stress the growth opportunities available and if there are incentives for completing growth initiatives.[28] It would help in the interview process to discuss a clear path for the millennials with attainable, measurable goals. Millennials have a strong inclination to use technology, and they need to hear how they will get to use the latest software to stay ahead of the technology curve.[29] It's essential that millennials feel they will be coached in their new job, so hiring managers should stress how they will be coached, who will do the coaching and the frequency of the coaching.

A competitive salary is a necessity to appeal to millennials. Many of them who were just beginning their careers in 2020 were set back by a tough job market because of the pandemic. The older millennials experienced the Great Recession of 2008, and it's estimated 17 percent of them were out of work in 2010.[30] The average college loan debt for millennials, some of whom are now in their 40s, is around U.S.$38,000, and 36 percent of millennials say they can't afford to buy a home because they're still repaying their loans.[31] Millennials and Gen Zers more likely to share salary information with their colleagues; 40 percent of millennials and 42 percent of Gen Zers have shared their salary with at least one coworker or other professional contact. By contrast, only 19 percent of boomers and 31 percent of Gen Xers have shared their salary information. What was once considered inappropriate discussions for older generations is becoming a more common practice among younger ones.[32]

To find their job openings, most millennials rely heavily on personal contacts and sites like LinkedIn, Zip Recruiter, Indeed, and Glassdoor.[33] One study found 48 percent, almost half, of millennials and Gen Zers had applied for jobs they found via social media.[34] Hiring managers need to understand that recruiting through social media brings a diverse applicant pool. Hispanic and Black Americans with work experience are far more likely than their white counterparts to say they have discovered job opportunities on social media (49 percent and 46 percent versus 28 percent). Additionally, Black and Hispanic Americans with work experience are more likely than their white counterparts to say they've used social media to apply for jobs (42 percent and 39 percent versus 21 percent), connect with recruiters and employees at prospective employers (42 percent and 35 percent versus 21 percent), and reach out to peers for job leads (42 percent and 37 percent versus 21 percent).[35]

Recruiting Gen Z

The opening of this chapter mentioned the importance of putting *you* in the recruiting process today, and this is especially important for Gen Z. They need to hear, "Here's what we can do for you...." When recruiting

Gen Z, it must be a very personalized approach, and it begins with face-to-face communication.

- Sixty percent of Gen Zers say their favorite way to find a job is through a personal reference from current or former employees of the company.
- Gen Zers put a high value on face-to-face communication, which means job fairs are important to them because they can sit down and talk with company representatives. Job fairs are twice as meaningful to them as to their older millennial counterparts.
- Gen Zers say the most important factor in choosing a job is the trust they build with their recruiter—which means the recruiter needs to be personable and able to relate to Gen Zers.[36]

Gen Zers are also less patient than older generations when seeking employment, and hiring managers need to speed up the hiring process when recruiting them. Seventeen percent of Gen Zers expect an offer a week after the interview. If the Gen Zer sought by a company is in this 17 percent of the applicants, it means the company needs to move quickly or risk offending or losing the applicant.[37] If a hiring decision will not be made within a week, the hiring manager should be sure to mention the timeline to the candidate, and if the hiring manager is interested in possibly hiring the candidate but no final decision has been made, it would be good to call or text the candidate in the week after the interview and to remain in touch until the decision is made.

The National Society of High School Scholars *2022 Career Interest Survey* (which also polled college students who were Gen Zers) found the three top priorities for Gen Zers when choosing a company are "fair treatment of all employees, quality of life and flexibility, and corporate social responsibility."[38] Consider how radically different these expectations are from the generation's expectations at the other end of the hiring spectrum, the boomers. Boomers would care about these areas, but they would not be at the top of their priorities. Gen Zers are signaling to the corporate world that inclusiveness, balance, and social responsibility are necessities. The study also found only 23 percent think being able to work remotely is important, and 63 percent would rather receive their training in person, not online.[39]

While the company's commitment to these causes might be important to Gen Zers, hiring managers should remember they are also seeking high wages. On an average, their college debt is not as high as it is for millennials, but like the millennials, they want to have money to live the lifestyles of their choice, which means they could be seeking money to use on vacations, housing, graduate-level degrees, advanced electronics, and health/wellness programs.[40] Highlighting growth opportunities and the ability to earn more money over time by gaining more experience and tenure with the organization will help Gen Zers understand what is expected over time to earn higher salaries.

Summary Tips for Hiring Managers

To summarize the topics to be covered in interviews, it's important to note that all generations could care about all the topics in the generational topics chart; however, some generations will place more of an emphasis on certain topics.

TOPICS	BOOMERS	GEN XERS	MILLENNIALS	GEN ZERS
Salary	✓	✓	✓	✓
Health Care	✓	✓	✓	✓
Paid Time Off/Vacation	✓	✓	✓	✓
Flexible Hours	✓	✓	✓	✓
Retirement Benefits	✓	✓	✓	✓
Opportunities for Promotions		✓	✓	✓
Professional Growth Programs		✓	✓	✓
College Loan Reimbursement		✓	✓	✓
Latest Technology			✓	✓
Wellness Initiatives			✓	✓
Transparency in Leaders			✓	✓
Diversity			✓	✓
Inclusivity			✓	✓
Equity			✓	✓
Civic Responsibility			✓	✓
Mentoring/Coaching			✓	✓

Figure 4.1 The generations are seeking some of the same benefits in their jobs, but the millennials and Gen Zers have additonal demands

Avoiding Generational Recruiting and Hiring Biases

Hiring managers have always had to overcome biases in hiring, some of which include seeking job candidates who:

- Are similar in background, interest, and race to the hiring manager
- Are of the same gender as the hiring manager
- Are able to confirm the hiring manager's pre-existing beliefs on key issues[41]

Other biases could negatively affect a hiring decision, like how an applicant looks if the applicant has an accent, or where the applicant went to school.

Effective 4-gen leaders should also be aware of a new sort of bias in their hiring: a generational bias (covered more extensively in Chapter 5). How they view the applicant's generation could affect how they view the applicant. Here are some steps 4-gen leaders can take to ensure hiring biases are removed from the recruiting and hiring process.

1. Examine the recruiting and hiring process to ensure that people of all ages are encouraged to apply for positions within the company. This includes not asking for birth dates or graduation dates on applications and focusing instead on the applicant's skill set.
2. Ensure the company website includes photos of all generations of employees.
3. Use age-diverse and culturally diverse interview committees.
4. Employ structured interviews that ensure all applicants have the same questions and opportunities to display their qualifications.
5. Track the types of new hires to ensure that all generations are being considered and hired.
6. Reflect constantly on hiring practices to ensure generational biases are not affecting who is hired or not hired[42].

Ultimately, it's not the age that matters. Four-gen leaders know hiring should be about skillsets and blending the generations into effective teams.

Do your company's job postings have any generational biases?

Voices From the Generations

Perry Fitzgerald is a Gen Xer and an executive for Hansen Lighting in Utah. He leads a multi-generational team, and he understands the need to recruit and retain outstanding team members. Fitzgerald has noticed a change in younger employees: as a group, too many of them have weak attendance or "show up dressed like they don't care." Around 50 percent of the people who show up for interviews don't dress appropriately. In the interview, he says you can "learn about their basics, but not their personality" so he's adjusted his interviewing techniques to learn more about their mindset to find the right fit. He asks questions like, "What matters to you? Who raised you to be a hard worker?" A key foundation in his field is to have a good background in technology, so Fitzgerald's company has hired a large number of millennials and "they are amazing!"

He wants his team to know he cares about them, so he regularly, proactively asks questions like, "What can we do to make you happier?" Fitzgerald says people of all generations who take pride in their work are more likely to stay with an organization, so one of his ways to build pride is to compliment his employees when they are successful. When he sees high-quality results, he makes it a point to tell them, "That was awesome!...Wow!" or "Thank you!" He realized several years ago a key part of recruiting and retaining employees was to rethink the meaning of the breakroom, so the company started to stock the room with free snacks. Now the break room is a community area where people can hang out, mingle, build relationships, and become a stronger team.

Fitzgerald wants to build people up, train them, and put them in a position to be successful. He believes in putting *aces in their places*. He values the unique skills and views of each team member, and

StrengthsFinder has been a tool in helping him understand his multi-generational team. During a reorganization several years ago, he stressed the need for improved interpersonal communication, a goal needed in many multi-generational teams, so that all the talents could be utilized. He doesn't believe in preaching to his team about improvement instead, he believes he as a leader has to lead through action, to *be the change*. He stresses *a goal mind* is better than *a gold mind*. Fitzgerald has realized a key point about how all generations view change: they are much more accepting of it when they see it is needed and it is viewed as a positive change. There are too many times when leaders don't take the time to explain why something is changing, or why a new procedure is being put into place to improve results.

Ultimately successful recruiting and retaining have always been about attracting and holding onto the right people, but Fitzgerald shows us that in recruiting and retaining today, a new tool is needed: a multi-generational leadership lens that understands, hires, motivates, and trains the right people across the generations.[43]

Your Real-World Connection

Consider this scenario: A Gen X vice president conducts a study of the organization and discovers most of the employees are Gen Xers and millennials. The Gen X vice president is seeking more generational diversity, so the Gen X vice president has a meeting with the Gen X personnel director and two senior-level hiring managers, one of whom is also a Gen Xer and the other one is a millennial. They tell the Gen X vice president that they have been interviewing highly qualified boomer and Gen Z candidates and making them job offers, but the boomers and Gen Zers are not accepting the positions.

The Gen X vice president tasks the personnel director and hiring managers with studying how to get more highly qualified boomer and Gen Z applicants to accept their job offers. The Gen X vice president instructs them to report back to her within a week of the steps they and the rest of the organization can take to recruit and hire a larger number of qualified members of these generations.

When the personnel director and hiring managers meet the next day to discuss the problem, they think about the conversations they've had with some of the boomer and Gen Z candidates and other feedback they've gotten from candidates who have rejected their job offers. They conclude the candidates acknowledged the pay was competitive, and the benefits, which included health care, paid time off, and retirement, were also good. The candidates cited other reasons for not taking the jobs. The three of them make a list of the comments they heard from the boomer and Gen Z candidates.

Boomer Comments

- "I don't know if your organization would be a good fit for me."
- "I'd be a little nervous about all the new software I'd need to learn."
- "I've never had to report to a millennial supervisor before."
- "I'd still have some questions about my responsibilities and exactly what you'd want done."
- "I don't know if I want to work in an office every day. I'd prefer more hybrid opportunities."

Gen Zer Comments

- "I'd be concerned about the stress of this position."
- "I'd like to know my company is dedicated to using the latest software and technology to be efficient."
- "I want to work in a place where my voice is heard."
- "I need opportunities to keep growing."
- "I want face-to-face interaction with my manager."

Solutions

The personnel director and the hiring managers report to the vice president the next week and make these recommendations for their interviewing and hiring process.

Recommended changes when interviewing boomers:

- To help the boomers feel like a good fit for the organization, they will stress the organization's desire to plug their experience into its structure and culture. Also, they will stress how the boomers will make many new friends in different generations and will be working with a wide range of people, which are things boomers like to do.
- To assist the boomers with technology concerns, they will stress that they will be mentored when learning new software and how to use new devices, and they assure them they will be patient as they get up to speed on using all technology.
- To help the boomers get comfortable with reporting to a younger supervisor, they will include the supervisor in the interview process so the boomers can get to know the supervisor. They recommend the millennial be the person to give the boomers the tour of the facility so the millennials and boomers could have some time to chat privately.
- To alleviate concerns or confusion about responsibilities and goals for the boomers, the hiring managers will be sure to clearly state the job description, what it looks like to be successful in the job, how timelines are implemented, and to whom the boomers can turn if there are questions or concerns.
- To help boomers who desire some days to work from away, they will stress that some days each week are reserved for hybrid work. (If the company doesn't do hybrid workdays, the hiring managers could be sure to show them the workplace and introduce them to coworkers to try to help them get comfortable in the space.)
- To help the boomers connect with other boomers, the hiring team will include current boomer team members in the hiring process.

Recommended changes when interviewing Gen Zers:

- To stress how they value diversity, the hiring team will be diverse, and it will give examples of how diversity and inclusivity have helped the organizations to thrive.

- To show its understanding of work/life balance, the hiring team will give examples of how the organization has provided time for team members to unplug and seek out their passions. Examples could include how the organization recommends sending and receiving e-mails only during working hours, providing a reasonable workload, and how the organization is setting a clear limit on the number of hours to be worked each week.

- To help with stress management, the hiring team will affirm to the Gen Zers that the organization recognizes its importance and has initiatives in place to assist employees. (If stress management initiatives are not yet in place, this could be the catalyst for implementing them.)

- To allay the Gen Zers' concerns about using outdated technology, the hiring team will be sure to mention the latest upgrades in software and technology used by the employees, and they will stress how the technology is used to be more efficient.

- To assure the Gen Zers that they have a voice in the company, the hiring team will have current Gen Z employees on the team. During the interview, it will ask for the candidates' opinions about technology, hybrid work, and other topics. The hiring team will give examples of how young employees have helped implement changes and improvements in the organization.

- To help the Gen Zers know how they will grow professionally, the hiring team will discuss some of the training initiatives underway in the company and give examples of the training and how it is delivered and its impact.

- To assure the Gen Zers that they will get face-to-face coaching and feedback, the hiring team will mention how the coaching and feedback are structured, and that they will occur frequently. As with the boomers, it would be good to have the supervisor be an active part of the hiring process so that the Gen Zers can begin to build a trusting relationship with the manager, which is a critical piece for Gen Zers.

Because Gen Zers rely heavily on the word of other Gen Zers, especially Gen Zers they know, Gen Zers currently in the organization will play active roles in recruiting other Gen Zers into the organization.

NEXT STEPS

4-GEN leadership

HELPING ALL YOUR GENERATIONS THRIVE IN THEIR TEAMS!

How do the values and expectations of each generation influence their approach to work and career choices, and how can you include this thinking in your job postings, interview process, and recruiting strategies?

What processes can you create to ensure future job postings are bias-free and recruit from a multi-generational talent pool?

How can you adjust your overall recruitment strategy to hire a generationally diverse workforce, and what multi-gen leadership traits need to be embedded into the recruitment process to ensure the organization remains generationally diverse?

Figure 4.2 Chapter 4 next steps worksheet

CHAPTER 5

Retaining the Four Generations

Key Points of This Chapter

1. Four-gen leaders need to help shape the overall employee experience in the organization.
2. Three new areas of concern for all workers, especially for millennials and Gen Zers, are hybrid work, establishing a work/life balance, and finding affordable daycare.
3. To retain millennials and Gen Zers, they must be allowed to play active roles in the organization.
4. Retention today requires a more personalized approach to the individuals of each generation.

Four-gen leaders do more than adjust their hiring practices to fit the needs of the generations; they also use their multi-gen lens to retain the generations. Four-gen leaders need to continue to offer the key benefits the different generations were seeking when they accepted the position: competitive salaries, affordable health care, paid time off, flexible hours, and good retirement and wellness benefits. Leaders must also understand the other new factors affecting employee retention—many of which have entered the conversation with new generation gaps.

A key step to retaining employees is for 4-gen leaders to embrace the evolving concept of the *employee experience*, also known as EX. The employee experience can be defined as everything the employees does, learns, sees, and feels while at the company. It's the summation of all the employee experiences in the organization. The EX will determine if the employee says, "I have a great job!" or if the employee says "I don't like it here!" and leaves.[1] To fully grasp the impact of the EX, it should be viewed through a multi-generational lens.

A Pew Research Center study in 2022 found the three top reasons employees leave companies are low pay, a lack of opportunity for advancement, and a lack of respect by management. Almost half of the people who quit their jobs also cited child care issues, a lack of flexibility in their work hours, a need for better health care coverage, and more paid time off.[2]

Consider how these reasons pertain to the generations.

- The top three reasons for leaving a company are issues around pay, advancement, and respect. This has been for decades for multiple generations and is relevant today for employees of all generations.
- The next three reasons for leaving a company—issues around flexibility in work hours, child care complexities, and wanting more paid time off—would be of particular importance to millennials and Gen Zers.

In summary, everyone wants good pay, a chance for advancement, and respect. These are universal job traits that won't diminish in importance in the immediate future. But child care, flexible hours, and more paid time off are relatively new job demands. They have seeped into the workforce as people began to take a closer look at their work and life balance. Gen Xers were the first to question the toll that work could take on their lives, millennials began to request more work/life balance, but Gen Zers now *demand* it.

To complicate things even more, in the post-COVID-19 2020s a new EX wrinkle emerged in the work landscape: remote and hybrid work. Companies are now balancing their need for employees to work in the office with the employee requests, or demands, to be allowed to work from home. Overall, the job landscape for managers has morphed into a more complex and competitive area where it is becoming increasingly more difficult to find highly qualified employees and almost as difficult to retain them.

The Great Resignation and the Need to Retain Employees

We can't look at ways of retaining employees in the 2020s without initially acknowledging how the shifting priorities of generations and the aftermath of the global pandemic brought about one of the greatest churns in the history of the U.S. labor market: the Great Resignation. Let's look at the Great Resignation through a multi-gen lens to see what it means to retain employees.

First, let's take a historical perspective. Some analysts believe the Great Resignation didn't begin with the COVID-19 lockdowns, but that it was a continuation of what began many years earlier. In 2009, a little over 20 million Americans quit their jobs. That number rose steadily every year until 2019, the final year before COVID-19, when a little over 40 million Americans quit their jobs.[3] This means the number of Americans quitting their jobs doubled within a decade. Looking at these numbers through a multi-gen lens; we can see these years as pivotal years for millennials and Gen Zers: They are years when these two generations were entering the workforce.

When the Great Resignation began, it was primarily led by the millennials and Gen Zers[4] who had less experience, less seniority, were less invested in their positions, were more mobile in their lifestyles, and tended to have fewer financial obligations than older workers; thus, they could more readily move to other positions, companies, and industries. Being the newest workers in the lowest positions, they were particularly vulnerable to layoffs and unemployment. The staffing issue became compounded when the economy reopened and employers had trouble filling jobs, which meant many of the employees who had stayed in their jobs were working in short-staffed environments, which exacerbated their stress. Millennials and Gen Zers saw their peers, and sometimes their managers, quitting, which made it more likely that they, too, would quit. When workers weigh whether to jump jobs, they don't just assess their own pay, benefits, and career development. They look around and take note of how friends feel about the team culture. When one employee leaves, the departure signals to others that it might be time to take stock of their options, what researchers call "'turnover contagion.'"[5]

The *quit rate* reached its highest level in 20 years in November of 2021 after the COVID-19 lockdowns.[6] One study at the end of 2021 predicted 70 percent of millennials and Gen Zers would consider leaving their jobs in 2022.[7] In 2022, over 50 million workers of all generations quit their jobs, which broke the record set in 2021.[8]

The majority of those who quit in 2022 were in the 18 to 29 age group.[9] A Gen Zer summed up the feelings of her peers when she said, "We don't owe any big businesses anything ..." as she quit her job in a large department store to take a job at her university alma mater where she could be mentored and give back to the community.[10] She summed up the sentiments of many Gen Zers who won't work for a company without having a clear picture of how they will benefit from the employment. Another study found millennials and Gen Zers felt they weren't learning new skills, and either had too much to do or not enough to do. In essence, they were bored.[11] So, they are turning their backs on many of the traditional corporate norms and seeking better lives. As put by another Gen Zer: "This is a revolution, not a resignation."[12]

Something else to know about Gen Zers, according to Karin Kimbrough, chief economist at LinkedIn, is that they are in "an experimental phase where they're still figuring out what they want out of a job .... But they're more passionate about finding a job that aligns with their values, and they're confident that switching jobs will help them get there."[13] If they don't see the purpose and how they can grow, contribute to a cause, and advance in their careers, they will be more likely to leave, which has led to some pundits giving them the moniker *Generation Quit*.[14] Some managers, especially boomers and Gen Xers, have complained that Gen Zers lack a proper work ethic. Gen Zers would counter that they have a strong work ethic, but that they need to be engaged to work their hardest. Employee engagement is essential for an organization to thrive; it's estimated a lack of employee engagement costs the global economy U.S.$8.8 trillion annually.[15] Gen Zers, and perhaps the younger millennials, would not see the Great Resignation as a time of quitting but more as a time of adjustment, a period some people refer to as the Great Reflection.[16]

What will the long-term impact of the Great Resignation (or Great Reflection) and new, remote and hybrid work environments be on Gen Z? One professor of sociology has some deep concerns for our youngest generation of workers. "What's really important here is that young adults are not getting the socialization to workplace norms, and they're also not getting mentoring," said Pamela Aronson, a professor of sociology and an affiliate of women's and gender studies at the University of Michigan-Dearborn. "There's so many more disruptions, and there's so much less of a sense that this is a place I want to be for a long time."[17]

Four-gen leaders should realize it's not just Gen Z and millennials who are quitting. While the younger workers might have led the way at the start of the movement, the Great Resignation has reached into Gen X. A survey in 2022 found that Gen Xers in knowledge fields like high tech and finance have also begun to leave their jobs in search of jobs with more flexibility and just as significantly, more meaning.[18]

What about the boomers? They are at the far end of the Great Resignation spectrum, but they, too, have been affected. Prior to the pandemic in 2020, one in eight boomers left jobs each year, but that number had gone up to one in three by April of 2020. Some left voluntarily for other jobs, and some were forced into retirement.[19]

> **What are some of the reasons cited by individuals who leave your organization to work elsewhere?**

A New Driver: Hybrid Work

As previously mentioned, one of the new elements affecting retention is the concept of creating a hybrid work environment. It is a recognition by companies that one size in the workplace doesn't fit all employees, and the option of working remotely has become critical for many workers today. A study by the *Harvard Business Review* found that 94 percent of the professionals surveyed worked at least 50 hours each week, and half of that group said they worked more than 65 hours each week,[20] With these sorts of hours, it's no surprise that employees of all generations, especially the younger ones with their desire for more work and life balance, would demand more flexibility in when and where they work. They want more control.

Hybrid work often manifests in three models.

- Everyone in the company works in the office on the same days and from home on the same days. For example, the entire staff could be in the building on Monday through Thursday, and everyone works from home on Friday.
- Some employees work onsite every day, and other employees work remotely every day.
- A mixture of the first two models could be used, depending on the company, its mission, and the ebb and flow of its work.[21]

The Gallup organization released survey data in 2022 that listed reasons why employees like the hybrid model. The most often cited reason is an improvement in work/life balance, followed by more efficient use of time, freedom to choose when and where the work takes place, less burnout and fatigue, and higher productivity.[22] It's estimated that 18 percent of the U.S. workforce worked in a hybrid model in 2023, which is up by one percentage point over 17 percent in 2022.[23] When looking at hybrid work through a multi-generational lens, we can see these five reasons could resonate with all generations today. Half of these employees have said they would seek other employment if they were forced to return to the office full time.[24]

When boomers entered the job market in the 1960s, 1970s, and 1980s, they were taught work should be done in an office. However, that attitude has dissipated for many reasons. A study released in 2023 found that 40 percent of boomers and 32 percent of Gen Xers preferred working at home or in different locations.[25] Hybrid work is popular with millennials and Gen Zers; research shows it is a top priority for them.[26] Their preferred model is one in which they work remotely with occasional trips at times of their choosing to an office or workplace so they can meet or mingle with colleagues, and a slightly less popular choice would be working for an organization when the employer has set requirements of how often and when they are to report to the workplace.[27] However, most millennials and Gen Zers feel it is important to have some sort of structure for reporting to a workplace; only 20 percent would want a fully remote job in which they never have in-person dialogue and collaboration.[28]

There are other reasons hybrid work is important for the younger generations; hybrid work allows millennials and Gen Zers, who make up the vast majority of working parents with young children, more child care options because the parents can be home on some days to watch their children or more easily get them to and from daycare and school.[29] Also, over half of millennials and Gen Zers say hybrid work is a positive for their mental health.[30] They actively seek ways to manage their stress, so a hybrid work environment in which they have more control of their setting could be of particular importance.

> As a 4-gen leader, are there ways you can accommodate a hybrid work environment for all generations?

Helping Employees Find Balance Between Their Careers and Their Lives

As 4-gen leaders work to retain their employees in all generations, they should establish a culture that promotes high productivity *and* work/life balance. A study in 2022 found workers valued balance over salary, which is a switch from the results of a prepandemic study in 2019 in which salary was more important.[31] American workers, however, are having trouble finding balance; 60 percent of them feel too much time and energy is given to their jobs.[32] Perhaps there's no other area where generational characteristics can be so evident.

Boomers are known for their work ethic. They grew up hearing tales of the Great Depression from their parents, so for most of their careers, balance was not as important as survival.[33] However, as boomers have begun to work more years and take stock of their lives after the global pandemic, they began to make a shift away from feeling their compulsion to work long hours each week. By the end of 2021, around 50 percent of boomers had retired, and 79 percent of boomers "would prefer to semi-retire rather than fully retire, citing unsustainable savings as their reason."[34] So, boomers will still work long, steady blocks of hours, but like the other generations, they are looking for more periods to step away from their jobs.

Gen Xers grew up watching their boomer parents work long hours, and they saw the resulting strain often put on their families. As adults, Gen Xers were the first generation to embrace flexibility and to use technology to be more efficient, which gave them more time for their personal lives. They also were the first generation to take a holistic approach to their well-being; they wanted to balance their climb up the corporate ladder with their desire to *maintain good mental and physical health*.[35] When helping Gen Xers, leaders need to remember Gen Xers are the *sandwich generation* because they are sandwiched between their boomer parents and millennial/Gen Z children—and they will need time away from their careers because they are sometimes caring for their parents and children in these generations.[36]

A study in 2022 found "just 14 percent of millennials agreed that work should always come first." They range in age from the late 20s to early 40s and have reached a period in their lives when they might feel torn between the need to cultivate a fulfilling career and start a traditional family.[37] Four-gen leaders can help them balance these two priorities in several ways:

- Establish a more flexible work environment that allows them to do some of their work remotely.
- Leverage the latest technology that embraces the ability to work remotely while also being highly productive and communicative with folks in the physical office.
- Align the corporate values with millennial personal values and encourage the employees to altruistically give back to the community and society.
- Provide onsite wellness opportunities and a holistic approach to health with digital access to programs that allow millennials to structure their entire lives in healthy ways.

- Almost half of millennials have children, so companies can assist with day care, family health care, and education funding.[38]

When helping Gen Zers find balance, leaders should remember Gen Zers do not believe working from home is the only way to have a balanced life. While they seek flexibility in their work environments, Gen Zers also seek face-to-face interactions, collaborative environments, and human connections found in traditional workplaces. Their goal is "to create a harmonious work-life balance, where work enhances their lives instead of consuming them."[39] Gen Zers want a mutually beneficial relationship with their employers.[40] For 4-gen leaders, this means they need to adjust their view of this manager/employee relationship; the older managers are still in charge, but the Gen Zers want more input into decision making and finding ways to structure their roles so that they can reduce stress and live the lives they desire. They want a strong emphasis placed on mental and emotional health; they are the first generation to refuse to accept high levels of workplace stress. Fulfillment for Gen Zers lies beyond their careers—they are seeking ways to integrate and balance their careers, personal lives, and dreams.[41]

One way of promoting work/life balance for all generations is to help employees limit the time they spend reading e-mails. A study in 2023 found 57 percent of Americans feel they are addicted to their smartphones, some of whom are checking their phones on average 144 times per day.[42] They might check their e-mails at the dinner table, as they crawl into bed, in the middle of the night, and before they get out of bed in the morning.[43] Some companies are trying to help their employees unplug from their e-mails by implementing blackout periods and guaranteeing time away from e-mail and the computer.[44] This could be particularly important for many Gen Zers who, as mentioned in Chapter 2, detest e-mail.

More employees are seeking wellness programs from their employers. It's an effective way to tap into the sought-after balance of work and career. A survey in the UK in 2022 found 89 percent of Gen Zers would quit their jobs if the company was not focused on well-being.[45] One of the most prominent aspects of a wellness program, both mental and physical, is to stress the importance of physical fitness and to make it a valued part of the corporate culture. Studies show that employees who weave physical activity into their jobs are more alert and more productive.[46] Leaders need to allow and encourage employees to work out, take a walk, or stretch during the workday, either by giving employees physical fitness time away from the job or by providing alternative options to workout facilities or memberships to private gyms. Physical activity also helps reduce "anxiety, depression, and negative mood"[47] and helps alleviate low self-esteem and withdrawal.[48]

Effective wellness programs do more than focus on the most obvious elements of emotional, mental, and physical health; they take a whole-person approach and incorporate elements that lead to an overall positive, affirming culture. Some of these elements could include the following:

- Financial education that helps employees eradicate debt and plan for long-term saving and retirement, which are often cited as areas of concern for millennials and Gen Zers
- A culture that consistently celebrates employee successes and promotes self-starting and workplace agility
- Collaborative workspaces that are designed to foster comradery and group brainstorming in a judgment-free environment
- Access on the job and away from the job to de-stressing activities like yoga, tai chi, and meditation that can be offered on a regular, daily basis[49]

Leaders need to understand that rested employees are better employees—and they're more likely to remain with a company. Employees should be granted paid time off (PTO), and they should be encouraged to take it. The Workforce Institute reports that up to 55 percent of American workers don't use their paid vacation time, and this adds up to 768 million unused vacation days. Employers who offer PTO and encourage their workers to use it see 6 to 8 percent fewer unscheduled leave days. Fifty-eight percent of employers say offering PTO helps them attract better talent.[50] While PTO is important for all generations, it's especially important for younger employees who want to be sure to have the time to do other things that are of high priority in their personal lives. For them, it should be part of the company's purpose and a commitment from leaders that empowers employees to explore their passions in their personal time.

An important and often overlooked aspect of promoting work/life balance and PTO is the modeling provided by the managers. Are they finding a balance between their own work and careers? Are they taking their PTO, or are they constantly working long hours and sending e-mails outside of business hours? Team members notice when their leaders are constantly working extended hours and sending midnight e-mails, and the team members often will think that's the expectation for their schedules. Effective leaders help to set the tone and culture of the workplace. Finding balance and taking PTO helps leaders to recharge, which enhances their own health and productivity, and it sends an important message to their teams: it's okay to step away.[51] To self-check their own balance and productivity, managers can ask themselves five questions:

1. At the end of the day, am I able to disengage from work?
2. While working, am I able to give my tasks my full attention?
3. Do I need to set more breaks and find PTO in my own schedule?
4. Are there any tasks or responsibilities I can delegate to others, especially to team members who might want to grow in new areas?
5. Am I setting a positive model for my employees in the hours I work and the efforts I'm making to find my own balance?[52]

Here's a fundamental shift that 4-gen leaders will have made over traditional leadership: they are leading in areas the traditional managers used to ignore or disdain. Traditional leaders would have wanted their employees to be overly attentive to their roles, checking their e-mail 24/7, not stepping away to exercise, spending their entire day on company tasks, and not taking all their vacation days. Four-gen leaders are enlightened leaders—they know the employees will be happier and more productive when they are given these options.

THE EVOLUTION
OF WORK

PAST   FUTURE

PAST	FUTURE
HIERARCHY	FLATTENED STRUCTURE
FIXED WORKING HOURS	FLEXIBLE WORKING HOURS
COMMAND & CONTROL LEADERSHIP	ENGAGING, EMPOWERING & INSPIRING LEANDERSHIP
CORPORATE LADDER	CREATE THE LADDER
SILOED & FRAGMENTED COMPANY	CONNECTED & ENGAGED COMPANY
WORK AT OFFICE	WORK FROM ANYWHERE

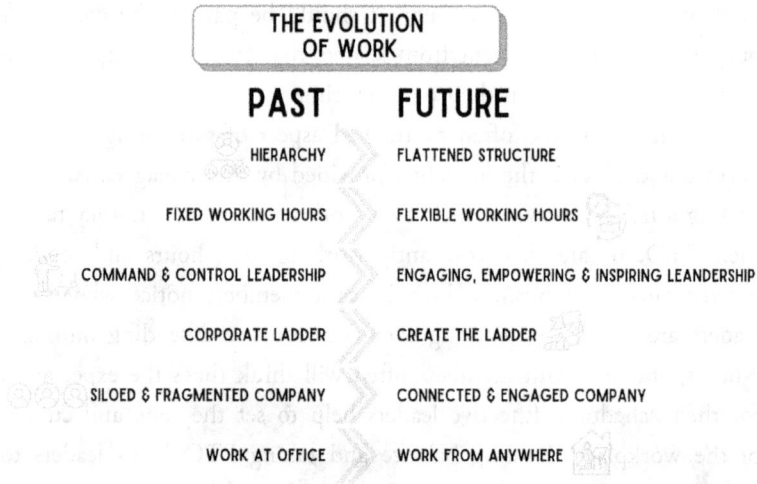

Figure 5.1 Work has evolved in many areas in the past two decades

A Growing Urgency for Childcare

For centuries, the mother was expected to remain at home and be the primary caregiver. However, that lifestyle began to shift with the late Silent Generation and early boomers as more mothers began to seek employment; the result was that Gen X became the first latchkey generation. Their mothers were no longer waiting for them when they got home; instead, they had to let themselves into their houses and wait for their parents to get home from work. While the need to care for young children keeps many women out of the workforce today, over 60 percent of women with young children—most of the parents are Millennials and Gen Zers—work outside the home.[53] This desire and need to work, combined with the high cost of childcare, make corporate-provided childcare or childcare allowances a priority and a prime reason for joining and staying with a company.

Childcare issues cause 45 percent of mothers to leave their jobs, and 24 percent of mothers with children under age five have considered reducing their hours or moving to a part-time job. Childcare factors considered by the parents are affordability, quality, reliability, convenience, and accessibility.[54] Finding these attributes in a childcare provider is both stressful and expensive for parents. One study of 2000 parents in 2021 found two-thirds of them would consider switching jobs to a company with childcare benefits.[55] These benefits can be offered in various formats.

- Companies can partner with established childcare companies to offer childcare onsite or remotely.
- The company can run its own independent childcare center.
- The company can offer a childcare allowance that parents can use completely or partially to fund childcare.
- The company can offer resources to help parents find childcare.
- The company can offer backup childcare for last-minute emergencies.[56]

Some companies that have onsite childcare even allow time during the day for parents to pop in to see their children.[57]

The U.S. government in 2023 recognized the importance of childcare by making it a requirement for some companies doing business with the government. These firms who receive federal contracts must provide access to affordable, high-quality childcare. The format is not defined, leaving it up to the company to find its own solution.[58]

Currently, only 6 percent of employers offer company-provided childcare. It is expensive and there is a fear of liability among corporate leadership.[59] However, one survey found 81 percent of millennial and Gen Z parents consider it an important issue and 72 percent of them said barriers to finding appropriate, affordable childcare for their kids would be a significant obstacle to achieving their professional goals. Employers should also note that having access to quality childcare is important for employees in almost all groups: gender, race/ethnicity, and political affiliation. Even employees without children recognize its importance: 76 percent of them say it's important for their peers.[60]

How would childcare benefits impact your retention strategy and how can you make small changes to support it?

Involving Millennials and Gen Zers at Every Level

An essential new component of retention of millennial and Gen Z employees is this simple idea: *involve them.* As mentioned in Chapter 2, younger millennials and Gen Zers have been raised in a parenting model that allowed them to be more like partners in the parent/child relationship. Thus, they are used to be a part of decision-making and influencing outcomes. They want to have this same impact when they join companies, and they will become frustrated when they feel they are being overlooked. Four-gen leaders can help retain millennials and Gen Zers by finding ways to include them in every level of the organization by plugging them in through a variety of ways.[61]

- They can support the interview process by screening the candidates for new hires on their team even if it is a more senior position.
- They can serve as reverse mentors by leveraging younger employees to mentor older employees in certain areas.
- They can help design training programs for all employees, especially in the new hire process.
- They can represent younger generations on advisory boards or play a role in shadow boards.
- They can run their own committees or focus groups to improve current workplace programs.
- They can assist with the design and implementation of advocacy programs.[62]

Involving young, less experienced workers in decision-making and focus groups runs counter to how many organizations have traditionally been run. Team members in the past gave input and had their voices heard only after they had earned experience, had been officially recognized for their work, and had risen through the ranks. If companies today wait for younger millennials and Gen Zers to follow this traditional path, these employees will be more likely to leave in search of a company that values their opinions *now,*[63] or they might become frustrated and engage in *quiet quitting*, a concept to be studied in Chapter 6: *Quiet Quitting: Generational Selfishness or Survival.*

The Big Take Away for Retention: A Shift From the Company to the Individual

In summary, to retain employees today, 4-gen leaders need to remember all generations are seeking some of the same qualities in a job: a safe, supportive culture; competitive pay; a work/life balance; paid time off; physical, emotional and mental healthcare; opportunities to learn and grow; and ways to have a positive impact. However, an important part of delivering these qualities is for leaders to consider the shift in emphasis from the team to the individual. The rise of the Internet and the resulting advent of the choice society (mentioned in Chapter 1: *From Boomer to Z*) and the change in parenting styles used to raise the four generations (mentioned in Chapter 2: *Different Generations, Different Parenting, Different Perspective*) has led to more empowered younger generations.

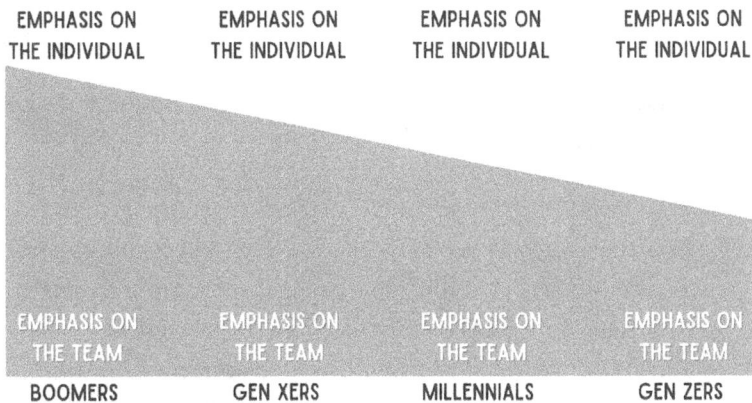

Figure 5.2 *The emphasis on the individual has grown dramatically and will continue to grow in the future*

This means successful 4-gen leaders today do more than provide profits for companies—they also find ways to personalize the employee experience for all generations on their teams.[64]

Voices From the Generations

The authors interviewed a 4-gen leader of an organization that has embraced many of these ideas. He is an executive at one of the largest banks in the United States with over 22,000 employees. He's also a boomer.

He and the organization are models of multi-gen leadership. One of his quotes summarizes his approach to helping generations bridge the generation gaps: "I'm not asking them to reinvent themselves. I'm just asking that you have a growth mindset. Be open to change. Try to be more accepting of differences and think more broadly about people."

The growth mindset manifests itself in numerous ways. First, he and the leadership team have embraced a philosophy that "everything evolves. We will be left behind if we don't keep up with the change." Part of the change for the organization has come in the generational makeup of its workforce. The bank's leaders know how the generations are represented throughout the organization. They know fifty-three percent of the workforce is made up of millennials and Gen Zers—while the majority of the leadership team is comprised of boomers and Gen Xers. With over half the team members in the younger generations, the bank's leadership team has adjusted its practices and culture to bridge the generation gaps.

> **Reverse mentoring**: When the COVID lockdowns occurred in 2020, the bank was able to quickly move to more online options for its customers. According to this leader, the speed and ease of the digital transition occurred in large part because of the number of millennials and Gen Zers in the company. The bank didn't wait for just the boomer and Gen X leaders to solve the problems; instead, the boomers and Gen X leaders turned to their younger team members for assistance in implementing solutions. It was a form of reverse mentoring. Today, reverse mentoring is an important part of the bank's multi-gen efforts: younger team members mentor boomers and Gen Xers on technology usage and forming a digital mindset, while the boomers and Gen Xers help the Millennials and Gen Zers learn about the banking industry

and how to communicate, especially in face-to-face communication, an area where the young generations may struggle.

Hybrid work: This leader's philosophy is that hybrid work is here to stay, and people will want more options in the future. He says, "We'll look back on this in ten years and ask, 'Why did we spend so much time debating this?'"

Leadership development: The bank has an Emerging Leaders program that helps millennials and Gen Zers to develop their leadership traits. About a third of the program is made up of boomers and Gen Xers who mentor the future leaders in the younger generations. This taps into the vast leadership experience of the older generations while giving the younger generations growth opportunities, which is a vital development goal for millennials and Gen Zers.

Conversations between generations: As part of their DEI efforts, he and his team have an open-door policy to seek out the opinions of employees. Constant conversations are occurring, which helps the leadership team stay in touch with all generations, including the millennials and Gen Zers who have a great interest in the bank's ESG.

A focus on the future: The leader and the leadership team are preparing for a future with more mobility in banking where people will be living longer and need more robust retirement plans that will last for more decades. He and the bank also know the demographics are changing; in ten years no one ethnic group will be majority of the American population. The leader, who is black, believes it will be easier for other leaders of color to break through the barriers that have held back marginalized groups. "Tech is the great equalizer," he says, "when all people have access to the same technology they can grow." Plus, he's excited about a future when more millennials and Gen Zers, the most inclusive generations, are in leadership roles and will welcome more diversity into their ranks.[65]

Your Real-World Connection

Consider this scenario: A high-level Gen Xer executive works in a mid-size technology company that prioritizes multi-gen leadership. The organization is:

- committed to understanding the generations
- aware of which generations are in its workforce
- tapping into the varied generational strengths to thrive
- intent on setting a foundation for future growth

The organization is committed to succession planning that will position it for success in the back half of the 2020's and into the 2030's. However, its leadership team realizes it has an area in which it can improve: it must do more to retain its top talent. The Gen Xer is tasked with launching a focus group that will research ways to hold on to the team members who are the most resourceful and have proven to be a good long-term fit. The executive includes boomers, Gen Xers, millennials, and Gen Zers in the focus group to leverage their multi-gen strengths.

The focus group does its due diligence and forms seven long-term goals. The group recommends that the organization:

1. Understand generational differences that may impact how the organization operates.
2. Determine critical roles and competencies within the organization and recruit appropriate individuals for those positions at all levels.
3. Collect data on team members' career aspirations to understand and bridge potential gaps in the future.
4. Implement a leadership development program to help individuals from different generations to develop their leadership skill sets.
5. Facilitate cross-generational mentoring programs so that experienced leaders can mentor younger employees and younger employees can mentor experienced leaders in key areas. Placing younger employees in mentor positions will also show that

everyone brings value to the organization, not just the older employees.

6. Establish a positive culture with open communication channels where employees throughout the organization can share their ideas about the succession plan without fear of reprisal or generational bias.

7. Periodically review and update the succession plan to align with changing organizational needs and goals. The organization should collect data and adapt strategies based on feedback, performance evaluations, and the evolving workplace landscape.

In leveraging an inclusive multi-gen focus group, the organization is positioned for success. This process not only helps plan for the future, but it also has deepened the collaborative, problem-solving skill sets of the focus group's members.

NEXT STEPS

4-GEN *leadership*

HELPING ALL YOUR GENERATIONS THRIVE IN THEIR TEAMS!

How does your current retention strategy balance the individualism of different generations with your company's needs, and how can you improve this for the future?

How can you leverage your 4-gen lens to identify gaps and ways to improve the employee experience (EX) for all generations?

How was your organization impacted by the Great Resignation, what strategies were implemented to remedy those issues, and how can you continue to evolve based on what you learned in this chapter?

Figure 5.3 Chapter 5 next steps worksheet

CHAPTER 6

Quiet Quitting

Generational Selfishness or Survival?

Key Points of This Chapter

1. Quiet quitting is a new term, but it's not a new concept.
2. All generations can be quiet quitters, but research is showing millennials and Gen Zers are less engaged than in the past.
3. Loud quitting is a term used to describe unhappy employees who are openly disenchanted with their jobs.
4. Four-gen leaders can take proactive steps to mitigate the effects of quiet quitting and loud quitting.

In early 2022, a new term began to circulate through the business world: *quiet quitting,* the act of individuals refusing to work beyond a 40-hour work week and doing the bare minimum to keep their jobs.[1] At 5 o'clock, or whenever the set workday ended, these individuals would close their laptops, leave the workspaces, and slip quietly into their personal lives, regardless of the amount of work left to be done or the number of colleagues still in the office. Some of these workers were searching for new jobs and didn't want to commit to more work in their current jobs. Others had no intention of leaving their current jobs but had no desire to take on any tasks that were outside of their job description.[2]

Quiet quitting is "a relatively new term, yet not a new concept."[3] Many employees in all fields have often been reluctant to work long hours in stressful environments, and some have pushed back in the past, but in 2022, this request for more life/job balance morphed into a demand and became a movement viewed by some as a necessity and others as a passive–aggressive protest against corporate expectations. A Gallup survey in 2022 found at least half the U.S. workforce consists of quiet quitters.[4] Some business analysts feel it could get worse in the future because more jobs are requiring "extra effort to collaborate with coworkers to meet customer needs."[5]

If you ask these quiet quitters themselves, according to Resume-Builder.com, "8 out of 10 people say it is simply because they are burnt out. There is good news though, 9 out of 10 people who consider themselves as quiet quitters can be persuaded to work to their full potential."[6]

What is the impact of quiet quitting in the workplace? Many of the managers who were boomers and Gen Xers viewed quiet quitters as selfish slackers who refused to sacrifice for the company the way they had done during their long careers. Kevin O'Leary, a successful business leader and star of the television show *Shark Tank* in which entrepreneurs push their ideas to successful investors, said quiet quitting is "a really bad idea… People that go beyond to try to solve problems for the organization, their teams, their managers, their bosses, those are the ones that succeed in life."[7]

Contrast this view with Maggie Perkins, a teacher who first began quietly quitting in 2018. She said saying, "No," to additional work and hours gave her more "personal happiness and satisfaction…It gave me more time with my family…It also gives me a sense of security at work, that I knew my answer would be 'no' if they said I needed to stay for something. I think of work in terms of hours and not in terms of the people that I'm affecting."[8]

It's worth noting that O'Leary is boomer, and Perkins is a millennial. O'Leary subscribes to the long-held boomer notion that you get ahead in your career and life through long hours and loyalty to the company. Perkins, on the other hand, doesn't buy into the *hustle culture* mantra that success is connected to working long hours and focusing on professional advancement;[9] for her, success is working effectively within the prescribed hours and having time to live a fulfilling personal life away from the job.

The views of O'Leary and Perkins represent broader views of their generations. When it comes to quiet quitting, older groups tend to view the younger groups as being *devoid of ambition.*[10] Yet, studies show millennials and Gen Zer are working hard, but maybe not in the traditional ways—a Lending Tree survey in 2022 found 62 percent of Gen Zers and 55 percent of millennials have side hustles.[11] They are barely getting by: a Deloitte study in 2023 found 51 percent of Gen Zers and 52 percent of millennials live paycheck to paycheck.[12]

In other words, as these groups will insist, they will work hard when they see the need to do so and often have career aspirations outside of their current full-time position.

It's safe to say all generations can be quiet quitters. Workplace disillusionment, and in some cases, laziness, have been constant threads in the workforce for many decades. However, a Gallup survey conducted in 2022 found engagement for workers under the age of 35 had dropped significantly since the prepandemic days of 2019. More young employees than in the past responded that no one in their organization cared about them or their professional development, and no one was giving them opportunities to learn and grow. Fully remote and hybrid young workers are feeling particularly disillusioned, with less than 4 in 10 of these workers reporting they were sure what was expected of them in their jobs.[13] The importance of coaching for millennials and Gen Zers was discussed in Chapter 3, so it's not surprising that they would feel disenfranchised in some of today's work environments if they were disenfranchised in their jobs.

A reason quiet quitting became such a well-known movement is that it quickly spread on various social media platforms around the world. It first went viral on TikTok in 2022, a platform popular with millennials and Gen Zers.[14] The hashtag #actyourwage was created for workers to share their quiet quitting stories. It's been viewed by millions around the world. An international Gallup poll in 2022 found that 60 percent of the global workforce could exhibit elements of quiet quitting. If this number is accurate, it could be costing the global economy almost U.S. $9 trillion per year.[15]

Quiet quitting is not confined to one group of the workforce; it is found in many different types of jobs. HR professionals say they've witnessed the following groups engaging in quiet quitting.[16]

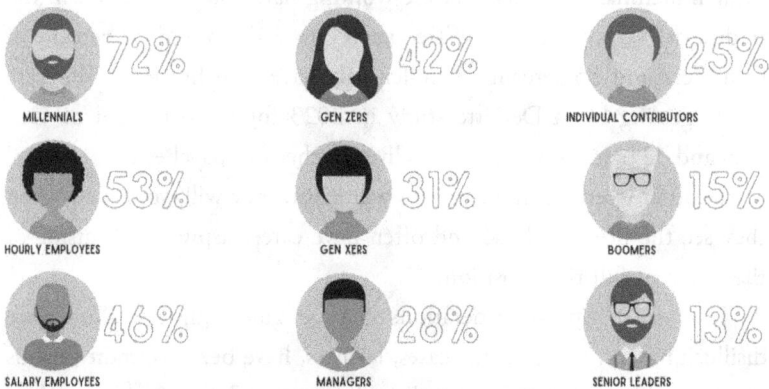

MILLENNIALS 72%	GEN ZERS 42%	INDIVIDUAL CONTRIBUTORS 25%
HOURLY EMPLOYEES 53%	GEN XERS 31%	BOOMERS 15%
SALARY EMPLOYEES 46%	MANAGERS 28%	SENIOR LEADERS 13%

Figure 6.1 Quiet quitting is found in many groups in varying degrees

The quiet quitting trend has created new tensions in the workplace. First, it has created a conflict with managers when they realize workers explicitly or tacitly refuse to take on new assignments or put in the extra hours to finish current ones. Second, quiet quitters have found themselves at odds with some of their coworkers who were not quiet quitters—these other coworkers are often the ones to whom management turned to pick up the work not done by the quiet quitters.[17]

Have you noticed quiet quitting in your organization, and in what roles is it most common?

So, what sparked this movement? Analysts point to several reasons, including workers feeling they are fatigued, have a poor work/life balance, are not recognized, are dissatisfied with their roles, and see no clear path forward to career advancement or a better life. Through it all, they feel undercompensated.[18] Resume Builder cited in a study that 46 percent of those surveyed said "they don't want to do more work than they're getting compensated to do" and 35 percent also said "it does not benefit my career enough to do so."[19]

The frustrations are compounded for millennials and Gen Zers, some of them are depressed because of their exorbitant college debts.[20] A survey in 2022 found most millennials and Gen Zers can't afford to own homes. In 2022, the average age of first-time home buyers was 36 years of age, which was a new record high.[21] It's such a barrier that over two-thirds of them reported they would relocate to another state if they could find an affordable new home or fixer-upper.[22] They, and all generations, are also having trouble paying the rent for apartments. A Moody's Analytics report found between 1999 and 2022, rent has increased by 135 percent, but income has gone up by only 77 percent.[23] It's estimated today, that one-third of Gen Z adults, including those with jobs, still are forced to live with their parents.[24] It should be no surprise that many millennials and Gen Zers, who grew up viewing life as a partnership and the need to be engaged and valued, have become so disillusioned that they are shutting down.

Loud Quitting: Open Discontent in the Workplace

A more concerning trend for leaders emerged in 2023: loud quitting. While quiet quitters subtly reject the company's requests or demands as they remain in their jobs, loud quitters are openly defiant or take action to undercut the success of their organizations before they resign from their positions dramatically. They might create a loud disruption in the manager's office as they announce they are leaving.[25] After they leave, loud quitters might continue to vent their frustrations to co-workers and denigrate their former company on social media.[26] TikTok videos posted by loud quitters have generated millions of views.[27]

Another form of loud quitting might not be loud; it might be silent. Sometimes, loud quitters silently walk out the door without giving notice, perhaps not even telling their closest coworkers they are leaving the company. They are just suddenly gone.[28] "I'm out of here" notices are simply being dropped on the desks of managers, or sent to their inbox, with an *effective immediately* signature. Or, in a scenario that could be even worse for managers and their organizations, loud quitters don't quit: they just stay in their positions and continue to complain.[29]

Loud quitting is more widespread than people realize: A study in 2023 found that 18 percent of global employees, almost one-fifth of the workforce, were loud quitters.[30] The report stated, "At some point along the way, the trust between employee and employer was severely broken. Or the employee has been woefully mismatched to a role, causing constant crises. Loud quitting can signal 'major risks' in an organization that should not be ignored."[31]

> **What examples of loud quitting have you observed, and what was its impact on the workplace culture?**

Solutions to Quiet Quitting and Loud Quitting

Organizations have responded to quiet quitting in different ways. Some companies have begun to monitor their employees' work habits more closely. For positions requiring computer usage, managers might use software that monitors work done at a computer keyboard, or they might check the amount of time the employee was logged into the company's digital platforms and tools. Some organizations have resorted to using more video surveillance in workplaces to monitor where and how employees spend company time.[32] They might also look for increased absenteeism and sick days or "a decline in performance, project completion times or productivity."[33]

Another way to respond and resolve quiet and loud quitting is to take a more proactive approach. Four-gen leaders should take steps to understand the core issues of workplace discontent and to find solutions. Leaders should view the issues through a multi-gen lens. Consider these strategies when addressing key issues:

- Leaders need to be in constant communication with workers. They might use companywide surveys to monitor feelings about compensation, benefits, and work conditions. Sometimes, a lack of clear communication is a huge demotivator.[34] Using appropriate communication styles for each generation will be pivotal in resolving issues.

- Leaders need to have one-on-one conversations and should consider using *stay* interviews, which are a structured discussion "with each individual employee to learn the specific actions they must take to strengthen that employee's engagement and retention within the organization."[35] These would be significant for millennials and Gen Zers who need to be heard, recognized, and coached.

- Leaders need to collaborate with employees to reimagine how work might look. This could include making organizationwide changes or helping workers prioritize their tasks.[36] This would appeal to all generations because they want to work efficiently and have an enjoyable workplace culture.

- Leaders should consider upskilling their teams to help them be more successful, engage them with innovative ideas, and assure them there is a path forward with new and better ways of working.[37]

- Leaders need to mitigate disenchantment when employees feel they are working beyond their max, either in hours or in tasks assigned, by communicating to them that the situation is short-term and solutions are being sought.[38] Even boomers and older Gen Xers, who are known for their work ethic, have breaking points, especially in a post-COVID landscape where work/life balance is highly valued.

- Leaders should "lean into *good enough*" to reduce stress. All leaders want to lead high-performing organizations that continue to improve, but they need to find the boundaries between motivating employees and stressing them out.[39]

- Leaders should examine the boundaries of the organization to see if they need to expand no-work times on weekends and evenings.[40] All employees need to know their personal time is respected.

- Leaders need to ensure employees are recognized not just for their achievements but also for their efforts.[41] This would appeal to all generations, but especially to Gen Zers who are gaining experience and need to grow their confidence and test out new skills obtained and not be afraid to fail.

- Leaders must recognize that while all generations like to advance, there could be individuals who do not want to move higher into the organization's structure because they are happy where they are, value their personal time, and want to manage their stress levels.[42]
- Leaders should be role models. They should monitor how they set the tone for the organization in their communication styles, when they communicate, how they react to stressful situations, how they recognize employees, the gratitude they show, and the overall actions they take to shape the organization's culture.[43]

Ultimately, reducing quiet quitting and loud quitting comes back to the depth of the employee experience (EX) mentioned in Chapter 5. When employees view their teams and organizations in a positive light, they will be more likely to engage in their work and make sacrifices for their colleagues and the company mission.

> How can you apply some of the strategies listed above to reduce quiet quitting?

Voices From the Generations

A Gen-X business owner and entrepreneur interviewed for this book, Bryce Ungerott, said one of his biggest challenges is "understanding Gen Z and adapting to their attitudes about work. Period." He is a co-owner of several late-night pizza restaurants and a few bars—and he has seen a huge change in the workforce since 2009 when he opened his first business. In 2009, he says the workforce was different, and individuals were *hungrier to work* and less focused on fighting the status quo. Ungerott says some changes are necessary, but they can be a challenge in the hospitality industry where it isn't always possible to guarantee tips, have a stress-free workplace, and maintain a positive mental health work environment.

Ungerott is well aware of the quiet quitting epidemic. He understands that communication and how he positions policy updates and changes can make a massive positive impact on the team and their loyalty. "When you don't handle communications well and clearly," he says, "people will make their own conclusions and that can be dangerous for them and the organization." He has prioritized coaching and training. He also says helping his younger employees learn more about their personal finances is very important, especially in today's economy.

His businesses are open late, and workplace safety is a major initiative for his entire executive team. They've made important adjustments, like adding armed guards to his establishments during late night hours. According to Ungerott, it's "a necessary expense to keep employees safe and give them peace of mind." At times, he's noticed how employees handle customer issues isn't a training issue—it's about a lack of experience. So Ungerott and his team provide coaching to employees on how to adapt to conversations and situations. He says this "can make a world of difference for employees and our customers." He adds it helps to have "respectful and kind managers who take a 'player-coach' approach and work alongside their teams because they are doing the same job daily."

While quiet quitting can be an issue, Ungerott remains positive and tries to focus on why his company is different and truly a unique place to work. His goal is for his employees to have careers and not just a job. He's proud of the diverse, inclusive workplace his team has created. Their motto is *One Human Family—Pizza for All*.[44]

Your Real-World Connection

Consider this scenario: A successful millennial manager has noticed one of her team members, a Gen Zer, has a high absentee rate, is not achieving his goals, participates minimally in meetings, doesn't want to take on any new responsibilities, and seems to be withdrawn from the rest of his team. The manager looks at the issue through a multi-gen lens, and she realizes several factors could be affecting the Gen Zer. He could be experiencing personal or professional challenges. He might even be a quiet quitter.

The manager wants to help the Gen Zer, so she uses her generational knowledge to prepare for a conference with him. Here is what she understands about the situation and the Gen Z generation. The Gen Zers:

- Want to be more involved with influencing decision making, especially about their place in organizations, and they want to understand why things are being done in certain ways
- Are sometimes stressed or depressed because they can't afford to move out of their parents' houses, have crippling college debt, and are worried about the economy and their futures
- Can be overwhelmed with the demands that come with learning how to navigate a professional workplace
- Are concerned about compensation to work ratio and other benefits offered by the organization to subsidize their personal spending
- Require balance in work and life
- Want meaningful and productive face-to-face interaction with their colleagues and coaching from their managers
- Use different communication styles and might be having trouble communicating with his peers and with her
- Must personally connect with the company mission, vision, and values
- Are just getting started in their careers, so they may be struggling because a new set of skills are required to complete the responsibilities of the role
- Value authentic, transparent managers

While the manager wants to find the cause of the Gen Zer's underperformance and to assist him, she also knows the Gen Zer might have become a quiet quitter because he feels he is underpaid and has bought into the #actyourwage movement. That, too, will be discussed if the manager feels the Gen Zer is not embracing the performance improvement ideas of their conversation.

The manager then prepares for the conversation around his recent performance. She obtains data and specific examples to share with the employee. To involve the Gen Zer, she will engage him in a discussion about how to implement steps for improvement and will avoid making it a one-sided conversation in which she simply tells the Gen Zer what must be done.

- To stress authenticity, she will assure the Gen Zer she is being transparent and will encourage him to be transparent.
- To address mental and emotional needs, she will express her concern for him and let him know of resources that are available within the organization and through the company's health plan if he wants assistance in dealing with managing his work–life balance.
- To build confidence in adjusting to the workplace, she will ask him if he has any specific areas of concern in completing his responsibilities and share training and learning opportunities that are available for upskilling.
- To learn about satisfaction with pay and benefits, she will ask him if he believes his pay and benefits are fair and competitive.
- To find balance, she will ask him if he is successfully unplugging in personal time from the demands of the job.
- To support professional development and interactions with colleagues and coaching, she will offer a mentor from the team and schedule more opportunities to connect one-on-one.
- To embrace different forms of communication, she will ask him if he feels he is being understood and will recommend effective ways of communicating with different people on the team.
- To connect with the company's mission, she will talk with him about the company's core values, and how she tries to live them, and ask how he can mirror them in his actions.
- To create an authentic and transparent relationship, she will recap the meeting's main points at its conclusion and ask him what he can do to be successful in the future based on this conversation.

- To develop accountability plans for professional improvement and track the specific metrics with him regularly and then provide acknowledgment and accolades for improvements made.

At the end of the conversation, the manager will have to determine her next steps as a leader. If the Gen Zer is actively engaged in their conversation, displays a positive attitude, and wants to improve, she will assist him in implementing the action steps. As a 4-gen leader, the manager will have recognized new, generational issues could be affecting the Gen Zer, and she will have actively included the Gen Zer in finding solutions. Traditional leaders, on the other hand, might have used the meeting as a vehicle for reprimanding the Gen Zer and telling the employee what would be expected in the future without understanding the generational causes and without involving the Gen Zer in his improvement plan.

However, if the Gen Zer is noncommittal, feels the pay or working conditions are not acceptable, and shows no enthusiasm for taking the steps they've discussed for improvement, the manager will deduce he could be a quiet quitter, or simply not a good fit for the position any longer. She will continue to monitor and document his performance and, if necessary, terminate. A supportive suggestion for this employee with limited work experience could be to suggest he find another position or organization that better aligns with his professional goals and work–life balance strategy so he can be happier and more successful.

NEXT STEPS

4-GEN *leadership*

HELPING ALL YOUR GENERATIONS THRIVE IN THEIR TEAMS!

How can your organization create an inclusive, purpose-driven environment that values the contributions of all generations and reduces the likelihood of team members resorting to quiet quitting?

How can your 4-gen leaders foster open communication channels within multigenerational teams to ensure that team members feel comfortable expressing their concerns before resorting to loud quitting and harming the workplace culture?

Has the #actyourwage movement created issues for your organization, and what solutions can you implement to control the narrative in a positive way?

Figure 6.2 Chapter 6 next steps worksheet.

CHAPTER 7

DEI and the Generations

Key Points of This Chapter

1. The success of corporate DEI initiatives can be determined by the initial rollout of the programs and how the different generations view them.
2. Studies show boomers and Gen Xers don't value DEI as much as millennials and Gen Zers.
3. Boomers and Gen Xers might have different understandings of the purpose of DEI.
4. Four-gen leaders should take steps to include all generations in the planning, training, and data tracking of DEI initiatives, not just the younger generations who will have the most interest in it.

Some of the most popular—and controversial—initiatives to sweep through American businesses in the last decade are those that promote diversity, equity, and inclusion (DEI) strategies into their cultures and operations. According to a study in 2021, 80 percent of over 650 companies surveyed said that they had begun to implement corporate DEI initiatives.[1] Besides wanting to promote fair practices for all individuals, these initiatives have a positive impact on the bottom line: one report found "75 percent of organizations with frontline decision-making teams reflecting a diverse and inclusive culture will exceed their financial targets"[2] in the coming years. Other studies have also shown that diversity when viewed through "the lenses of race, ethnicity, ability, gender, sexual orientation, neurodiversity, and beyond, can help strengthen organizations."[3]

While many companies are placing more value on DEI, it's clear that there is still work to be done to create diverse, equitable, and inclusive work environments. According to a 2022 study by Boston College in which it partnered with SHRM to poll 1,062 businesses:

- 28 percent of the companies reported their employees had experienced gender bias in the past two years.
- 27 percent of organizations reported that their employees have experienced racial bias in the past two years.
- 26 percent of organizations reported that their employees have experienced bias against older workers in the past years.

The majority of these businesses, 64 percent of them, noted that DEI was either important or very important; yet, only 38 percent of them reported they were giving their DEI initiatives support needed to be successful.[4]

DEI efforts have been present in American businesses for decades, but the efforts might not have been called DEI. Some would even say DEI has its roots in American business in the 1960s with "the Equal Pay Act of 1963, Title VII of the Civil Rights Act of 1964, and the Age Discrimination in Employment Act of 1967. Efforts at that time were focused on Affirmative Action and nondiscrimination. Diversity (as in the inclusion of under-represented groups) in the workplace started to become part of the conversation, at least for large US companies."[5]

Today, the political times have changed, and implementing DEI has become an extreme challenge for many business leaders who must grapple with the backlash against the implementation of programs that "teach about white supremacy, privilege, and bias"[6] while leading the two most politically strident generations—millennials and Gen Zers—in a super-charged political environment.

On one side of the issue, most employees expect leaders to promote business cultures that promote DEI. A Pew Research Center report in 2023 found 56 percent of American adults believe focusing on DEI in the workplace is the correct thing to do.[7] However, 28 percent have no opinion on the topic, and 16 percent feel DEI initiatives should not be a part of the workplace environment.[8] For this latter group, DEI might be threatening and could stand for other words: discrimination, exclusion, and indoctrination.[9]

People form beliefs around DEI based on several factors, like where and how they grew up, what they've encountered in their lives, and the conclusions they've formed around their own experiences. Their personal and professional views often lead them to accept or reject DEI initiatives—and four-gen leaders understand these views are often generational.

How can you lead conversations about DEI with all generations?

According to an article published by LinkedIn by Julia Kratz, an experienced leader of DEI training programs with Next Pivot Point, research is showing "those of the Baby Boomer generation view DEI lower on their list of workplace priorities, members of Generation X have mixed views, Millennials recognize its importance, and Generation Z, the most diverse and most-educated American generation yet, believe that workplace equity is imperative."[10] To complicate matters even more, the "leaders grappling with how best to execute, measure and share their progress on DEI are often Gen X and baby boomers—but it's younger workers who are leading the charge for better efforts."[11]

As stated earlier, just because a person is in a certain generation doesn't mean he or she has that generation's most common views. If boomers and Gen Xers are more likely to question or reject DEI initiatives, it doesn't mean all boomers and Gen Xers will reject them. On the contrary, some boomers and Gen Xers have been life-long champions of DEI. If millennials and Gen Zers are more likely to promote DEI causes, it doesn't mean all millennials and Gen Zers will buy into this philosophy. Some of them might be opposed to DEI initiatives. Another thing to consider is when and how DEI initiatives are released. Many in the younger generations want DEI to be woven into the corporate culture, not rolled out as a single corporate initiative that was in response to a negative workplace experience, or something that has massive media coverage due to a recent event. While the change in corporate policy can be good, the essence of where it stemmed matters.

In looking more closely at these generational views of DEI, the support for DEI grows with each generation and divides itself along the Internet generation gap; the boomers and Gen Xers have more of a neutral stance, while the Millennials and Gen Zers are much more vocal about the need for making DEI a nonnegotiable pillar of the operating culture. Consider the contrast found in one study: 57 percent of boomers said DEI had little or no impact on their decisions to leave or stay with a company, while 76 percent of millennials said they would leave their company if it didn't offer DEI initiatives.[12]

One reason for this breakdown could be boomers and Gen Xers grew up being told to make their own way in the world, but the millennials and Gen Zers grew with access to the Internet, which gave them visibility into seeing many people who didn't have that equal opportunity. Boomers and Gen Xers see everyone as starting at the same starting line, while millennials and Gen Zers realize not everyone gets to start in the same spot and some people have more obstacles and equality issues to overcome. Older team members are more focused on their own careers and job security, and while those things are also important to younger team members, they, and especially Gen Zers, rank DEI above compensation and flexibility in priority.[13] Gen Zers and millennials want action on DEI, not just words, and the "companies who are not positioning themselves strongly on DEI will struggle to find top talent"[14] in the younger generations.

Corporate leaders need to understand DEI is not a normal adjustment in policy or actions; it represents a profound shift in generational thinking. In a multi-gen training workshop in Texas in the summer of 2023, a black Gen Z female verbalized its importance when she said to the group, "My mom is a Gen Xer. When George Floyd was murdered, I went to the protest even though she told me not to go. I had to be there. I had to speak up. If I don't speak up today, I feel like I'm letting myself down."[15]

This is a powerful message for traditional leaders. If they view their DEI efforts through a normal leadership lens and don't grasp DEI's generational importance, the initiatives will be more likely to fail. The leaders, who might have treated implementing and leading DEI initiatives as just another thing to check from a long list of goals, will be left searching for reasons their employees are not buying into the efforts, or in a worse scenario, will be dealing with employees who are openly hostile to DEI. Instead, leaders must use their multi-gen leadership lens to understand how generations view DEI to create diverse, equitable, and inclusive cultures. Like this Gen Zer who feels she must be heard, other young employees also feel they have no choice; they feel compelled to participate and speak up. They can't ignore these deeply ingrained principles. They expect workplaces and society to be diverse, inclusive, and equitable.

Your Teams and DEI

As mentioned earlier, 4-gen leaders need to know how the generations are represented in their teams. This is of particular importance when implementing DEI initiatives. Here are some generational questions leaders can ask as they implement and assess their DEI efforts.

- Are there four generations in the teams? If so, the leaders need to understand there could be different views about DEI by each generation.
- Which generations form the majority? The dominant generations might be setting the corporate culture. An older team might not be as acceptive of DEI, but a younger team will expect DEI to be respected and acted upon.
- How are the minority generations treated? For example, if there are small numbers of boomers or Gen Zers, do they feel they are included and given equitable treatment?

Cultures that marginalize individuals can lead to a constant stream of microaggressions by the majority members directed toward the minority members. These microaggressions intentionally, or often unintentionally, exclude the feelings, efforts, and results of the minority members.[16] As part of the DEI efforts, leaders will have to ensure all voices of all generations are heard. To see if all team members are including all their peers, leaders can study how the team members of different generations communicate, show each other respect, develop common goals, and support each other's growth and development.

Leaders can remind the generations that a great culture will have "open communication, mutual respect, shared goals, and a commitment to employee growth and development,"[17] and that DEI should be woven into the fabric of their culture and professional growth.

Multi-gen leaders should take steps to include all generations in the planning, training, and data tracking, not just the younger generations who will have the most interest in it. When boomers and Gen Xers have a voice in the efforts, they will feel respected, and that the DEI efforts are being done *with them* and not *to them*. While corporate policy and governance cannot include everyone's thoughts and opinions, some of which could be conflicting, it should be said that employees had a voice and were asked to support the efforts of leadership to create a positive, productive, and safe work environment and culture centered around DEI of all people.

When possible, all generations should have options in how they participate in the DEI initiatives. Boomers and Gen Xers are more likely to resent all types of mandatory training sessions, and if they are opposed to DEI, they will have particularly harsh feelings about participating in mandatory DEI training sessions. Having options would give them more autonomy in how they take part. If boomers and Gen Xers can work independently or in small groups with readings, online training, or other options of their choosing, then they will be more likely to align the training to their values.[18]

Some leaders make the mistake of asking or forcing individuals in the least represented groups to lead the DEI initiatives. If a person is of a certain generation or is Black or Latino or LGBTQ, it doesn't mean he or she should have to lead or wants to lead, the workplace DEI efforts. For example, leaders shouldn't assume the lone boomer or lone Gen Zer will want to spearhead the discussions or planning around generational awareness. Research also shows women of color can feel particularly vulnerable. According to Erika Hines, a DEI consultant and the founder of Every Level Leadership, data show that "when women and people of color bring up issues around DEI, the impact is that they can be considered troublemakers."[19] Hines has this advice for Black women: "workplace DEI is a company issue, not yours."[20] This can be said for all marginalized groups, including generations that are underrepresented in an organization. DEI leadership among team members should be a personal choice and not a responsibility. It should not be assumed someone will be willing to maintain their regular duties while also taking on the additional burden of leading reform around age, race, and gender while possibly taking the criticism from peers that comes with shifting mindsets.

Leaders should clearly articulate their DEI goals and metrics because generations sometimes begin with different perceptions of DEI. Often, these perceptions are divided by the Internet generation gap. Boomers and Gen Xers tend to focus on diversity, but millennials and Gen Zers are more focused on inclusion and behavior.[21] The boomers and Gen Xers tend to think the goal is to just hire more underrepresented individuals to increase the ratio of people in team diversity, while the millennials and Gen Zers want diverse teams and want to be sure to include all team members in conversations, projects, and social gatherings.

> **Who in your organization is leading DEI initiatives, and are all generations appropriately represented?**

Sometimes, multi-gen leaders must help the team form a common vision of DEI. They must educate the older team members, who have not had as much experience with inclusion and equity, on DEI's broad meaning. In some of the minds of boomers and Gen Xers, DEI simply means hiring from a more diverse labor pool and then allowing the newly hired team members to forge their own paths through the workplace culture just like they did when they were hired decades ago. In their minds, the playing field is level, and success will come to those who exhibit a strong work ethic, loyalty to the company and cause, and talent in getting the job done. For some millennials and Gen Zers, who tend to come from more diverse backgrounds and have had more diverse experiences, might mistakenly assume the boomers and Gen Xers have moved beyond the D and also understand the E and I of DEI.

Ten DEI Questions for Multi-Gen Leaders

When beginning DEI work with their teams, leaders must consider age, gender, race, cultural background, sexual orientation, individuals with disabilities, and other diversity factors. Most questions standardly asked in surveys and efforts to promote DEI are centered on these areas. However, because the new generation gaps have now entered the workforce, 4-gen leaders should ask some new types of DEI questions and add a generational component to traditional DEI questions. Here are ten questions leaders can use to begin or to assess their current DEI efforts.

1. Which generations are in our teams?
2. Are there any generations that dominate our team culture because of their numbers, leadership, or personalities?
3. How will the teams feel about DEI work, and are the generations affecting their views?
4. How have the teams, especially the boomers and Gen Xers, been educated about the importance of DEI for individuals, for the teams, and for the overall success of the company?
5. Do all generations have a common definition and understanding of DEI?
6. Where does the company need to improve the most in its DEI efforts, and are the generational efforts adequate?[22]
7. How diverse is the leadership group in gender, race, cultural background, sexual orientation, individuals with disabilities, and generations?[23]
8. How is diversity promoted and celebrated in the organization, including celebrations to honor different milestones of different generations?[24]
9. What does the evaluation and promotion process look like, and is it equitable for gender, race, cultural background, sexual orientation, individuals with disabilities, and generations?[25]

10. Is there a DEI group of team members assisting the leadership team as it promotes DEI, and does this group include the different generations?[26]

Beyond using these DEI foundation questions to grow, leaders can also use them to help determine why DEI efforts might be failing within an organization. It might be a generational failure.

A Generational Shift: More Young Employees Who Identify as LGBTQ

An area of DEI that has grown in importance over the past few decades is the promotion of LGBTQ policies in the workplace. Consider these data from a Gallup poll in 2022 that reported the percentages of adults who identified as lesbian, gay, bisexual, transgender, or other:

- 1.8 percent of the silent generation
- 2.6 percent of boomers
- 4.2 percent of Gen Xers
- 10.5 percent of millennials
- 20.8 percent of Gen Zers[27]

What does this mean for employers in the 2020s? Social attitudes toward LGBTQ issues have evolved through the decades. More adults are feeling more comfortable identifying as LGBTQ today. The number of Gen Zers and millennials who identify as LGBTQ today, 20.8 and 10.5 percent, respectively, are already much higher than previous generations. This number is expected to grow as more Gen Zers, followed by Gen Alphas who will be entering the workforce in 2028, become proportionally larger parts of the population and workforce in the decades ahead.

Employers should also remember that while the number of people who identify as LGBTQ is growing, there is significant anti-LGBTQ pushback occurring in American society and politics—and this could affect the mental and emotional well-being of team members of all generations who identify as LGBTQ. According to CNN, a record number of anti-LGBTQ bills were addressed in the first three months of 2023, which already doubled the previous total, 180, that were filed in 2022.[28] The number of anti-LGBTQ legislation has risen steadily since 2019: 530 anti-LGBTQ bills were filed in states across America through the first six months of 2023.[29]

ANTI-LGBTQ LEGISLATION

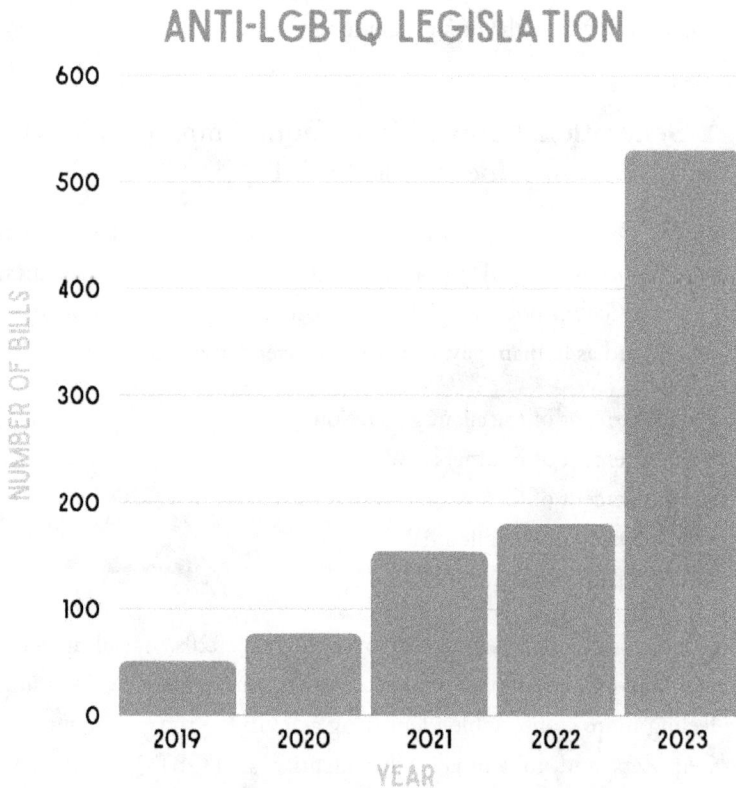

Figure 7.1 Anti-LGBTQ legislation

Most of the bills fall into two categories: education and health care. Legislatures taking action in these areas are restricting what can be taught and read in schools, and they are prohibiting some forms of health care for transgender youth. However, other bills pertain to civil rights, public accommodations, and create other types of new barriers for the LGBTQ population.[30] These could be bills in which millennials and Gen Zers take particular interest, especially the ones who are LGBTQ.

Four-gen leaders should recognize their LGBTQ employees might feel they are now living in a more hostile society. In March 2023, Logan Casey, a spokesman for the Movement Advancement Project (MAP), which is a think tank that researches LGBTQ issues, summed up the fears of anti-LGBTQ sentiment when he said,

> It's clear that we are in a disturbing new era of attacks on our communities, and especially on transgender people…This dramatic rise in political attacks clearly illustrates how emboldened anti-LGBTQ activists seem to feel. Over the years we've seen many attacks on LGBTQ communities, but this moment is very different and frankly terrifying for many people.[31]

A report released by MAP in 2023 summed up this anti-LGBTQ sentiment by stating, "In reality, this is a war against LGBTQ people in America and their very right and ability to openly exist."[32]

If LGBTQ employees feel threatened when they are away from work, 4-gen leaders need to ensure these employees feel welcomed in the workplace. Part of improving the company's EX and DEI efforts should be committed to ensuring LGBTQ individuals work in a safe, inclusive environment, which means it's important to have a strong LGBTQ component in DEI plans and company culture.

How are your organization's EX and DEI strategies synergistic?

Spotting Ageism in the Workplace

The average age for retirement has risen in the past two decades from 62 to 66 years,[33] which means boomers are staying in the workforce longer. However, this also means they are interacting longer with people of other generations, which increases opportunities for them to experience ageism, which is when a bias is held against someone because of that person's age. A survey in 2022 found that 93 percent of workers over the age of 50 believe age discrimination is a common occurrence in the workplace.[34] However, while ageism most commonly impacts employees over 45 years of age, it is experienced by workers of all generations, including younger ones.[35] Research published in 2019 asserted workers between the ages of 18 and 35 felt they experienced age discrimination at even higher rates than the boomers and Gen Xers.[36] Boomers and Gen Xers might think millennials and Gen Zers are too young or inexperienced to understand or take on the responsibilities of certain jobs, while millennials and Gen Zers think boomers and Gen Xers are too old, unwilling to lean into more modern ways of operating or too backward in their thinking to get today's jobs done. Attitudes and actions that discredit people because of their generations are more than hurtful. They lower morale, reduce mentoring opportunities, negatively affect corporate branding efforts, and might even violate state and federal laws.[37]

Here are four common areas ageism can be found: job descriptions, the hiring process, meetings, and social corporate sponsored events.[38] More specifically, here are some examples of how ageism manifests itself.

- A team member makes a remark, critique, or joke about someone's age, which could be a series of microaggressions that undercut another individual's self-esteem or standing within the team. These actions, even jokes, could create a hostile environment.[39]
- Learning opportunities are only given to younger or older employees, including access to courses and programs, reimbursement, and professional development conference attendance.[40]
- Some generations are constantly left out of critical meetings and succession planning for the organization.[41]
- Surveys conducted by a company might show older or younger employees express concerns about being treated fairly.[42]
- The human resource department gets a steady stream of complaints about ageism.[43]
- Managers frequently ask employees about their plans to retire or to have children.[44]
- Younger, less qualified employees receive promotions over more senior, more effective, and more qualified applicants.[45]

Groups of people who have been historically marginalized are more likely to recognize ageism or be its victim. One research group has written:

Racial biases also play a pivotal role in shaping the experiences of older workers. People of color may encounter a unique set of challenges that intersect with ageism. Stereotypes about certain racial groups, coupled with ageist assumptions, can lead to discriminatory practices in hiring, promotions, and compensation.

Older workers of color often face the "invisible worker" phenomenon, where their contributions are overlooked or undervalued. Additionally, these workers may experience isolation and exclusion in predominantly white work environments, which can hinder their professional growth and well-being.[46]

Women are more likely than men to spot ageism. According to one study, 72 percent of women between the ages of 45 and 74, which would be today's boomers and Gen Xers, believe ageism is a problem at work. This percentage is greater than the number of men in the same age group who notice ageism, which is 57 percent.[47]

DEI Considerations

Finally, here are strategies 4-gen leaders can take to ensure workplaces are diverse, equitable, and inclusive for all individuals, including team members from all generations:

1. Commit to long-term growth around DEI. Educate employees. Reassuring employees it's not about judging them, but it's about helping them and the organization.[48] Be sure to add a generational component to the DEI initiatives.
2. Build a DEI committee.[49] Leaders can't shoulder the entire DEI workload alone, and a diverse implementation and activation team can offer advice, help plan training, and be a sounding board for both the leaders and team members.

3. Ensure all types of individuals are actively recruited, including members of all generations, and ensure that these metrics are tracked by hiring managers and human resources to adjust accordingly.

4. Create inclusive policies. More precisely, consider explicitly using "all individuals...LGBTQ...persons of color...persons with disabilities ... all generations..." in the text of policies when spelling out the protections and rights of employees.

5. Create networks of underrepresented groups or groups that could use extra support from their peers. When individuals have similar colleagues with whom they can converse, they feel less alone, and when they know their company cares about their well-being, they feel more comfortable and are more likely to grow. This includes the different generations.

For this to occur, a 4-gen leader must take the essential first step: remove internal biases. The road to diversity and a stronger, more effective culture begins with the inclusive thoughts of the leaders. Also, 4-gen leaders should tap the passions and strengths of millennial and Gen Z workers as they transform their culture into one that is more LGBTQ-friendly. While all generations should be included, the younger generations of workers have a particularly strong desire to implement change designed around inclusive practices and can play critical roles in assisting the leadership in its LBGTQ initiatives. Younger team members should not be forced to lead, but their voices and efforts can be invaluable, especially in the decade ahead as more Gen Zers and Gen Alphas enter the workforce.

Voices From the Generations

Reggie Henry, the Chief Information and Performance Excellence Officer at the American Society of Association Executives (ASAE), has decades of experience in the association field and brings a unique mission-driven approach to his use of his multi-gen lens. When interviewed about his work, the word *legacy* was frequently mentioned.

"While the word 'legacy' is positive," he says, "it sometimes can bring legacy 'baggage' that is negatively impacting the organization." His organization makes a conscious effort to review policy and programs to replace the attitude of "this is the way we've always done it" with one in which team members consider "the effort it takes and the value it brings to the organization and its members." He says this mindset switch has resulted in "a mentality focused on 'the good of the order'" and they now have a prism "where every generation can influence change and see the value."

In its focus on generationally diverse and inclusive programing, ASAE launched several internal initiatives, one of which was to create working groups in which the group members represented different generations and backgrounds. This step, according to Henry, "led to many 'a-ha' moments" that deepened connections across teams and set the stage for powerful change.

Reggie is known throughout the association space for his empathy and his passion for his work, and his moral compass is what drives his partnerships with vendors in the community. "It's important to find a shared vision, mission, and values in your partners to build something great," he says. Another ASAE initiative of which Reggie is proud is the Diversity, Executive Leadership Program (DELP), which supports "individuals from under-represented identity groups (i.e., people of color, lesbian/gay/bisexual/transgender people, people with disabilities) to advance into the ranks of leadership in the association management profession."[50] The program has made a difference in the association community and has increased access to a more diverse pool of talented leaders.

Your Real-World Connection

Consider this scenario: A Gen Z leader has started her own high-tech company, and it has 12 employees. Most of them are millennials and Gen Zers, but there is one boomer and one older Gen Xer on her team. In meetings, the leader notices the millennials and Gen Zers are quick to offer ideas and to discuss new ways of moving forward, but the boomer and Gen Xer, who the leader knows have excellent ideas, are reluctant to offer their opinions. She also notices they do not participate as often in lunches in the office breakroom and in company happy hours that take place once each month at a popular bar down the street from the office. The leader is afraid the two older team members are feeling excluded.

When she speaks to them both individually, the boomer and Gen Xer admit that they don't feel included in the office culture. They both say they like and respect their coworkers, but the millennials and Gen Zers have different interests and are much more willing to run with new ideas before fully vetting them. The leader realizes she needs to expand the office culture to include these two team members, so she takes the following steps:

- The leader begins by asking herself if she has modeled inclusivity through her own interactions with the boomer and Gen Xer. She resolves to work to eliminate any internal biases.
- In team meetings, the leader does more to stress the importance of all opinions and experiences, and she makes a point of trying to include the boomer and Gen Xer in team discussions.
- The leader works with the entire team to create group norms that are inclusive for all individuals, including all generations. As a group, they stress all opinions matter. She asks for ideas from the team on how to make the norms a daily part of their culture.
- The leader suggests they rotate through different bars for their company happy hours because the current bar is extremely popular with millennials and Gen Zers but not as popular with other generations. She asks the group, including the boomer and Gen Xer, to recommend new places.
- The leader checks the company hiring procedures, terminology used throughout their operations, and steps in their review process to ensure she and the others are being inclusive.

Throughout the process, the leader continues to deepen her relationships with the boomer and Gen Xer through listening and valuing their opinions. She resolves to do more to recruit boomer and Gen Xer talent to continue to diversify the team.

NEXT STEPS

4-GEN
leadership

HELPING ALL YOUR GENERATIONS
THRIVE IN THEIR TEAMS!

Are the current generational DEI initiatives in your organization a result of a workplace problem or were they created proactively to strengthen your corporate culture?

Who in the organization creates the culture and are there dominant generations setting the tone and direction? If so, how can you make this a more balanced culture that is inclusive of all generations?

If you've experienced any negative responses to DEI initiatives in your organization, is it because of personalities, because of generational views, or because of something else, and how will you address negative responses in the future?

Figure 7.2 Chapter 7 next steps worksheet

CHAPTER 8

Welcoming Gen Z to the Workplace

Key Points of This Chapter

1. Gen Zers continue to present new challenges in today's workforce that are forcing leaders to rethink how to cultivate a more supportive, positive workplace.
2. Gen Zers know they are different from other generations, feel misunderstood, and want to be given the space to develop and thrive.
3. Four-gen leaders are looking for new strategies to support and connect with their Gen-Z employees so that their youngest employees can continue to be an asset to the organization.
4. Four-gen leaders want to help Gen Zers tap into their passions and understand accountability as they make their professional dreams a reality.

Research is showing that it's difficult for many traditional leaders to connect with and lead Gen Z. Supervisors of Gen Z are in "a unique—and in some ways unprecedented—position"[1] of leading a generation that is expecting more of its employers as it also tries more than previous generations to balance its work/life needs.

A top business headline in 2023 stated: *three in four managers find it difficult to work with Gen Z*. In the survey released by Resume Builder of over 1,300 managers and business leaders, 49 percent of them stated it was difficult to work with Gen Zers "all or most of the time." Sixty-five percent of the leaders said that they fired more Gen Zers than any other generation, and 12 percent had fired a Gen Zer less than one week after the start of their employment. Most of those same managers prefer to work with millennials.[2] The survey also found that two of the biggest reasons Gen Zers are difficult employees are their lack of effort and motivation. A third reason Gen Zers are difficult new hires, and the reason that got the highest percentage of responses, might surprise some people: too many Gen Zers lack technology skills they need to be successful at work. In addition, the managers consider Gen Zers to be more sensitive than other generations; they don't respond well when being critiqued about their work or effort.[3]

Leaders should look closely at this data about Gen Z and link the findings with some of the points already presented in this book. Four-gen leaders will know that Gen Zers, more than any other generation, are driven by passion and a need to make a difference. If the Gen Zers lack passion and motivation, is it because they don't find their jobs, many of which are at the entry level, fulfilling? It's not a new concept for employees of any generation in the workforce to question how they got into mundane 9-to-5 jobs and to complain about their working conditions and low pay; what's different is that today's Gen Zers are less likely to tolerate being in an unfulfilling position. In addition, social media plays a significant part in how Gen Zers form their vision of work, and it might distort their reality when they only view amazingly positive job posts other Gen Zers share on TikTok and Instagram.

It must also be remembered that Gen Zers, as mentioned in Chapter 2, have grown up at the center of their families. They are used to being respected and active participants of the family. Four-gen leaders will also understand Gen Zers have grown up in a world of choice where if they didn't like one option, whether it was a video game, a club sport, type of food, or how to spend their free time, they moved on to another option, often with the full support of their parents. They are bringing this mindset and shared expectations into their jobs.

If Gen Zers are more sensitive than other generations, as indicated in one study,[4] does it mean they need a different approach from their supervisors? The necessity of coaching, not managing, was discussed in Chapter 3. Leaders must develop relationships with Gen Zers and offer timely, authentic, personalized feedback to reassure the Gen Zers that the leaders are interested in their development. According to other data, a significant number of Gen Zers consider themselves to be hard workers who have had to overcome obstacles thrown in their way by the older generations. A survey of Gen Zers found:

- 32 percent of them say that they are the hardest working generation.
- 36 percent of them think that they have it the hardest of any generation
- 39 percent of them feel high school did not prepare them for their jobs
- 42 percent of them feel that college did not prepare them for their jobs.[5]

> **How are you helping Gen Z become a valuable asset for the organization?**

A study found in 2023 that 78 percent of Gen Zers were likely to look for a new job in the near future,[6] which means they are constantly looking for new opportunities. It's also one reason Gen Z has been nicknamed Generation Quit.[7] They are leaving their jobs for a variety of reasons. A Cigna global health report in 2022 reported that stress plays a key role in Gen Z's job performance. According to the survey, 91 percent of 18- to 24-year-olds say they are stressed, and 87 percent of 25- to 34-year-olds say they are stressed. The hybrid work environment, while welcomed by Gen Zers, has also meant they are not mingling with their more experienced team members as much as previous generations, and they worry that this is slowing their professional growth. It also found 18- to 24-year-olds are seeking more trust and more engagement from their managers.[8]

These conflicting data coming from the opinions of Gen Zers and the opinions of their supervisors are troubling for numerous reasons. More Gen Zers are entering the workforce each year, and they will play a vital role in the global economy. The data show that Gen Zers are having trouble fitting into a business world where they need to be successful for their prosperity and growth. It won't be good for them, the economy, or society if they bounce from job to job seeking a place where they fit. Plus, research shows Gen Zers, because of both their talents and challenges, have a disproportionally larger influence on their organizations than other generations,[9] meaning their success or failure could have a disproportionally larger impact on their team members and the company's productivity. The Gen Z employment puzzle needs to be solved.

An essential question asked today is "Who needs to adjust their practices to support more Gen Zers to be successful in the workforce, the business leaders or the Gen Zers themselves?" Perhaps, the answer can be found through compromise. Many business leaders need to do more to understand their youngest employees, and Gen Zers need to do more to understand what's needed to be successful in the workplace.

How can you help Gen Zers have a clear understanding of what is expected of them?

If one were to ask Gen Zers which steps their supervisors could take to help them acclimate to the workplace, they'd give some of the practical advice mentioned in previous chapters, like helping them align their passions with their careers, coaching them through the steps they must take to continue to develop and grow, offering competitive pay and benefits, and helping them find a good work/life balance. Here are some other strategies 4-gen leaders can use to help Gen Zers in acclimate to the workplace.

Prevent Misunderstandings With Generational Awareness Training for All

Sometimes, Gen Zers don't understand the views or actions of their older leaders to the point that the Gen Zers become angry or disillusioned. As mentioned in Chapter 3, organizations should develop cultures that are open and accepting of the four generations in the workplace—which means all generations need to study the characteristics of other generations to understand who they are and how they view the world, including how they view work, and point out the connection from experience to behavior. The development of a multi-generational lens should be a priority to help alleviate Gen Z's frustration with their colleagues and supervisors,[10] helping other generations to learn about their Gen Z colleagues in a respectful and educational way.

Rethink the Onboarding Experience

With the evolution of hybrid and exclusive remote employees due to the pandemic, the onboarding experience has continued to be an area of concern and frankly a source of high turnover because of the employees' lackluster experiences. Leaders should create an experience where Gen Zers can thrive by focusing on empathy, belonging, and community. Leaders should allow Gen Zer to build the connections they need to feel supported and the network they can lean on to grow and learn as they continue to develop their careers. Leaders should remember to ask for feedback post-onboarding and adjust accordingly.

Communicate More Effectively, Share More Information, and Involve Them

Gen Zers, more than previous generations, want to be heard.[11] When they enter the workforce, they expect to be informed, consulted, and coached by their supervisors. When it comes to engaging Gen Z, leaders need to be sure to inform them of what is happening and why it is happening. When Gen Z understands the leaders' reasoning, they are more inclined to be supportive of their initiatives, changes, and strategies.[12] This is especially important for those Gen Zers starting their careers in a fully remote environment. It can be isolating, and these new professionals are not organically connecting with colleagues to have an open dialogue about the organization and what it means for their role specifically.

Ditch the Analog Mindsets

One of the most frequent and annoying issues for Gen Zers is the inability of some boomer and Gen X leaders to adopt a digital mindset. Gen Zers are the first truly digital generation. For them, technology isn't a new thing—technology's just another part of life they've always had, have always used, and will expect to use in its various forms forever.[13] They become frustrated when they see processes that could be made more efficient with technology usage.[14] Boomer and Gen X leaders, who have spent most of their lives adjusting to new technology, should commit to constant digital growth for themselves and their employees. They should ask, "How can I use technology for this, and are my employees getting the best training on how they can more efficiently use technology?"

Leverage the Latest Software and Provide Tech Training

One of the surprising results of the 2023 Resume Builder survey, that Gen Zers lack the technology skills to be successful in the workplace, means 4-gen leaders must not assume that just because Gen Zers grew up with social media and devices that they know how to use business software.[15] They have a digital mindset, but they might not have professional digital skills. They, too, will need to be trained alongside the other generations. Consider weaving commonly used software and technology platforms into the onboarding experience from Day 1. It is also important to highlight that new training efforts need to be bite-sized and present in the flow of work. Learning should be done in a short-video presentation style, while individuals are in the process of their daily work and not as a standalone 45-minute lesson where learning is disconnected from the actual work experience.

Eliminate "Could This Have Been an E-Mail?" Meetings

Millennials and Gen Zers, tend to want to move, sometimes for better and sometimes for worse, at a faster pace than Gen Xers and Boomers. They want to get things done. When they attend meetings, they want the meetings to run efficiently so that they can get something accomplished and then get back to their responsibilities for the day. Leaders should balance the need to foster relationships with the need to honor the time of all attendees.[16] Put another way, the pleasantries shouldn't take up too much time. Also, meeting agendas are good in that they show proof of planning, help the attendees know what will be covered, and help them organize their thoughts; however, the leaders shouldn't spend so much time explaining the agenda that the meeting becomes boring and perfunctory.

Avoid Age-Related Advice

Older generations should be aware of *how much* advice they are giving Gen Zers. Younger generations in the past have tolerated some of the tips passed to them by older colleagues, but today's accelerated rate of change and the vastly different generational experiences mean some of the traditional advice passed down from older generations could be outdated and offensive to Gen Zers. Here is some traditional generational advice that should be questioned in today's hyper-change world.

- "When you get older, you'll agree with me."[17] Being older doesn't make someone right, especially when the world is changing so rapidly. Gen Zers will be in their 50s and 60s in the 2050s and 2060s, and society and the working landscape will be radically different, which will call for new ways of thinking, not necessarily the thinking of today's boomers and Gen Xers.
- "Pull yourself up by your bootstraps."[18] The boomers were told hard work would help them advance in the world, but Gen Zers disagree and often are stressed because they see themselves working hard in a rapidly evolving global economy as they

have trouble finding affordable housing, face new uncertainties because of advancing AI, and are already seeing the effects of climate change brought about by previous generations. They don't want to be told to work their way through their troubles, many of which are new and feel extremely oppressive.

- "All of you young millennials... ."[19] Many boomers and older Gen Xers don't realize their youngest colleagues are Gen Zers and refer to all young people as millennials. While millennials and Gen Zers have commonalities, they also have differences.

Realize Power and Titles Don't Mean as Much to Gen Z

An irony of this point is that Gen Zers care deeply about their titles at work while not giving as much credence to the titles of more senior positions. Sometimes, when Gen Zers can't get a pay raise they seek a *title bump*, which has led to *job title inflation*. Since 2019 and the Great Resignation, which was led by Gen Zers, the word *lead* is used three times more, *principal* is used 57 percent more, and *junior* 50 percent less in job descriptions.[20] Another irony is Gen Zers' extreme confidence in their own ability to solve problems means they don't put as much stock in the abilities, or titles, of experienced leaders. They question traditional norms in the workplace, and their confidence (or overconfidence as some leaders would say), can be unsettling or annoying to older leaders.[21] Leaders of Gen Z should understand that Gen Z (and probably Gen Alpha and other future generations) will need to be coached and not be put off by their confidence or willingness to question established attitudes and procedures.

Implement Swift but Thoughtful Organizational Change

One millennial who has worked with Gen Zers made this observation: "Ideas from boomers and Gen Xers tend to be safe, but millennials and Gen Zers often have more ambitious ideas... Older generations tend to be more risk-averse. Gen Zers would rather ask for forgiveness than permission."[22] However, the millennial points out that the rapidly formed, big plans of Gen Zers and millennials sometimes don't have the feasibility needed for implementation or the needed return on investment. A proper mixture of the four generations in a team could result in a combination of vision, risk, caution, and success. The challenge for leaders is to quicken the pace to accommodate impatient younger team members while also listening to older team members and doing a thorough benefits and risk analysis.

Question and Adjust the Dated, Established Professional Norms

As mentioned throughout this book, Gen Zers are less likely to accept the status quo, and this includes questioning some of the most basic of business norms, as they see the world becoming more digitized, more diverse, more complicated, and more casual.[23] Business leaders of all generations are currently asking, "What does professionalism mean today?" Boomers and older Gen Xers who entered the workforce in the 1960s, 1970s, and 1980s were trained with long-established business norms, such as what it means to keep professional hours, to have professional attitudes, and even what it means to dress professionally (covered more extensively later in this chapter). These boomers and Gen Xers inherited these norms from their mentors in the Silent Generation and from the early boomers—norms that had been used in business for centuries. Gen Zers, more than any other generation, are dismantling many of them.

Understand Work–Life Priorities, and How It Is Connected to Wellness

Some critics of Gen Zers say they are unprofessional and need to develop more professional attitudes. However, when these critics take a closer look at some of the professional issues involving Gen Zers, they'll see it might be a matter of having new priorities—and not a case of lacking the will or talent to be successful. For leaders, these new priorities can fall into new areas that create new types of problems with new types of generation gaps to bridge.

For example, a millennial leader told the authors a story about a Gen Z team member and technology usage. The company had its most important programs downloaded onto its computers, and all team members needed to have access to the company devices. This leader ensured the Gen Zer was given a top-of-the-line computer; in this case, a new one that had never been used. But, there was a problem: it was a PC and not a MacBook. The Gen Zer had used a MacBook her whole life and didn't want to use the PC. The Gen Zer was initially adamant that she be allowed to use her MacBook. Her devotion to Apple products (or perhaps her inability to move out of her comfort zone) caused her to come across as inflexible and unwilling to compromise on behalf of the organization and on behalf of the team.[24]

In another example related to the authors, a Gen X principal approached a Gen Z teacher and asked to see her during the teacher's conference period, the time of the workday assigned to the teacher for planning, grading, and meeting.[25] The Gen Z teacher responded, "But that's when I do my yoga. Can we meet some other time?" Previous generations of young teachers would not have suggested a meeting with the principal be put off for a personal reason, especially for an activity that stresses mental balance and emotional well-being. A principal is often busy before school days, during lunch periods, and after the school day is completed. Teachers are also busy throughout the day, so the teacher's conference period might be the best opportunity to meet. When the Gen Zer balked at giving up her yoga time to meet with her superior, she (like the other Gen Zers) appeared to be placing her personal wishes over the welfare of the organization. However, in fairness to the Gen Zer, stress and burnout levels remain high in teachers,[26] and new ways of thinking, including adding more stress reduction activities, need to be incorporated into schools today.[27]

Another story about stress was related to authors by a Gen X school principal who had to talk with a Gen Z teacher about the Gen Zer's excessive absences. The teachers in that school system were given 10 sick days to use in a 183 day school year, and this particular Gen Zer had used almost 20 sick days. The principal was concerned for the health of the teacher but also had to worry about the missed days of instruction for the students (a substitute teacher filling in for the teacher could not bring the expertise of the regular teacher or have the essential relationships fostered with students). The young teacher told the principal the primary reason she was missing school was that she felt stressed, and she referred to her sick days as *stress leave*. Then the teacher asked the principal, "Isn't that why we're given the sick leave? To use as we see fit, including for days when I feel so stressed I can't do my job?"[28] The Gen X principal urged her to improve her attendance.

In previous generations, the youngest members of the team (with the least amount of seniority the ones easiest to terminate) would have gladly accepted the new computer, put off the yoga session, buried their stress, and reported to work. They wouldn't have questioned the decisions of their leaders or wanted to create their own paths. But these are Gen Zers, and they have been raised in ways that encourage them to be individuals. Four-gen leaders will understand Gen Zers don't blindly follow the wishes of their leaders—they need to be coached and supported in new ways.

In each of these examples, transparency on role norms and expectations is crucial. There are times when 4-gen leaders can bend and flex to new generation gaps, and there are times when corporate policy is set. This is not to say that corporate policy cannot change, but for the current organizational state, there is a precedent and that takes effort and process to change. Those norms must also be communicated to Gen Zers to find that compromise in the workplace.

> **How can your organization better communicate role norms and expectations to avoid generational conflict?**

Define the Workplace Dress Code

As the world becomes more casual, employees of all generations must ask what is accepted and not accepted in the office. Dress code—if the office still has a dress code—is often a hot topic. Prior to the COVID19 lockdowns of 2020, around one in five companies were operating with no dress codes,[29] and that number has probably increased post-COVID-19 as companies work harder to retain more team members in an employee-friendly, more relaxed work environment. It's especially hard sometimes for the casually inclined Gen Zer to know how to dress. Sometimes it's necessary to have one-on-one conversations with Gen Zers who might not understand the dress code or just don't want to follow it. One millennial leader interviewed for this book cited an issue in her organization in which a Gen Zer was joining online meetings with upscale clients where the other members of the organization and the clients were in business casual—while the Gen Zer was constantly dressed in a hoodie. The organization recognized the importance of coaching the Gen Zer, so it addressed this issue by having a popular leader discuss it with her person, not through text or e-mail with the Gen Zer. "It's important how you approach them," said the millennial leader.[30]

Gen Zers often don't see a link between dress and success. As one Gen Zer put it, "I don't think you need to be in a suit to look professional and be taken seriously."[31] Boomers also have trouble understanding some of today's business dress requirements—especially when it comes to dressing down or dressing more casually. To understand business casual, boomer leaders should look at it this way: what they often wear on the weekends is now acceptable as daily business wear.[32] It can be expected dress codes to become even more relaxed in the future as Gen Zers move into management roles and will be the ones setting the dress code—or eliminating it.

Understand Gen Zers Are Resetting the Conversational Boundaries

While Gen Zers are helping to push business norms in new directions, boomer and Gen X supervisors need to understand Gen Zers are more "open than any generation before them,"[33] and are "more likely to talk casually...about aspects of their personal life in the workplace,"[34] including topics that were once taboo. For example, they are less afraid of telling managers what the managers are doing wrong and discussing their compensation with their colleagues.[35] They are also more willing to discuss their mental health (which might first have been destigmatized by millennials[36]). In 2023, Gen Zers expanded the boundaries around a topic once considered taboo: menstruation. In that year, numerous TikTok videos featuring new types of sanitary pads provoked discussion about their effectiveness while also sparking debate about women's genital health.[37] While this would not be a work topic in most companies, Gen Zers' need for authentic conversations could bring it and other topics into the workspace, especially in conversations between other Gen Zers. If members of older generations overheard talk about menstruation, they might find it inappropriate. They, and their leaders, need to understand the Gen Zers were not trying to be offensive—they were just being authentic.

Marketers understand this authenticity needs to be exhibited when targeting this generation.[38] Companies, too, are redesigning their branding to be clearer and to have fewer euphemisms because Gen Z isn't afraid to say or do things previous generations shied away from.[39]

Help Gen Zers Understand the Need for Grit

Finally, 4-gen leaders will help Gen Zers (and members of all generations) understand the power of grit in the workplace. In 2016, Dr. Angela Duckworth released her best seller, *Grit: The Power of Passion and Perseverance,*[40] in which she identified grit as being able to identify what drives us and possessing the will to follow through on commitments. While the need to possess grit is not a new requirement for success, the book's message connected with readers of various age groups in an era of hyper-change and generational shifts. Determination and perseverance still matter.

Think of how 4-gen leaders can use the grit philosophy to assist Gen Zers. The Gen Zers already want to connect with their passions, so the first part of the grit mentality is a natural fit, but do they always understand the follow-through needed to turn those passions into success stories, especially a generation like theirs that has been raised with a myriad of choices in how they can live their lives?

It's clear some Gen Zers, including the ones who are successful entrepreneurs, have exhibited grit. They had dreams and worked hard to make their dreams a reality. Not all Gen Zers can be entrepreneurs; however, 4-gen leaders need to understand the dreams of the Gen Zers on their teams. The leaders need to try to find a way to connect the Gen Zers' passions with the organization's goals and reinforce the need for hard work and perseverance. They need to stress to the Gen Zers that they should never stop learning and must strive to do and be better daily. Gen Zers want to see paths to a better future, so their leaders should help them design their paths and connect how exhibiting grit can lead them to success.[41]

Voices From the Generations

Landen Stacy, an 18-year-old Gen Zer, interviewed for this book, went directly from high-school graduation into the workforce—and he's pursuing his dreams. Stacy has always had a passion for the outdoors, specifically being on the water and boating. As a child, he grew up on water and loved everything it offered. For him, it was a fun way to spend time with friends and family, an outlet for stress, a connection to physical activity, and a unique way to meet people. Today, Stacy is a full-time employee for a well-known marina based in Ohio, but he works out of the company's Tennessee location. He says, "I worked my way up in the company, first pumping gas in boats over the summers, then selling apparel and watersports equipment in the store, next traveling with the company to dealer boat meetings and boat shows. I love being on the water showing customers everything a boat has to offer. Now I've got a full-time job in the sales department selling boats to customers." He credits both his parents for affording him the opportunity to grow up on the water and the marina owner, a millennial, who saw he had passion and drive and knew he'd be a great fit for the organization long term.

In addition to his career, Stacy is an entrepreneur. He loves teaching people new things about watersports. He gives private lessons, teaching others how to wake surf, wakeboard, and a crucial factor on the water—how to safely operate a boat. He says, "When you are knowledgeable at something, it doesn't feel like work. I enjoy seeing the accomplishments and joy in others." When it comes to working with other generations he says, "Between my team and customers, I connect with all the generations. In sales, it's important to know your audience and listen to what they are saying. For older generations, I focus on selling points they care about, like comfort and affordability. For younger generations, I bump up the music and show off the light system and appeal to their wants and needs." Stacy recognizes "social media is a huge part of brand awareness for the marina, and oftentimes the initial sale starts because kids see our boats and share the videos and pictures with their parents and next thing you know they are all in the showroom." Stacy supports the social media channels for the marina too.

As for career aspirations, Stacy would one day love to own his own dealership. For now, he is just getting started and says, "It's about the process, learning, building connections, and doing the work to gain the skills I need to get there." In his career, he wants to feel connected, make a difference in the world, and have fun along the way. Stacy is an example of a Gen Zer who knows what he wants and is working hard to reach his goals.[42]

Your Real-World Connection

Imagine this scenario: A Gen X leader has recently hired two new Gen Z employees to join a team of boomers and Gen Xers. However, after they have been working for six weeks, the two Gen Z employees tell the leader they don't know if they fit into the organization. They both say they are considering taking jobs elsewhere. The leader doesn't want to lose these two Gen Z employees because they are hard workers, have good attendance records, have positive attitudes, and are assets to the team. The leader meets with them individually and asks why they are not satisfied with their jobs, and they give these reasons:

- They don't like the dress code.
- They think the department meetings are too long.

- They see areas where the organization needs to be better; yet, they don't see progress being made in these areas.
- They are dissatisfied with the technology they are using; they want newer devices and better software.
- One of the new Gen Z employees says the two of them have compared salaries, and this employee is upset the other employee makes more money per hour, even though they were hired at the same time. The Gen Z employee making more money is also upset about this discrepancy and thinks it's unfair that the other person makes less money.

A traditional leader would have told the two young employees:

- They are to follow the dress code whether they like it or not.
- The meetings are long because they have a lot of important information to cover.
- It's not their job to identify where the organization needs to be better.
- The organization's technology is the best they can afford, so they should stop complaining and use it.
- It's the boss's prerogative to set salaries, and salaries are best not discussed.

However, this leader is a multi-gen leader who understands Gen Zers, so the leader responds to the two Gen Zers in this way:

- The leader explains the reasons for having the dress code but assures them the dress code is periodically reviewed and adjusted. The leader assures the Gen Zers, who want to be heard, that they will be included on the committee that will review the dress code in the near future.
- The leader is looking for ways to make the meetings more efficient, so the leader asks the Gen Zers for ideas. They tell the leader that they'd like to see the meeting's agenda before the meetings so they can be more prepared to participate, and they also suggest the team use an online polling system to gather

information before the meetings to save time gathering input during the meetings. The leader agrees to consider implementing their ideas.

- The leader asks the Gen Zers for their ideas of where the organization can be better and assures the Gen Zers they all have the same mission and improvement goals. The leader realizes the Gen Zers don't have a complete picture of all that is happening within the organization, so the leader shares information about progress being made at different levels of the organization. The leader agrees to keep them informed of future improvement steps and will ask for feedback on these changes.

- The leader acknowledges the devices and software could be better and assures them that upgrading technology is a priority. The leader shares the timeline for the next upgrade and asks if they would be willing to form a committee to research and pilot potential new tech that could improve job performance. In full transparency, the leader tells them it would not part of their day-to-day roles but would need to be done outside of normal business hours. The Gen Zers are given the opportunity to advance in the organization if they can show they are willing to go beyond normal job expectations.

- The leader discusses the discrepancy in pay. To protect the privacy rights of both employees, the leader doesn't provide specific information about individual qualifications. However, the leader assures them both the pay was set fairly and based on experience, education levels, and specific skillsets. The leader also reminds them they both can move into more challenging and impactful roles in the future and will receive pay raises based on their new responsibilities.

In summary, the multi-gen leader dignifies the Gen Zers and includes their ideas (when practical) by encouraging them, helping them to focus on the future, and reminding them they can eventually move into new, higher impact roles in the organization.

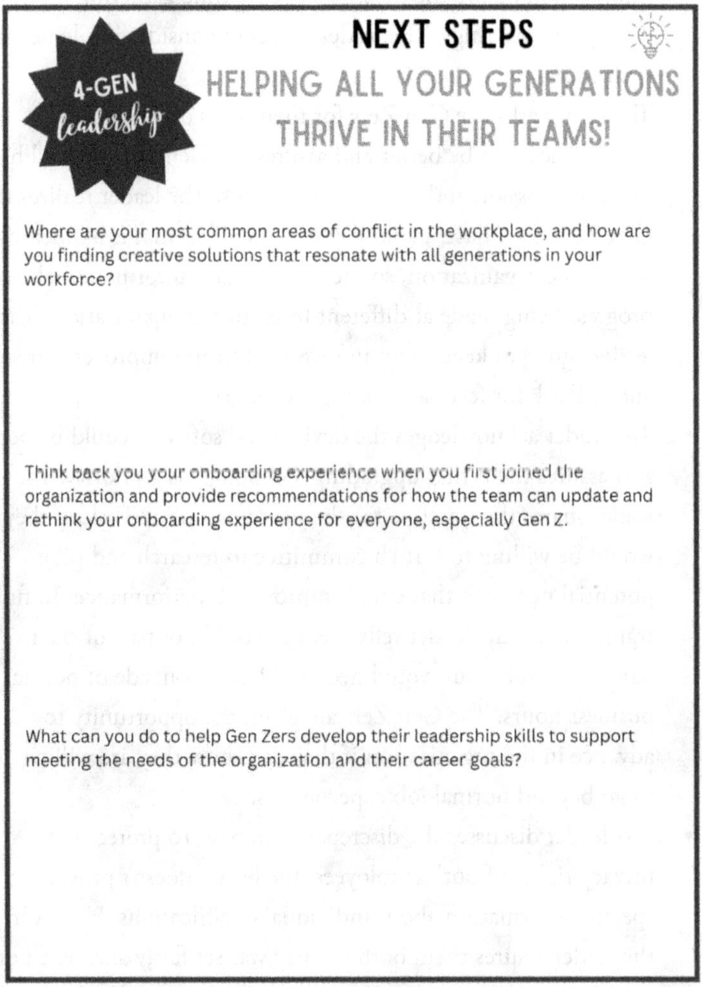

NEXT STEPS

4-GEN *leadership*

HELPING ALL YOUR GENERATIONS THRIVE IN THEIR TEAMS!

Where are your most common areas of conflict in the workplace, and how are you finding creative solutions that resonate with all generations in your workforce?

Think back you your onboarding experience when you first joined the organization and provide recommendations for how the team can update and rethink your onboarding experience for everyone, especially Gen Z.

What can you do to help Gen Zers develop their leadership skills to support meeting the needs of the organization and their career goals?

Figure 8.1 Chapter 8 next steps worksheet

CHAPTER 9

Personal Brands for Each Generation

Key Points of This Chapter

1. Individuals of all generations need to develop their personal brands.
2. When leaders and team members align their brands, the organization is more successful.
3. Boomers and older Gen Xers might be reluctant to form personal brands.
4. Millennials and Gen Zers feel personal branding is an important part of who they are personally and professionally.

One of the most important professional goals of the past decade has been for individuals to develop their personal brands, which is "the conscious crafting of a person's public identity, which includes their image, their story, and their position within particular communities."[1] In a mobile, transforming workplace, it's important for individuals to be known for who they are, what they stand for, what they can do, and most importantly, how others view them. In the past, personal branding was more commonly known as a tool only used by celebrities and top-tier executives, but now branding has become a way for job seekers and employees who want to market themselves.[2] However, a personal brand is more than how a person is perceived. It can also be a useful, personally crafted tool for self-growth because it can be used to build trust, improve self-promotion, refine an elevator pitch, expand a network, and advance a career.[3] A personal brand is not just who the person is, but just as importantly, it's who that person aspires to be.

It's no surprise that the generations take different views on branding. Some generations embrace the idea of showcasing singular talents and accomplishments, while other generations are hesitant to embrace a concept that promotes the individual. Leaders need to know the basics of branding so they can build and use their personal brand—and these leaders need to use a multi-gen lens to know how to help the different generations develop theirs.

Branding Basics

Here are essential questions 4-gen leaders can consider:

1. What do I stand for?
2. What are my skills?
3. What are my goals?
4. Where does my brand show up?
5. How can my brand help me to grow and achieve higher levels?[4]
6. How do I get the different generations on my team to identify with my brand?

These questions are profound. They push individuals to reflect and dig deep into their personal and corporate souls. Do they stand for helping others? Are they motivated by making money? Does corporate success drive them? This first question about taking a stand in life is sometimes the most difficult—and most exciting—question to answer. In the hustle of day-to-day life, between the job, personal commitments, stress, challenges, and successes, it's sometimes easy for a person to lose track of what he or she stands for, or it could be the vision has changed with age and experience, which brings up another point: personal brands evolve as a person ages, changes jobs, and gains new life experiences.

After people narrow their vision to who they are now and what they aspire to be, they need to ask which skills they currently have and which skills they must acquire to fulfill their mission. Are they technical skills or interpersonal skills? Are these the primary skills they've used to be successful? Do some of them need further development? The world is moving toward a skills-based workforce.[5] Success in finding work and advancing in an organization will depend upon skills, and these skills need to be showcased online and offline, during all sorts of actions and interactions, and on a daily basis in personal and professional settings.

> **Has your personal brand evolved since the beginning of your career?**

When establishing goals for a personal brand, it's important for individuals to ask, "How am I measuring my success in achieving those goals?" This question also calls for extreme soul-searching. It pushes people to get a truer picture of who they are and what they have achieved in their personal and professional lives. It's important to remember this question can be answered through various metrics in professional and personal lives. Sometimes, goals are something measurable like getting a degree or job title, but sometimes, they could be more abstract and involve helping others on their team, raising children, or volunteering in their local communities.[6]

In forming a brand, people of all generations need to know where their brands are seen by others. They sometimes mistakenly think a personal brand is only found online on social media sites or in the bio section on the corporate website. These areas are, indeed, important for sharing a brand, but a brand is also found in how people live their lives, which is why personal branding can be such a powerful motivating tool: when people want to live their brand, it guides them in positive ways that help them become who they want to be in life.

Leaders of all generations need to have brands. One study found three out of four Americans were "more likely to trust someone who has an established personal brand."[7] Personal brands also help attract young talent, as stated in a Forbes article:

> The personal brands of your company's leaders and employees have a major impact on the organization's ability to hire, engage, and retain top talent. In fact, for millennials who are looking

to join your company, the brand of your organization and the brand of its leaders are equally important (in terms of recruiting) to the job that is being offered. In the hiring process, leaders and other team members are being googled. In the war for top talent, it's essential that the company brand and the brands of your people stand out from the competition to attract the best.[8]

Four-gen leaders should build brands that appeal to each generation. While the different age groups might have different ideas of what to place in their brand, all of them respect honesty and transparency. Regardless of what elements the 4-gen leaders want to place in their brands, the brands need to come across sincerely and with kindness and professionalism.

Managers should empower employees to build personal brands for the welfare of the company. Employees do a great deal to form the company's collective identity, which means their personal brands help comprise the corporate brand. Also, when employees align their brands with the company and with their managers, they remain more engaged with the company, even when they are away from the workplace. Ultimately, personal branding, when promoted, valued, and recognized, can help create a more cohesive, effective organization.[9]

After 4-gen leaders commit to developing their brand and helping their team members develop theirs, they need to use their multi-gen lens to see the challenges and benefits the different generations will encounter when branding.

Personal Brands and the Generations

To understand the generational approach to personal branding, it's easiest to start with the first generation to take advantage of the concept of forming a brand: the millennials. Some researchers believe the personal branding concept began in 1997, which happens to be around the time the millennials were entering the workforce when Tom Peters wrote an article titled *The Brand Called You: You Can't Move Up If You Don't Stand Out.*[10] Peters wrote that society had entered the "Age of the Individual," and it was "time to take a lesson from the big brands" to "prosper in the new world of work."[11] Millennials, who had been raised to be more individualistic than their boomer and Gen X parents, were happy to oblige. As the last of the millennials entered the workforce in the early 2010s, the Internet was more firmly built out and social media platforms were established that allowed them to carve out their unique online spots to showcase their brands. Today, personal branding is still associated more with millennials than with other generations. They are the first generation to grow up on this side of the Internet generation gap and in an era of hyper-change; thus, they are best suited to lead the way in understanding the requirements for showcasing personal attributes in a rapidly evolving, more personalized world.

Millennials have advanced in their branding from managing social media posts to using more sophisticated methods to establish brands. Their brands today might feature:

- Storytelling that allows the individuals to share their triumphs, struggles, and even their vulnerabilities
- Video and images that connect with the audience and reinforce their brand
- A focus on a certain area (a niche) that sets the individual apart from others
- Use of a variety of social media platforms that are most often used by the target audience[12]

Four-gen leaders who want to assist millennials (and other generations) with their branding need to help them answer these questions: Have they found a niche, a specialty, at which they excel? Are they using social media platforms to target a particular audience? Are they using videos and images to connect, especially on their LinkedIn pages? Unfortunately, too many LinkedIn profiles often lack adequate personal photos and *About Me* sections, two of the most important parts of any LinkedIn profile. Do their brands tell a story? People today want to connect with meaningful stories, so over-arching questions for creating personal brands include, "Does your brand have a positive tone, and is it helping others?"[13] Again, this goes beyond social media posts. It includes all sorts of actions and interactions.

The ancient Japanese concept of ikigai is a great baseline to leverage to start thinking about personal brands. Ikigai in Japanese translates into *reason for being*[14] Four-gen leaders can study these areas to build their own brands and to help their teammates as they build theirs.

IKIGAI (EE-KEY-GUY)

A Japanese concept that combines the terms iki, meaning "alive" or "life," and gai, meaning "benefit" or "worth." When combined, these terms mean that which gives your life worth, meaning, or purpose.

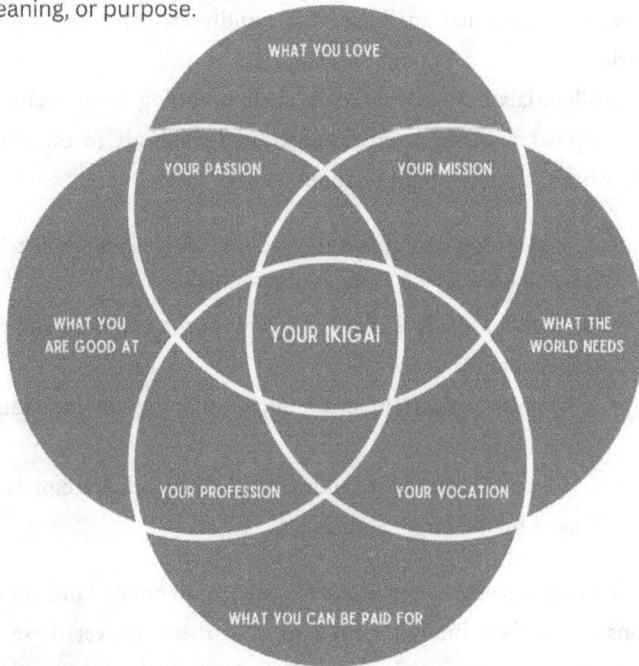

WHAT YOU LOVE

YOUR PASSION

YOUR MISSION

WHAT YOU ARE GOOD AT

YOUR IKIGAI

WHAT THE WORLD NEEDS

YOUR PROFESSION

YOUR VOCATION

WHAT YOU CAN BE PAID FOR

Figure 9.1 The ikigai can be used to form the basics of a personal brand

Boomers and Gen Xers: The Reluctant Branders

Branding is an area that boomers and older Gen Xers, who have been feeling increasingly left behind by a more technology-driven, rapid-paced world, find particularly challenging. Many of them don't care about branding, don't understand it, or are not interested in doing it. Often, they think of personal branding as how someone portrays themselves on social media. Because these generations did not have social media channels during their formative years, they sometimes don't see the value of personal branding the same way as millennials and Gen Z. Some boomers who place a greater emphasis on teamwork and conformity could even be opposed to the idea of developing a brand that promotes the individual because showcasing personal talents is the antithesis of how boomers were taught to be part of a team.[15] Plus, the personal branding movement began long after boomers and Gen Xers had settled into the workforce, and many of them have not seen a need to showcase their personal brand. When they sought new jobs or wanted to showcase their achievements, they referred to their resumes, which were pieces of paper that listed their achievements in chronological order. However, boomers and Gen Xers need to understand their degree, and many of their accomplishments were garnered decades ago—but the business landscape has changed so rapidly in the past decade that many of the resume points feel like they were achieved in another world that no longer exists. Those honors should not be forgotten. They often show the character of the boomer and the Gen Xers and their long history of success, but their attributes are most useful to companies today when they showcase how they help that company in today's world. The question becomes: Has this person evolved and developed the skills to help us now? A personal brand can help them do this.

> **How can you use your personal brand to help others understand the value of having a strong personal brand?**

Reluctant boomers and Gen Xers need to know this key point about personal branding: People of all generations have a brand, whether they know it or not.[16] This includes boomers and Gen Xers. A boomer or Gen Xer can be viewed as either someone skilled, talented, compassionate, and up on the latest trends—or as someone who appears to be lacking in those areas. The key word is *appears*; these experienced individuals who have not developed their brands might not be accurately showcasing to the different generations who they are or what they can do.

If boomers and Gen Xers have begun to job hunt late in their careers, including moving to new positions within companies, they have begun to realize they are competing with younger workers, many of whom have established their personal brands and stand out because of them. The boomers also begin to see that hiring managers might be millennials who value personal branding and are identifying potential new hires because of what is appearing in the applicants' LinkedIn profiles, which are extensions of their personal brands.

It's never too late for a boomer or Gen Xer to establish a personal brand. Boomers and many Gen Xers who develop their brands have a broad career of experience from which to draw and showcase, which in some ways gives them an advantage over millennials and Gen Zers. The younger generations might be aspiring to do in their personal brands what the boomers and Gen Xers have already accomplished in their careers; put another way, the millennials and Gen Zers are seeking success while the boomers and Gen Xers have already had it but must learn to amplify it. The boomers and Gen Xers need to reflect and focus on these accomplishments, but just as importantly in today's workforce, they need to identify the skills that made them successful. They need to tell their story in a way that is appealing in the 2020's.

As 4-gen leaders work with boomers and Gen Xers to establish their brands, they need to stress these points.

- Boomers and Gen Xers must be willing to showcase their strengths and experience and not undersell who they are or what they have achieved. Again, this is sometimes difficult because it runs contrary to how many of them were raised,[17] especially boomers. Highlighting skills and abilities doesn't have to come across as bragging about it. Boomers can think of it this way: Bragging is boasting about abilities, but branding is showing someone, like a teammate or prospective client, how those abilities can be of use to them.[18]
- Today's rapidly evolving economy and the companies wanting to thrive in it require team members who are up to speed on today's

demands, not the demands of yesterday. Boomers and Gen Xers should focus on the skills they possess today that allowed them to be successful through the decades.[19]

- Boomers and Gen Xers need to show they're humble and willing to learn, and this trait should show up in their brand. This means they need to value professional development and not discount it, and their brand should reflect how they have grown through recent professional and life experiences. They must also acknowledge the rapid rate of change and their need to evolve through constant reflection and upskilling.[20]

- While much of society places an emphasis on youth and vitality, boomers forming a brand shouldn't fall into the trap of pretending they are younger than they are. Transparency is essential in branding, and this includes boomers and Gen Xers owning their age and the experiences they bring to the position.[21]

- While a brand goes well beyond social media, boomers and Gen Xers should be careful not to neglect their online presence. They don't have to be social media experts, but they need to acknowledge they live in a digitally connected world and their brand can be showcased on various platforms.[22] Professional boomers and Gen Xers should at least have an up-to-date, attractive LinkedIn page, which is often the most visible and initial point of contact for other professionals who want to learn more about them.

Here's another point for boomers and Gen Xers to remember as they use their brands to apply for new positions: they shouldn't dismiss younger hiring managers because the managers do not have the same depth of experience. Besides having the authority to hire and promote, the millennial and Gen Z managers will have a firm grasp of what is needed to be successful in different positions and within that organization. The boomer and Gen Xer brands should show they can work well with people of all generations, including when being subordinate to younger managers. Ideally, the boomer and Gen Xer brands will mesh well with the brand of the person doing the hiring.

A final point for Gen Xers is that unlike the boomers who are retired or approaching retirement, the Gen Xers have a longer amount of time left in the workforce. As they develop their brands, they should be thinking ahead to how it might look and be used in their remaining years of work, some of which might stretch to well over a decade.

Gen Z and Branding

Personal branding is a natural fit for Gen Zers, the most individualistic of all generations.[23] One study found Gen Zers consider personal branding to be an essential key to job success[24]. When 4-gen leaders begin to work with Gen Zers on establishing their personal brands, they will probably find that Gen Zers have already begun to define who they are as individuals.

For example, one part of personal branding is using social media effectively, an area in which Gen Zers will excel. While Gen Zers grew up with social media, they need to remember their use of social media should be professional and consistent with maintaining a professional brand identity.

One of the most important goals for Gen Zers is the development of their skills. They should take courses, seek out mentors, and volunteer for projects that help them grow. Because they are at the beginning of their careers, they should constantly seek out networking opportunities by attending industry events, joining professional organizations, and interacting with key associates and leaders on social media.[25] LinkedIn is the world's largest professional networking site with over 950 million users in over 200 countries.[26] LinkedIn can be a powerful resource for Gen Zers to both expand their network and find the best practices used at various levels of business in multiple regions around the world.

Gen Zers forming their personal brands have a new challenge not faced by previous generations: avoiding the trap of striving to be just like the hugely popular influencers they follow on social media. Gen Zers should be striving to be authentic in their brands and not a clone of someone else's brand. They should act, dress, and develop the skills that fit who they are, not their influencers.[27] They shouldn't feel guilty if their brands are not as flamboyant or engaging as the handful of successful influencers who make their living off their brands. Their brands don't have to make money; instead, their brands should help them, during the span of their careers, to land new positions and live the professional and personal lives they desire. They need to be true to themselves, which means their brands might not be flashy, but they'll be authentic.[28]

Being authentic also means Gen Zers should avoid impulsivity in forming their brands. Just because friends or colleagues are putting some new trend in their brands does not mean everyone should do so. Gen Zers need to critically reflect on who they are today and where they want to go in the future to determine which elements should be in their personal brands. This will also help the Gen Zers be consistent, which will lead to a stronger brand.[29]

A final tip to help Gen Zers form their brands is to remind them of the importance of being intentional. For example, they could determine what they need to do in upskilling, networking, and promotion seeking that will help them become the person they desire to be.[30] After reflecting and forming a vision for the brand, the Gen Zers could form short- and long-term goals. For example, they could resolve to make three or four new connections each month and follow up with previous connections. They could commit to consistently searching for opportunities that help them grow and achieve their vision of who they want to be. They could also set benchmarks for their short- and long-term goals and be committed, perhaps in January at the beginning of the new year when people often make resolutions, to checking their brand for possible adjustments and updating.[31]

What realistic, measurable goals will you set for your team members as they begin to form their personal brands?

Branding will be even more important for Gen Z and generations in the future. Today, millennials are the largest group in the American workforce, and by 2028, millennials will comprise a majority of the global workforce,[32] which means the world is moving toward a society in which the majority of the workforce will have strong personal brands. In addition, more Gen Zers will enter the workforce each year, Gen Alpha, the next wave of workers, will be in the workforce in 2028. Because these younger generations are even more in touch with who they are and how they want to stand out, the personal branding movement is here to stay.

Voices From the Generations

Tara Harland is a 37-year-old millennial mom of two children, and she is a 12-year tenured employee of one of the world's largest banks. She knows what it takes to create an authentic personal brand, relate it to company values, and leverage it to rise through the ranks from an entry-level position to a highly valued senior relationship manager in the retirement division of her bank. Tara is a firm believer in transparency, honesty, integrity, and hard work—which are also all values prized by her bank. She is committed to work–life balance, but she says, "It doesn't come without sacrifice. You have to make commitments, stick to them for a set timeline, and then make adjustments when it comes to personal, family and career goals. Pulling too many levers at once isn't healthy for anyone."

When interviewed for this book about sharing advice for other generations in developing their personal brands, she has this advice: "Boomers, it's accountability. Don't forget why you started. You may be on the way out the door but don't bail on the rest of us yet. We are all working hard to make this organization a great place so continue to set up for success before leaving. Gen X, it's about being a visionary. You are about to be or already are our fearless leaders. Own it and take it very seriously. Be open to changes previous boomers weren't, and make sure you hold the younger generations accountable for a better tomorrow. Millennials, own your perseverance. Yes, at times you need to work harder to prove yourself and gain experience, but it won't go unnoticed in the long run. Don't forget to be proud of what you've already accomplished. Gen Z, embrace patience. We know you're an entirely new generation with access to things the rest of us never even could dream technology would be like. You need to give us time to catch up and learn the best way to approach your new ways of handling things."

Though Tara has a strong personal brand and a successful career, she also offers these words of advice: "It's important to have fun, be a life-long learner—don't get too frustrated when you make a mistake—and most importantly, never take yourself so seriously that you prohibit yourself from personal and professional growth."[33]

Your Real-World Connection

Imagine this scenario: A boomer leader has worked diligently to establish her personal brand. In forming her brand, she has identified her personal and professional goals, what she stands for personally and professionally, defined her unique qualities, skills, expertise, and values, and how she wants to be perceived both in-person and online to convey a memorable identity. However, she knows it's important that her brand aligns with the team members she leads, and she also wants to ensure their brands all align with the organization's corporate brand. So, she asks members of different generations to voluntarily join her in an upcoming focus session to discuss personal brands.

Prior to the session, the multi-gen leader takes these steps:

- She monitors who has volunteered to take part. She knows millennials and Gen Zers, who are enthusiastic about branding, will participate, but she makes sure boomers and Gen Xers are also represented in the session.
- She asks the participants to think of their brands and how they will describe them in the session.
- She wants to support her team members, push them to grow, and help them learn from each other, so she asks them, "What evidence do you have you've lived your brand?" She asks them to be prepared to voluntarily present ways their branding has shown up online and in person.
- She shares the main attributes of their organization's corporate brand and asks, "Do our individual brands align with our

corporate brand? Let's be prepared to discuss how our brands can support each other and the organization."

During the focus session, the multi-gen takes these steps:

- She understands the importance of modeling, especially for younger team members, so she leads the way in showing the steps she has taken to build her personal brand and how it aligns with the corporate brand. She strives to be authentic by discussing both her successes and challenges in building her brand.
- She understands team members, especially millennials and Gen Zers, want their opinions heard, so she asks for feedback from the group about her brand.
- She wants to involve the youngest Gen Zer in the group, so she asks the Gen Zer to make notes of the meeting on Dotstorming, a digital board all team members can access later on a 24/7 basis to add content, ask questions, give compliments, and vote on ideas.
- She asks for team members to share their branding stories, and she monitors the participation of her boomer and Gen Xer team members to ensure they feel comfortable developing and discussing their brands.
- She honors the boomers and Gen Xers for their decades of success and encourages them to capitalize on their accomplishments when cultivating their brands.
- She asks the group to find common strengths and weaknesses within the group in their brand development and how their brands are aligned with the organization's brand.
- She finishes the session by leading the group to a consensus around next steps for the individuals and for the entire group in strengthening their brands and providing more alignment.
- She asks for feedback on when to meet again, and they set a date for their next meeting.

After the focus session, the multi-gen leader takes these steps:

- She follows up with each team member individually to address his or her needs, especially from what she knows about their strengths and challenges and how they fit into their generations.
- She asks the boomers and Gen Xers, who might be struggling with the branding concept, if they have any questions about branding and offers, if needed, to team them with a millennial or Gen Zer who have successfully built their brands.
- She asks the millennials and Gen Zers, who often are intent on seeing progress, for feedback on the meeting and again asks what they would recommend for next steps in case they have any new ideas that formed after the focus session.
- She knows the Gen Zer who formed the Dotstorming board responds well to praise and coaching, so she will thank the Gen Zer in person and offer ideas on how the Gen Zer can take on an even greater leadership role in future meetings.
- She constantly monitors the Dotstorming board for ideas and who is using it and not using it, including the different generations within the team. She notes if the boomers and Gen Xers are participating or if the millennials and Gen Zers are dominating the online conversation.
- As she prepares for the next focus session, she forms an agenda based on progress, challenges, and the generational needs of her team.

NEXT STEPS

4-GEN *leadership*

HELPING ALL YOUR GENERATIONS THRIVE IN THEIR TEAMS!

How can you launch a personal branding initiative in your organization and what impact on the culture of your workplace might this have?

What did you learn about yourself when building your own personal brand, and how can you leverage these takeaways with other members of your team to encourage them to build their brand on and offline?

How do you balance the unique individual traits of your brand that may not completely match those of the organization?

Figure 9.2 Chapter 9 next steps worksheet

CHAPTER 10

Professional Development for Four Distracted Generations

Key Points of This Chapter

1. Upskilling has never been more important than it is today.
2. Only 25 percent of all funding for learning and development produces positive results.
3. All generations today have shorter attention spans, which makes training harder than in the past.
4. Presentation styles need to be adjusted to fit the needs of each generation.

Leaders must use their multi-gen lens in another critical area today: learning and development (L&D).

A 2022 LinkedIn survey found that the number of skills needed to be successful in many positions had grown by 25 percent from 2015 to 2021, and that the number of new skills would increase to 40 percent by 2025. Upskilling is a new necessity if employees and the company are going to keep pace with a rapidly changing workplace.[1] Learning professionals in the survey had these observations about today's training:

- 74 percent of them said L&D had become more cross-functional.
- 72 percent of them said L&D had become more strategic.
- 62 percent of them said L&D is playing a major role in reshaping the organization.[2]

It's not just the people who create our corporate learning programs who value professional development: the LinkedIn survey also pointed out 94 percent of employees want to work for a company that helps them develop as individuals. This means this desire for development is arching across the four generations. Almost everyone understands the need for growth and constant improvement.

Two key areas receive the primary focus for development today: (1) leadership and management training and (2) upskilling and reskilling employees. Corporations understand their challenge: an emphasis is being placed on developing leadership to lead in a new work environment, and they need to deepen employees' skillsets in a changing workplace.[3]

Professional development now plays a key role in forming company culture. According to another survey on learning and development, "Opportunities to learn and grow" was the top driver of work culture. Its rise in importance since the pandemic has been meteoric—it was ranked #9 in 2019.[4] When employees stayed home for parts of 2020 and watched part of the world unravel, they looked inward and realized they wanted to grow. They also saw their organizational operations transforming and wanted to stay ahead of the transformation. Two powerful motivators are driving the employees: a personal desire to fully develop as an individual and a professional realization they need to grow to stay relevant in a continuously reinvented workplace. An important note from the survey is that "Opportunities to learn and grow" was ranked ahead of other drivers, some of which are also related to corporate training. These include:

- Belonging
- Organizational values
- Support for well-being[5]

But, professional development is not just for the rank and file employees; the LinkedIn survey also indicated this new emphasis on training is forcing all the learning pros to continue to grow as leaders of learning and development. Eighty-five percent of learning pros expect to see at least the same amount of growth in themselves or perhaps even more growth as they complete projects and other tasks in their day-to-day operations.[6]

When companies place a high priority on developing the skills in their teams, they are also promoting a sense of belonging, reinforcing one of their key organizational values, and showing their support for the employee's well-being. Team members are happier and feel more motivated when they feel the company is investing in them, and they will be more prepared for future success. Plus, money and time are saved when current employees are upskilled instead of bringing in new ones.[7] It's a win/win for employees and the companies.

Almost half the development leaders say this need is showing up in budget allocations for training. In 2022, 51 percent of development leaders reported that they expected greater allocations, while 40 percent of the development leaders in Europe, the Middle East, and Africa expected increases in funding and 57 percent of the development leaders for the Asia-Pacific region expected increases in funding.[8] They are reporting they expect to see a continued increase in the money dedicated to development in the years ahead.

> **In which areas has your organization devoted more time, money, and resources for learning and development?**

Wasted Time and Wasted Money

Unfortunately, while the data show that organizations around the world are placing a heavy emphasis on training and are willing to fund it, much of it is ineffective. Each year companies spend U.S.$130 billion globally to develop their employees. However, it's estimated only around 25 percent of the training produces positive change, which means around 75 percent of this funding, or U.S.$97 billion, is wasted. Written another way, that's *97,000,000,000 dollars* spent without an adequate return on the investment. That's a lot of zeros representing money that could be better spent elsewhere.[9]

New Questions for Multi-Gen Professional Development

What's happening, or not happening, in corporate training that leads to this much waste? It can be "attributed to a range of factors including the quality of delivery and uninspiring content."[10] However, another factor should be considered: the different generations are bringing different perspectives on learning and goals into their training sessions. When designing goals, presentations, and tactics for training, learning leaders need to think of how they are going to deliver the content in ways that can appeal to different generations.

Four-gen leaders should ask new generation-based questions when planning professional development:

- "Which generations will be taking part in the training?" Most learning groups today will have a mixture of generations, but learning pros should analyze the group to determine if it is predominantly an older group, a younger group, or a group with an equal number of participants from the generations.
- "How will the training be designed to fit the needs of each generation?" Designers should then tap into their multi-gen leadership knowledge to determine the best tactics to use for that group. For example, the learning leader might design one training for boomers and a different training for Gen Zers. If the group is mixed, the training design will have a mixture of activities and scenarios that appeal to the different generations.
- "Which generation gaps might be exposed during the training?" For example, a heavy reliance on technology in the training, especially some parts of online training, could be challenging for boomers and older Gen Xers. On the other hand, younger millennials and Gen Zers might request more technology-based training.
- "How will those generation gaps be bridged?" A key part of all training has always been the *support* provided to learners as they learn and apply new concepts. Four-gen leaders will know the strengths and weaknesses of their generations and

the steps the leaders can take to help them through difficult passages, including the support needed after the initial training is concluded.

- Another critical element when designing training is the level of experience. This can directly apply to generations and their years in the workforce, but at times it does not correlate and should be considered as an important element of multi-gen professional development efforts.

Different Generations and Different Approaches

While 4-gen leaders should use their multi-gen lens to design and implement training, they should also remember not all members of the same generation have the same learning tendencies. However, the authors have noted in their research and their training of thousands of people in all generations that generational characteristics often become evident when training groups with mixed generations.

Boomers want the training to be successful for the welfare of the team. However, boomers have experienced decades of training sessions, and if 75 percent of their training has been unsuccessful, or perhaps even harmful, they could bring a cynical attitude into the latest training initiative. For too many boomers, training is not something to help them or the organization to be successful, but it is instead something that must be endured. Plus, they are now sitting in rooms or are online in training sessions with millennials and Gen Zers with very different views on a variety of topics. It's easy for them to become disengaged. Here are five steps multi-gen trainers can take to engage and help boomers:

1. Set clear goals for the training. Boomers want to know the expected outcomes.
2. Be organized. Have a clear agenda with objectives. Share the timeline for training and implementation. Be precise in the steps to be taken.

3. If technology is used, be prepared to assist the boomers. Some boomers would be more comfortable using paper than using their devices (if paper is an option).

4. Mix the boomers with other generations, especially younger generations. Boomers like to share their experiences and learn from younger team members.

5. Provide a clear picture of how success will look when the ideas are successfully put into place. Boomers want to be able to visualize it as they work toward it.

While boomers have become cynical with their approach to corporate training, Gen Xers grew up with more of a *prove it to me* attitude about life, and they, too, need some differentiated approaches to training:

1. Be clear on how the training will help the organization. Try to alleviate their cynicism.

2. Help the Gen Xers, who are beginning to peer into the future at their retirement, see how the training can help them be more successful individually in this latter part of their careers.

3. Allow them to be bridges between the boomers and millennials. Gen Xers have some tendencies of each of these groups, and they can help relate new ideas to these groups.

4. Be prepared to assist them if technology is used. While some Gen Xers were among the first to begin to use technology, the older Gen Xers might be more like the boomers and not comfortable using it.

5. Dignify the Gen Xers by reminding them they and their experience are needed to help the training to be successful.

When training millennials, it should be remembered they grew up on the digital side of the Internet generation gap. Devices and being online shaped their view of the world and how they want to get things done. These five steps can help millennials in their training:

1. Help them tie the training concepts to their personal branding. Millennials were the first to use branding, and if they see the connection between the training and their brands, they will be more engaged.

2. Let them see why the training is important. Millennials don't want their time wasted and want to see the purpose in what they are doing.

3. Use technology in most parts of the training. While millennials will want some face-to-face interaction, they will want to use technology to make the training more efficient.

4. Let millennials assist in leading the session or the initiative. They bring a digital, global mindset to the training and into their jobs, and their ideas need to be heard.

5. Consider how the millennials might be able to assist the Gen Zers when implementing the objectives. They are closer in age and philosophy to the Gen Zers, and the Gen Zers might be more comfortable working with them.

Gen Zers are still entering the workforce, but there are enough of them present now that learning leaders should be sure to use methods that fit their learning needs. These five steps will appeal to Gen Zers when designing training:

1. Be very clear about what the Gen Zers will get out of the training. They want to see explicitly how the training will help them grow as individuals.

2. Connect the learning goals with the overall mission of the organization. Let the Gen Zers know how the improvements brought about by the training will improve their efforts to make a better company culture.

3. Coach the Gen Zers. They want to learn and be guided. Reduce their stress. Reassure them during the training and implementation of ideas.

4. Involve the Gen Zers by calling on them, including them in planning, and listening to their ideas before, during, and after the training.

5. Gen Zers, who are the most digital of generations, will want the training to have a strong digital component.

> **What steps does your organization take to develop training that is a fit for all generations?**

Again, the suggestions for each generation could also appeal to members of other generations. Also, depending on the content and timeline, it might not be possible to work all the suggestions into the training. There could also be differences based on in-person and online formats. However, the wide disparity in generational views warrants, when possible, a new generational approach. Learning designers must be 4-gen leaders.

Training Methods to Engage Today's Hyper-Distracted Audiences

While learning and development leaders must use their multi-gen lens to differentiate for each generation, they must be able to balance these new generational needs with a common challenge in training all the generations: all generations today are hyper-distracted.

Researchers have noted how Gen Zers learn differently, but those leading multi-gen learning need to understand the other three generations—boomers, Gen Xers, and millennials—are also living in the same connected, digital world that has shaped Gen Z and is shaping Gen Alpha. These other generations, who have also adapted to a life of constant connectivity, and digital-first mindsets, are now taking in information in the same fast-paced ways as Gen Z. In the 2020s, the brains of all generations are being reshaped by digital interactions.[11]

Neuro-researchers have known for decades that the brain has the ability to rewire itself, an attribute known as neuroplasticity. Today's brains are changing because of their constant interaction with screens and apps, and it's affecting learning:

Pings, alerts, rings, and notifications can shift our focus in a way that can lead to long-lasting difficulties with paying attention. Difficulties paying attention can lead to poorer performance on academic, personal, and professional tasks. In fact, researchers from France and the United Kingdom found that frequent media multitasking may contribute to diminished gray matter in the anterior cingulate cortex, an area of the brain where attentional control resides.[12]

Effective training today begins with holding the attention of all the distracted generations—as attention spans are getting shorter. A Microsoft study in 2015 found that attention spans had dropped to eight seconds (from 12 seconds in 2000), meaning there are only eight seconds to engage the participants before the participants grab their cellphones or allow their minds to drift away to rehash the movie they watched the previous night on Netflix. That study was done almost 10 years ago. Microsoft found the attention span had shrunk by as much as 25 in just 15 years.[13] Today's trainers and content creators must wonder:

- Have attention spans continued to shrink?
- What is the length of today's attention spans?
- How long do we really have to engage an adult before the adult tunes out the message?
- Is the attention span even shorter for Gen Zers who grew up with a digital-first mindset?
- What will the Gen Alphas' attention span be when they join the workforce?

Regardless of exactly how long attention spans are today, it's safe to assume they are short. This doesn't mean employees can't concentrate; it just means they become distracted more easily and at a faster rate.

Sometimes the challenges run deeper than just attention spans. When creating new learning initiatives, it is also important to be aware of *Content Shock*, which occurs when people have so much content coming at them in all parts of their lives from various sources that they don't want to absorb any more new information because they are in a type of information shock.[14]

This is not a new concept. In 1970, the futurist Alvin Toffler famously made a similar prediction that people in the future (which could be now) would go into a state of *Future Shock*, a mental haze in which people would be unable to process all the information being presented to them and would mentally shut down.[15] Boomers and Gen Xers, who grew up on the far side of the Internet gap, could be struggling the most with the rate of change, the amount of new information, and the number of new skills they must acquire to stay relevant in the 2020s.

An uncomfortable reality of funding, planning, and delivering professional development is that while the importance of the content has never been higher, it's also never been as difficult to keep participants engaged. Individuals creating these programs need to recognize boomers, Gen Xers, and millennials are morphing into hybrid versions of Gen Z—to develop today's audience, they should think of it as having a new, collective moniker: *Audience Z.*

> **How can you reframe your professional development to better fit the needs of all generations?**

Ten Methods to Engage Audience Z (All of Us)

Remember we are all Audience Z. Besides catering to the generational needs and working Hattie's ideas into today's professional development programs, 4-gen leaders can use other tactics to engage Audience Z. Here are 10 tips the authors have successfully used in their multi-gen training sessions:

1. The importance of culture has already been stated, but 4-gen leaders need to create a positive learning culture where relationships are valued and all participants feel safe in voicing their opinions, including their unique ideas and solutions.

2. Present the agenda with learning goals at the start of the professional development initiative. When the participants have a clearer picture of how the learning program will unfold, they can absorb its content more easily.

3. Use simple, easy-to-understand language to match the more casual world of the 2020s.

4. Introduce the learning program with an essential question or a high interest activity that focuses the participants on the objectives. This will let the more cynical boomers and Gen Xers see an immediate link between the training and their work, and it will allow millennials and Gen Zers to participate as they report out and interact with their peers.

5. Use a digital tools to gather data in the training and a digital posting board to allow participants to share ideas. This will engage the learners and deepen their learning.

6. Use a diverse and inclusive mix of images, colors, videos, and movement on the screen.

7. An imperative aspect of training for Audience Z is the pacing—the activities must keep moving because of the shortened attention spans. In other words, if direct instruction is being used, the activities need to vary to hold the audience's attention. A person leading training might spend most of the session using direct instruction, but direct instruction should be chunked in 7- to 12-minute increments, and these increments are broken up by turn-and-talks, the use of a digital tool, a video, or some other activity to give the participants a break from the direct instruction.

8. A neglected tool is physical movement. We are all human and need to move around. At key times, especially in the afternoons after lunch, to have learners stand up, stretch, move around, and go across the room to share ideas with someone else. The act of moving keeps participants awake and more engaged.

9. Rigor is essential in training. Use questions and activities at the upper end of Bloom's Taxonomy, a hierarchy of thinking

developed by Benjamin Bloom in the 1950s to help organize levels of thought. Even though this tool was first developed 70 years ago (and revised in 2001 to place Create at the top of its hierarchy), it is still an effective tool to use to engage learners in the 2020s—and will be for decades to come. High rigor makes workshops more interesting and engaging. Audience Z wants/needs to be challenged to think.[16] Here are the levels of Bloom's Taxonomy:

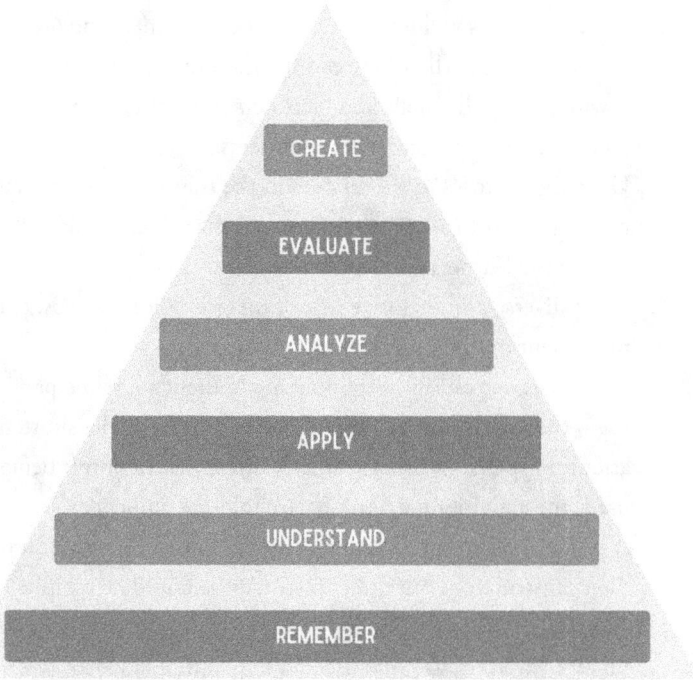

CREATE

EVALUATE

ANALYZE

APPLY

UNDERSTAND

REMEMBER

Figure 10.1 Trainers should be aware of the rigor of their training

10. Make the content relevant. Audience Z needs to see a purpose for participating. Remind learners how the activity will help them grow, help people in society, and help the company be successful. Put the *You* into the training, as in "This training is about YOU!" A way of measuring the relevance is to gauge the interest level of the participants.

A Framework to Measure Rigor and Relevance for Audience Z

The Corporate Need/Personal Interest (CNPI) framework is a tool designed by the authors to measure both the rigor level of the activities and the interest level of the participants in their learning programs. If the content is presented in a way that gets participants to analyze, evaluate, and create, and the participants find the content interesting (if they make a deeply personal or professional connection with it), then the learners will be more engaged and more likely to understand and successfully implement the ideas.

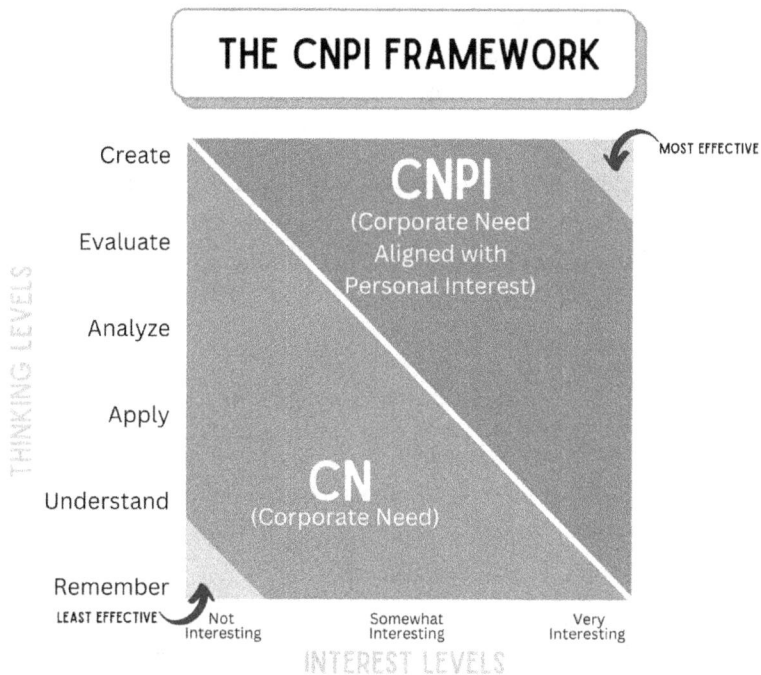

THE CNPI FRAMEWORK

MOST EFFECTIVE

CNPI
(Corporate Need
Aligned with
Personal Interest)

CN
(Corporate Need)

THINKING LEVELS

Create
Evaluate
Analyze
Apply
Understand
Remember

LEAST EFFECTIVE

Not Interesting   Somewhat Interesting   Very Interesting

INTEREST LEVELS

Figure 10.2 The CNPI Framework

After the Training

A necessary, and often neglected, part of a successful implementation is to provide generational support for the participants after learning has concluded. Many times, the participants are expected to go back to their jobs after the training session to immediately and smoothly begin to use the content. Sometimes they stumble and become frustrated when there are no clear paths for assistance. A step to take during the planning of the training—before the training even starts—is to form follow-up activities and announce that there will be support for the participants in days and weeks after the training has concluded. While professional development is meant to provide continuous improvement for team members throughout the organization, it's also important to gather feedback so that programs can continue to evolve and improve. An easy way to assess how the participants liked the training and to get ideas to improve future learning initiatives is to send out a quick survey (using a digital tool, perhaps something like Google Forms) that can be completed quickly and easily by the team members and can be quickly understood by the reviewers. Audience Z likes to be included, and getting feedback also models how the trainers wish to be coached like the team members.

An important generational component will be to examine professional development success through a multi-gen lens. If possible, the learning leaders need to determine if the training and implementation worked equally well for all generations.

Voices of the Generations

Mike Taylor is a Gen Xer who helps design training for over 30,000 employees at a global insurance and financial services company. Taylor is also a world-renowned speaker on professional development and has spent his entire career building his personal brand to support others in creating great training programs. He's a huge believer in the idea of marketing professional development. He says today you must "leverage that thinking when creating training because you have to get people to want to learn." Taylor also reminds us we can't get so caught up in the design of the content and the establishment of timelines that we forget we are dealing with people. He constantly asks, "What are good approaches to take with humans?" He tries to make "some simple tweaks to make along the way" to make training more engaging.

Taylor is excited to work with younger generations, and he has accepted some of their viewpoints. "They have different perspectives and ideas," he says. "It can be a two-way street when it works well." He finds hope in the millennials and Gen Zers. "The younger ones are so much more progressive," he says. "They've grown up in a more diverse society and haven't known any other world. They have an awareness I was never exposed to." He also believes the younger generations "just get technology easier" and aren't as afraid to try new things. As he puts it, "They are not afraid to break it." Taylor jokes, however, that sometimes their willingness to try new things can be problematic if they don't take the time to prepare. "My son says he's going to fly a space shuttle. I hope he doesn't say, 'I don't need training for this! I'll just play with it!'"

Taylor encourages team members across all levels to invest in their continued learning and education, especially in the workplace. The world is moving at rapid speed and the power of AI is only making it faster. He says, "The ability to continuously learn, update your knowledge, and even let go of outdated information will help you avoid falling behind."[17]

Your Real-World Connection

A millennial manager is hearing complaints about the quality of the organization's recent training session about a new process to be used in the future. When he speaks to team members of all four generations on the team, they tell him it is boring and not useful. Part 2 of the training will take place in five days, so the millennial manager speaks with the person who will lead the training and makes these multi-gen training suggestions:

1. Consult team members of all generations who will attend the training to hear what can be done to improve the upcoming session. Let them know their voices matter. Try to incorporate some of their ideas.
2. Be aware of which generations are in the room because they like to learn differently:
   a. Boomers will want to know how this process will be better than the previous process. They will want to know step by

step how the new process will look when it is implemented, and they will want to know the timelines and exactly what is expected of them so that they can be sure to do it correctly.

b. Gen Xers will be more open to using the new process than the boomers, but they, too, will have some questions about the need for the new process. If technology usage is required to implement the new process, the older Gen Xers who are closer in age to the boomers could be more apprehensive than the younger Gen Xers who are closer in age to the millennials.

c. The millennials, who will probably be the largest group in the training because they are the largest group in the workforce, will be more willing to use the new process than the older groups. Being more open to taking new steps, they will offer ideas throughout training on ways to successfully transition into the new process. They will be open to having a technology component present in the training and in the process because they know technology can make their work faster and more efficient.

d. The Gen Zers will want to know how the new process helps them grow as professionals, improves the company, and aligns with the company's mission statement. They might have more questions than other groups because they want more coaching and want to understand more about *the why* behind the process and its steps. They will also want less direct instruction than the older groups and will instead want more time to explore the process on their own.

3. Use strategies that engage all generations (Audience Z):
   a. Be sure to state the objectives and steps of the training to help all generations form a structure in their minds of how the training will unfold. Try to address the generational needs for its purpose.
   b. Start the training session with *a hook* that grabs the attention of the audience. It might be an image that is related to the new process or a highly rigorous and relevant question like,

"What do you think this organization could achieve if this new process is implemented on time and successfully?"

    c. Involve the audience throughout the training. Ask the members to respond to the whole group and the people they are sitting with.

    d. Use technology at key times to deepen learning and engage the learners, especially the millennials and Gen Zers.

    e. Vary the activities and keep the pace moving. Audience Z needs to move more quickly than the audiences of previous decades.

    f. At the end of the session, be sure to clearly articulate the next steps and timeline for implementation.

4. After the session, the organization should take these steps.

    a. Provide support for those team members who need it. Know how the different generations respond to coaching.

    b. If necessary, use traditional mentoring or reverse mentoring to tap into the talents of team members of different generations to help individuals grow.

    c. Take the individual personalities and needs into mind and check-in more frequently with team members who might need it.

    d. Be sure to celebrate the success of the team as the new process is implemented, because all generations like to be a part of a successful effort.

NEXT STEPS

4-GEN leadership

HELPING ALL YOUR GENERATIONS
THRIVE IN THEIR TEAMS!

How do your professional development efforts appeal and resonate with the
four generations in your workforce, and how are you adjusting the approach
when they are not making an impact?

Have you solicited feedback from your recent professional development
programs and adapted the current training into something more fitting for your
Audience Z employees?

How can you use the CNPI Framework to evaluate an upcoming professional
development initiative and increase its effectiveness?

Figure 10.3 Chapter 10 next steps worksheet

CHAPTER 11

Generations of the Future

Key Points of This Chapter

1. New generation gaps will emerge as the millennials and Gen Zers grow older and work alongside the Gen Alphas and Gen Betas.
2. Today's challenges for millennials and Gen Zers could impact them for decades into the future.
3. The boomer approach to work is fading into history and will never return.
4. Success in bridging generation gaps in the future will depend upon multi-gen cooperation and maintaining the finer attributes of being human.

What are the major generational issues of the future? In this era of hyper-change, it's imperative that multi-gen leaders see how the generation gaps of the past and present might impact the future. As one wise boomer, Francesco C. Leboffe, interviewed for this book so eloquently stated, "We need to understand what the previous generations have done, what the current generation is doing, and what the next one needs to do...Unless we take action, what good is knowledge?"[1]

Let's broadly summarize the accomplishments of the generations.

- The Greatest Generation and Silent Generation laid the foundation of many of the business and societal norms that dominated life for decades.
- Their kids, the boomers, refined and adjusted many of the norms.

- Then Gen Xers became the first generation to begin to question the norms.
- Today, millennials and Gen Zers are questioning even more of these established norms and are resetting expectations for office hours, work locations, environmental and inclusionary practices, work/life balance, and even the meaning of work in the 2020s.

How will future generations continue this evolution in how we live and work? First, we need to ask, "Which generations will be driving the change?" Most changes today are being brought about by the younger generations, the millennials and Gen Zers, partly because the millennials make up such a significant part of the workforce and partly because they and the Gen Zers bring new attitudes into their work and how they prefer to live. Will these generations continue to be the pacesetters of change, or will the Gen Alphas (who will begin to enter the workforce in 2028) and future generations transform the millennial and Gen Z norms as they stamp their different views on their world? Will the younger generations who will be growing up in the future with new, increasingly more powerful technology be the ones who have a vision for how businesses and the world should function?

In 2050, the ages of the millennials and Gen Zers will range from 45 to 74. They will be either approaching middle age or into their senior years. Will the Gen Alphas and Gen Betas look upon them the way the millennials and Gen Zers look upon the boomers and Gen Xers today, and will new generation gaps emerge as millennials and Gen Zers look over their shoulders and try to understand the new mindsets of the Gen Alphas and Gen Betas? Or, will the millennials and Gen Zers, who have grown up on this side of the Internet generation gap, have the flexibility to stay ahead of the waves of change?

Or, will we even have newly titled generations? Generations are now being labeled every 15 years. However, the acceleration of technology advancements means AI and new devices could be arriving at such rapid rates and life and work could be changing so quickly that it would be nonsensical to try to label a group as a generation growing up within a certain period. Technology could render generational labeling obsolete.

Future Challenges for Millennials and Gen Zers

According to a study by Deloitte in 2023, millennials and Gen Zers today are most concerned about four areas: financial security, work/life balance, mental health, and climate action[2]—and all these areas could impact them for decades to come.

The study found the high cost of living was the top concern of these two generations. Half of them live paycheck to paycheck, and they have been forced to take on side jobs to make ends meet. Many of them report they are postponing or abandoning the idea of buying a house, starting a family, or starting a new full-time job because of the uncertainty they feel in their economics.[3] How will these missed opportunities today affect their future mindsets and actions? Will they eventually be able to acquire property and start families, or will they be the first generations in which large numbers permanently lose these parts of adulthood?

Another area of concern is the balance of work and life; 62 percent of millennials and 49 percent of Gen Zers say work is central to their identity. Yet, they want options in where and when to work. At least 75 percent of them who are in remote or hybrid work roles say they would consider looking for a new job if they were forced to work full time in an office. They are also seeking more opportunities for part-time employees to advance in the organization.[4] Is there any reason to think these priorities will shift in the future, especially as Gen Alpha and Gen Beta join the workforce? Hybrid and remote work will remain necessary options for future employees.

Climate change is a major stressor for Gen Zers and millennials, and it's already impacting some of their actions and career decisions. About 15 percent have already changed jobs because of how their employers were addressing (or not addressing) climate change, and another 25 percent say they are planning to change jobs for similar reasons in the future.[5] In the decades ahead as the world experiences more extreme weather associated with global warming, it can be expected that a company's environmental record will be even more closely scrutinized by even more employees.

Dealing with stress is a significant challenge for millennials and Gen Zers. Nearly half of them say they "feel stressed all or most of the time,"[6] and many of them feel they can't talk with their employers about their mental health issues.[7] Stress will likely be compounded in the future as they deal with ongoing threats stemming from financial insecurity, finding balance, and a warming planet. For companies to stay competitive, they will have to offer various wellness programs for their team members.

Finally, Gen Zers see a new challenge that has entered society and the workforce, a challenge that will grow in intensity as it dramatically reshapes society and many parts of the business landscape during their lives: AI. A 2023 survey of younger Gen Zers shows that while over 75 percent of them have used AI, they have deep concerns about how it will affect them in the future:

- 45 percent of them think AI will replace their parents' jobs or reduce opportunities for them in their future professions.
- 45 percent are concerned that AI could be used to impersonate them
- 59 percent are worried AI will collect too much of their personal data.
- 55 percent fear AI could allow their personal photos to be used in making sexually explicit or inappropriate images.[8]

There's no reason to believe these concerns will be alleviated for the Gen Alphas, Gen Betas, and Gen Gammas who will be living in the latter part of the 21st century. Or, if these generations get lucky, perhaps they will find ways for the latest iterations of their AI to correct the mistakes and transgressions of the previous AI.

Questioning America's Current Role in the World

As they move forward, multi-gen leaders should recognize that millennials and Gen Zers have such a different view of America that they even question what it means to be American. When 1,026 adults were asked in a 2021 poll about their feelings toward America, 69 percent said they were proud to be American. But, notice how these numbers break down by generation:

- 84 percent of boomers said that they were proud to be American
- 71 percent of Gen Xers said that they were proud to be American
- 52 percent of millennials said that they were proud to be American.
- 58 percent of Gen Zers said that they were proud to be American.[9]

Only a little over half of the millennials and Gen Zers answered in the affirmative, which means almost half of them were *not* proud to be American. They were not buying into the America they have seen and experienced in their lifetimes. That number of disillusioned Gen Zer's grew dramatically over the next two years. Another poll, this one taken in 2023, showed that *only 16* percent of 18- to 25-year-old Gen Zers said they were proud to live in the United States.[10]

Boomers and Gen Xers were raised with the post-World War II philosophy that espoused the idea of American exceptionalism, but millennials and Gen Zers grew up watching the world on their devices. Their global view has allowed them to view America from afar, and not from just beneath the American flagpole. A summary released by the polling firm Morning Consult said, "COVID-19 lockdowns, social unrest, and graphic images of police brutality may be causing them to abandon" their faith in the American way of life, "especially in terms of respect for civil liberties at home compared with less democratic countries."[11] This lack of belief in American exceptionalism means many millennials and Gen Zers don't view American leaders, American companies, American culture, or American history as even remotely exceptional.

Will Gen Zers and Gen Alphas be able to reshape America and its politics as more of them become voters and politicians? The voters of Florida's 10th Congressional District became the first electorate in America to pass the leadership torch from an older generation to a Gen Zer in November of 2022 as 25-year-old Maxwell Frost became the first Gen Zer elected to Congress. Frost is a progressive. Like many other Gen Zers, he places social issues at the top of his priorities. Over a third of American Gen Zers are politically active, and over half of them are "extremely interested in environmental issues,"[12] and early evidence about young voters shows they tend to be more liberal, and remain liberal, than previous generations.[13] Key elements of Frost's campaign platform were meant to appeal to millennial and Gen Z voters: addressing climate change, ending gun violence, protecting abortion rights, and providing health care for everyone.[14] Frost has been active in the *March for Our Lives* organization, the national group formed after the Parkland High School shootings in 2018. He's also a member of the American Civil Liberties Union. He refers to Gen Z as the "school shooters generation."[15] Frost hasn't finished college; he's been busy community organizing and driving for Uber to pay his rent. The opponent he defeated? Calvin Wimbish, who is a 72-year-old former Green Beret and a conservative activist. Wimbish is also a Baby Boomer.

As a 25-year-old, Frost is much younger than his Congressional peers, who in 2024 average 58 years of age, which would place them at the end of the boomer generation and beginning of the Gen X generation. This means Frost could be separated in life experiences, views, and dreams by up to *two or three generations* from many of his colleagues. Over half of Americans are in its younger generations: the millennials, Gen Zers, and Gen Alphas. Yet, they are woefully underrepresented in political offices. This is especially true for females and people of color.[16] The U.S. Congress tends to be made up of white males who are boomer and Gen Xers. For now, Frost is an extreme outlier, but it's only a matter of time before Congress will be reshaped by the younger, more diverse generations. America has over 68 million Gen Zers, and more of them reach voting age each year. This is the message to Congress: Gen Zers are coming, and they're bringing new attitudes. Members of Congress today should be looking beyond their own life experiences to connect with them. Multi-gen leaders will know their employees might be interested and involved in politics, but they could be wanting to steer America in a new direction.

A Crisis and a New Beginning?

As we look to the future of the generations, we should also consider another role they could be playing: cyclical agents of change. William Strauss and Neil Howe, in their 1997 book *The Fourth Turning*,[17] say that history, especially American history, moves in cycles called saecula that repeat every 80 to 100 years—and these cycles are driven by generations.

According to their theory, each 80 to 100 year saeculum consists of four periods of 20 to 25 years called *Turnings*. Each Turning plays a critical role in the cycle of the saeculum and history. In the First Turning, called the High (or spring period), society experiences a new beginning, meaning it is experiencing prosperity and seeing itself and the world differently. In the Second Turning, called the Awakening (or summer), a period of unrest begins when the children begin to reject their parents' views. In the Third Turning, called the Unraveling (or autumn), the unrest grows and various institutions begin to decay. In the Fourth Turning, called the Crisis (or winter), many of society's institutions, norms, and cohesion begin to fall apart.

According to Strauss and Howe's theory, America's current saeculum began after World War II in the 1940s. When considering the 80- to 100-year timeline for the saeculum, it means in the 2020's, America has entered this saeculum's Fourth Turning, the Crisis. More precisely Howe writes in his sequel *The Fourth Turning Is Here*[18] that the Fourth Turning, which always has a climactic event, began with the financial crisis of 2008.

In addition to naming the Turnings, Strauss and Howe have given the generations distinct names that correspond with the roles they play in the saeculum: the first generation born into the saeculum is the Prophet generation; the second generation is the Nomad generation; the third generation is the Hero generation; and the fourth generation is the Artist generation.

Consider how Strauss and Howe's theory aligns with what we are experiencing today: wars being fought around the world, a global decline in faith and in traditional institutions, a deepening fear of the future, and a feeling that governments and society are not functioning as well as they should in a fraying global community. As Strauss and Howe's projected, our world has indeed moved from an Unraveling into a Crisis. Furthermore, their naming of the generations aligns well with what we know about today's generations.

- The boomers are the Prophets; they are the wise ones who have presided over a world of their making that is now rapidly decaying.
- The Gen Xers are the Nomads; they are the cynical generation that will assume more prominent leadership roles in the final turbulent years of the Crisis.
- The millennials are the Heroes; they are the first generation born on this side of the digital generation gap and poised to play a heroic role in providing fresh ideas as the world enters history's first digital-based saeculum.
- The Gen Zer's are the Artists: the world's first digital natives who have grown up with a global mindset that could make them the most creative and most progressive generation in history, attributes that could lead to a new Renaissance of thought in future Turnings.

A positive note in these troubled, disruptive times is that Howe in The Fourth Turning is Here asserts the world should be headed into a new saeculum in the 2030s—and into the next positive first Turning, a Spring of new beginnings—from which will emerge "a new egalitarian, outward-facing, confident and unified America, a high-tech version of the Eisenhower era...."[19] This will be the time (if the theory continues to function in an era of hyper-change and the world survives the end of the Fourth Turning without experiencing a global nuclear war) when the millennials, Gen Zers, and Gen Alphas begin to leave their mark on global history.

The Demise of the Boomer Education System

If generations of the future are going to reach their full potential, a boomer legacy in a key area must be replaced: the education systems used around the world to educate the younger Gen Zers and the Gen

Alphas. As the global society moves deeper into a connected, rapidly evolving economy, education systems must adjust their philosophies, goals, and actions to help their graduates develop entrepreneurial mindsets to help them thrive in a constantly evolving world. This is not a new concept; it's been said by countless American education leaders since the advent of the global economy in the 1990s that they were going to reinvent education. While progress has been made, Gen Zers and Gen Alphas are still being educated for the most part in the same obsolete boomer system used to educate their grandparents: the school years are still the same length, many of the same methods are still being used, much of the same content is still being taught, and a 20th-century testing model with its one-size-fits-all mentality is still the measuring stick of success or failure at the national, state, and local levels. Gen Zers believe the education systems have failed them; one study showed they don't think they've been adequately prepared to enter adulthood.[20]

In Chapter 10, the need for rigorous thinking was stressed in professional training. The same rigorous thinking in which students work in the upper levels of Bloom's Taxonomy is needed in classrooms at all grade levels today. The rigor of the education standards being used in the classroom, or what is being taught and how much creative thinking is involved, is too low. Today's Gen Zers and Gen Alphas are spending too much time memorizing the facts of the boomer world as current jobs disappear or change and new jobs emerge.[21]

This is not meant to be an overly harsh criticism of educators; professionals in all fields in all parts of the world have struggled to remain in front of the tidal wave of technological and societal change. Educators have a particularly hard time with their small training budgets, lack of time for training, stream of mandates from state education agencies, and the demoralizing weaponization of school boards. Yet, if education doesn't evolve, it will doom Gen Z, Gen Alpha, and Gen Beta to gain a set of knowledge that is woefully inadequate for success in the 2030s, 2040s, 2050s, and beyond. Today's Gen Alpha students will be the first generation to live into the beginning of the 22nd century,[22] which means the skills taught today will be used into the 2070s, 2080s, and 2090s. Young people today need to develop flexible, problem-solving mindsets to thrive in their hyper-change futures.[23]

Some millennial and Gen Z parents aren't waiting for their schools to change. They're forming their own education vision and expectations of K-12 schooling through their home-schooling initiatives. According to a 2023 article in *The Washington Post*, "Home schooling has become —by a wide margin—America's fastest-growing form of education, as families from Upper Manhattan to Eastern Kentucky (and beyond) embrace a largely unregulated practice once confined to the ideological fringe."[24] According to the article, the number of home-schooled students has jumped over 50 percent since COVID-19 school closures in 2020s, and there are now between 1.9 and 2.7 million home-schooled students in the United States. Parents are now beginning in larger numbers to reject the current traditional education models. More Gen Zers and Gen Alphas are staying home. These parents understand this about their Gen Z and Gen Alpha kids: they are being raised to be unique and don't fit into one-size-fits-all school systems.

Whether it's more home schooling, a reworking of public schools, or a creation of some other new types of schools, it's abundantly clear a new model is needed. In 2021, one of the authors of this book wrote "the education system we need doesn't exist yet."[25] It still doesn't exist, but it could be that the millennials and Gen Zers who have ditched significant parts of the boomer business mindset will be able to ditch the boomer school model for one that works better for the Gen Alphas and Gen Betas.

Boomers: Fading Into History

The first words of this book were, "OK, Boomer...." It's appropriate that one last look at the boomers is taken in this book's final chapter, and more significantly how the boomer mindset and approach to work —with all its blind loyalty and willingness to sacrifice for the team—are fading into history.

An emotional and significant generational milestone was reached on September 1, 2023, when boomers mourned the death of a generational peer who was one of the most successful and influential boomers to ever strum a guitar: Jimmy Buffett. He was born in 1946, which was the first birth year of the boomer generation, placing him among the oldest boomers. His life spanned the entire era of boomer influence.

And his demise is a symbol of the passing of the boomer work philosophy.

To understand the significance of Buffett's passing for an entire generation is to understand an epic battle involving their work, a sort of internal civil war that no generation will ever experience again—the battle that raged for decades within the boomer psyche. Boomers have lived lives of dueling priorities: one voice in their head told them to do what they were taught by their Silent Generation parents, to throw themselves blindly into their jobs. But, another internal voice was also speaking to them, urging them to slow down and to do more to enjoy life. In many boomers, the voice advocating for work was loudest. They have been among the hardest working of any generation, but Buffett's music, and his success, were evidence of a boomer angst that permeated their conflicting attitudes toward work and life.

While Buffett's music was popular with all generations, it resonated most deeply with boomers and older Gen Xers who dreamed of escaping their 9-to-5 jobs, mortgages, and commitments. In his life and his brand (as he accrued millions of dollars in profits off his music, restaurants, resorts, clothing, and all things Buffett), he was a boomer rebel. Buffett didn't wear dress shoes; he wore flip-flops, and many times on stage, he didn't even wear shoes but was barefoot. He didn't have a traditional job; he lived on tropical islands and hung out in beach bars and on sailboats. He didn't live a sedentary life; he flew a massive seaplane around the Caribbean. For boomers, the world was a place for work; for Buffett, the world was a place for play. He followed his heart. When Buffett made the beach a part of his career, he became a boomer hero. Boomers wanted to be like him. They had been taught to pay their dues to get their one week vacations, but Buffett was their pied piper of escapism. When they went to Jimmy Buffett concerts on Saturday nights, they could take one-night vacations and forget the jobs awaiting them on Monday mornings. Who else could get these normally staid boomers to wear grass skirts, brightly flowered Hawaiian shirts, and inflatable flamingo hats? For boomer Parrot Heads, the affectionate nickname given to Buffett's fans, his music helped them survive their internal civil war.

When Buffett's death was announced, Buffet's boomers felt a part of them had also died. They went to their Facebook pages and posted memories of attending his concerts and what his music had meant to them. His influence was so large that his death was also felt by the younger generations. The kids of these boomers and older Gen Xers in the millennial and Gen Z generations had grown up hearing Buffett's *Margaritaville* playing on their parent's home stereos and CD players at the beach. His music had been part of the background soundtrack of their lives. To them, Buffett's passing wasn't the demise of *their* dreams—their generations had already rejected the weight of blindly sacrificing too deeply for the sake of a job and career—but they recognized his significance to their parents, and they offered their condolences. Buffett's passing brought a stark reality into clearer view: Buffett was a boomer, but his mindset was Gen Z. Boomers who toiled endlessly and wanted to be like him were in some ways wanting to be more like millennials and Gen Zers.

Another way to see Buffett's passing is to view it as a window closing on the boomer-led world and the boomer work philosophy. As of this book's publication in 2024, the youngest boomers are 60 years old and reaching the end of their careers. While many of them are choosing to work later into their lives because they are living longer and want to stretch their dollars, millions of them have retired. An estimated 10,000 boomers reach retirement age in America *every day*.[26] The civil war in the boomer psyche is coming to an end, not because boomers have found a way for the priorities of work and leisure to coexist, but because the conflict is being resolved through retirement. The boomers have paid their dues. The last of them can now slip quietly off to their beach to watch their sunset at peace.

For the older Gen Xers, most of whom are still in the workforce, they are looking at retirement with trepidation: the majority of them think they will not be financially prepared for retirement.[27]

The dueling voices of work and leisure in Gen Xers are more tempered because Gen Xers were the first generation to openly question the role of work in their existence. They led the way in disavowing a blind loyalty to work, companies, and authorities, and this need for balance has grown stronger in each successive generation. Future generations will no longer blindly throw themselves into their careers and sacrifice their happiness for a paycheck. That era is gone forever. Multi-gen leaders of the future will have to cope with the new work ethos: millennials and Gen Zers will work just as hard as their predecessors—but they will continue to seek jobs that align with their mission and desire to make a difference. Of course, most of the managers will be millennials and Gen Zers, so many of them will share this need for balance. A looming question for them to answer as they advance in their careers is: Will they find balance as they advance through the leadership ranks, or will they eventually succumb to the pressures of time and responsibilities that come with organizational leadership as many of their boomer and Gen X predecessors did before them?

Gen Z: The Hope for the Future?

Finally, let's consider the finer attributes of Gen Z and how it might lead the world into a more peaceful, inclusive future. It is the most digitally capable, most diverse, most socially conscious, and most accepting generation in history. Gen Zers don't care as much as earlier generations about who people date, where they are from, what they do, how they identify, or what happens to be the color of their skin.[28] They are ready to lead: a poll of over 3,000 Gen Zers in 2023 found 82 percent believe they will achieve their goals.[29] Martin Luther King wrote "the arc of moral universe is long, but it bends toward justice."[30] Perhaps the finer attributes of Gen Zers and their younger Gen Alpha siblings will bend it faster.

To lead Gen Z and future generations, multi-gen leaders should heed the advice of a millennial leader interviewed for this book, Heath Ritter, who has a history of successfully managing startups. When asked how he would continue to stay relevant in the future as he worked with young people, he offered this advice: "Make time to connect with younger generations. Know their ideas might be big. Listen to them. Don't just discount them. People will need open discourse so people can still debate and agree or disagree on new ideas. Ultimately," he says, "people will need to find ways to be human."[31]

Notes

Chapter 1

1. Thebault (2019).
2. Anglesey (2022).
3. Brower (2022).
4. Ensign (2023).
5. Ibid.
6. Smith (2023).
7. Career Guide (2022).
8. Lynch (2015).
9. Nativ3 (2022).
10. de la Mora (2019).
11. McKenna (2023).
12. Purdue Global (2024).
13. Zelazko (2024).
14. Lowrey (2020).
15. de la Mora (2019).
16. Entrepreneur (2019).
17. Iqbal (2018).
18. Gianfagna (2021).
19. DiNardi (2023).
20. Calm Business (2023).
21. White and Scarpitti (2023).

Chapter 2

1. White (2022).
2. White (2023).
3. ResumeBuilder.com (2023).
4. Kim (2022).
5. Scarpitti (2023).
6. Kim (2022).
7. Focardi (2021).

8. Williams (2023).

9. Smith (2021).

10. Literary Devices (2020).

11. Spector (2019).

12. Russell (1993).

13. Frommer (2023).

14. McKenna (2023).

15. Currier (2018).

16. Smith (2021).

17. Currier (2018).

18. Turpin (2023).

19. Nulsen (2021).

20. Cottrell (2023).

21. Cottrell (2023).

22. Brindle (2021).

23. Pollak (2023).

24. Doran (2023).

25. Zelazko (2024).

26. Fuscaldo (2023).

27. The Garage (2021).

28. KinderCare (2022).

29. Gauthier (2019).

30. Scarpitti(2024).

Chapter 3

1. Cain (2018).

2. Ibid.

3. Knights (2021).

4. Bloznalis (2022).

5. Graniello (2023).

6. Dunlop and Pankowski (2023).

7. Italie (2023).

8. Ibid.

9. Ferland (2023).

10. UPCEA (2019).

11. Cooks-Campbell (2023).

12. Pelta (2023).

13. Vervent (2023).

14. Ibid.

15. Ibid.

16. Gupta (2023).

17. Jha (2023).

18. Wilmes (2023).

19. June (2021).

20. Ibid.

21. Jha (n.d.).

22. Morrison (2022).

23. Leading Effectively (2023).

24. Holland (2023).

25. Manik (2023).

26. Jones and Munday (2020).

27. Manik (2023).

28. Jones and Munday (2020).

29. Ibid.

30. Parker and Patten (2020).

31. TriNet (2015).

32. Stange (2021).

33. Jones and Munday (2020).

34. Jenkins (2019).

35. Jones and Munday (2020).

36. Burg and Mann (2007).

37. Carnegie (1936).

38. Scarpitti (2023).

Chapter 4

1. Hetler (2023).

2. Meister(2022).

3. Sull, Sull, and Zweig (2022).

4. Meister (2022)

5. De Smet et al. (2022).

6. Hyatt (2023).

7. Lobosco (2022).

8. Delgado (2019).

9. Rasp (2020).

10. Ibid.

11. Kumar (2023).

12. Perry (2023).

13. Akhtar (2019).

14. Morrow (2016).

15. Davidson (2019).

16. Llarena (2018).

17. Engstrom (2024).

18. Carlson (2022).

19. Christ (2023).

20. Hangsterfer (2020).

21. Ibid.

22. Digital Information World (2022).

23. Morse (2020).

24. Ibid.

25. Hangsterfer (2020).

26. Leading Effectively (2021).

27. Tannian (2022).

28. Tolan (2016).

29. Tannian (2022).

30. Leonhardt (2022).

31. Tan (2022).

32. Fox (2022).

33. Raid (2022).

34. PR Newswire (2022).

35. Ibid.

36. Hangsterfer (2020).

37. Ibid.

38. 2022 Career Interest Survey (2022).

39. Their (2022).

40. Bump (2021).

41. Daly (2022).

42. SHRM (2019).

43. Scarpitti (2023).

Chapter 5

1. Hastwell (2022).
2. Parker and Horowitz (2022).
3. Iacurci (2023).
4. Zinkula (2022).
5. Goldberg (2022).
6. Parker and Horowitz (2022).
7. Smith (2023).
8. Iacurci (2023).
9. Prackash (2023).
10. Kaplan (2023).
11. Stahl (2022).
12. Bruner (2021).
13. Smith (2023).
14. Kaplan (2023).
15. Kelly (2023).
16. Brand (2022).
17. Kaplan (2023).
18. Molla (2022).
19. Stahl (2022).
20. Perlow and Porter (2021).
21. Fowell (2022).
22. Wigert and White (2023).
23. Anders (n.d.).
24. Christ (2023).
25. Ibid.
26. deloitte.com (2023).
27. Ibid.
28. Ibid.
29. Anders (n.d.).
30. deloitte.com (2023).
31. Aviva (2022).
32. Cooks-Campbell (2023).
33. Rook (2019).
34. Brown & Brown (2022).

35. Larsen (2023).
36. Hoffower (2022).
37. Forbes (2020).
38. Ibid.
39. Hoier (2023).
40. Ibid.
41. Ibid.
42. Dreibelbis (2023).
43. Epperson (2014).
44. Ibid.
45. Brand (2022).
46. Boehike (2019).
47. Sharma, Madaan, and Petty (2006).
48. Ibid.
49. DiNardi (n.d.).
50. Levine (2021).
51. Schroeder (2023).
52. Ibid.
53. Seeberger et al. (2016).
54. Gitlin et al. (2022).
55. Dow (2023).
56. Ibid.
57. Ibid.
58. Chen (2023).
59. Ibid.
60. Bohanan and Cohen (2020).
61. Martic (2023).
62. Ibid.
63. Ibid.
64. Ibid.
65. Scarpetti (2023).

Chapter 6

1. Robinson (2023).

2. Ibid.

3. Ibid.

4. Daugherty (2023).

5. Harter (2023).

6. ResumeBuilder.com (2023).

7. Tong (2022).

8. Ibid.

9. Carnegie (2023).

10. Pittinger (2023).

11. Davis (2022).

12. Brown (2023).

13. Harter (2023).

14. Pan (2023).

15. Kayser (2023).

16. Stanchak (2022).

17. Espada (2022).

18. Perry (2023).

19. ResumeBuilder.com (2023).

20. Onque (2022).

21. Kodé and Hanley (n.d.).

22. Huddleston (2022).

23. Kodé and Hanley (n.d.).

24. Ibid.

25. Madell (2023).

26. Kelly (2023).

27. Harter (2023).

28. Madell (2023).

29. Harter (2023).

30. Tong (2023).

31. Ibid.

32. Czerwonka (2023).

33. Roller (2023a).

34. Ibid.

35. Roller (2023b).

36. Gostick (2022).

37. Veras (2023).

38. Roller (2023).

39. Gostick (2022).

40. Robinson (2023).

41. Ibid.

42. Ibid.

43. Gostick (2022).

44. Scarpitti (2023).

Chapter 7

1. WorldatWork (2021).

2. Sakpal (2023).

3. McKinsey & Company (2022).

4. SHRM (2022).

5. Williams (2020).

6. Creary (2023).

7. Minkin (2023).

8. Ibid.

9. Diaz (2023).

10. Kratz (2023).

11. Hawkins (2022).

12. Ibid.

13. Kratz (2023).

14. Hawkins (2022).

15. White (2023).

16. Falcone (2023).

17. Hastwell (2023).

18. Kratz (2023).

19. Jackson (2022).

20. Ibid.

21. Kratz (2023).

22. Focht (2022).

23. Ibid.

24. Ibid.

25. Ibid.

26. Ibid.

27. Jones (2023).

28. Choi (2024).

29. Walker (2023).

30. Choi-Allum (2022).

31. Miller (2023).

32. Ibid.

33. Urwin (2022).

34. Choi-Allum (2022).

35. Indeed (2024).

36. Dill (2019).

37. VANTAGE Aging (2020).

38. Indeed (2024).

39. Nezich (2023).

40. Autenrieth (2021).

41. Ibid.

42. Callaham (2023).

43. Ibid.

44. Ibid.

45. Simmons (2023).

46. Polles (2023).

47. Palmer (2022).

48. Wolfe (2018).

49. Ibid.

50. ASAE (2024).

Chapter 8

1. Kaplan and Knight (n.d.).

2. ResumeBuilder.com (2023).

3. Ibid.

4. Welcome to SHRM (2023).

5. Lomu (2023).

6. Gillespie (2023).

7. Chandler (2023).

8. Cigna (2022).

9. Segal (2023).

10. Kuligowski (2023).

11. Dunlop and Pankowski (2023).

12. Forbes (2023).

13. Scholl (2023).

14. Roberto Torres (2023).

15. ResumeBuilder.com (2023).

16. Gallaga (2023)

17. A Dime Saved (2023).

18. Ibid.

19. Ibid.

20. Siu (2023).

21. Kaplan and Knight (n.d.).

22. Scarpitti (2023).

23. Segal (n.d.).

24. Scarpitti (2023).

25. White (2023).

26. Will (2023).

27. White and Carter (2021).

28. White (2023).

29. Randstad USA (2019).

30. White and Scarpitti (2023).

31. Young (2023).

32. Ibid.

33. Hall (2022).

34. Rubin (2023).

35. Teo (2023).

36. Khan (2021).

37. Holman (2023).

38. Emiliani (2023).

39. Holman (2023).

40. Duckworth (2016).

41. Schroeder (2022).

42. Scarpitti (2023).

Chapter 9

1. Smith (2022).
2. Phys.org (2023).
3. Herrity (2023).
4. Love (2021).
5. Hancock et al. (2022).
6. How to Measure Your Personal Brand Effectively (2023).
7. Brand Builders Group (2021).
8. Arruda (2022).
9. Ibid.
10. Giridharadas (2010).
11. Peters (1997).
12. Kaminskaya (2023).
13. Bochantin (2018).
14. Perry (2021).
15. Marx (2022).
16. Miller (2019).
17. Marx (2022).
18. Goodgold (2021).
19. Smith and Kissell (2023).
20. Marx (2022).
21. Ibid.
22. Ibid.
23. McKnight (n.d.).
24. Phys.org (2023).
25. Cornelius, "How to Build a..."
26. About LinkedIn (n.d).
27. Mashao (2022).
28. Ibid.
29. Ibid.
30. Ibid.
31. Ibid.
32. Batchelor (2023).
33. Scarpitti (2023).

Chapter 10

1. LinkedIn Learning (2022).
2. Ibid.
3. Ibid.
4. Employee Well-being Report (2021).
5. Ibid.
6. Ibid.
7. Brush (2020).
8. Ibid.
9. Business Wire (2020).
10. Ibid.
11. Korte (2020).
12. Loh and Kanai (2014).
13. Chokhani (2023).
14. Ranieri & Co (2022).
15. Toffler (1970).
16. White and Carter (2021).
17. Scarpitti (2023).

Chapter 11

1. White (2023).
2. Deloitte (2023).
3. Ibid.
4. Ibid.
5. Ibid.
6. Ibid.
7. Ibid.
8. Carufel (2023).
9. Jarvis (2021).
10. Sachs (n.d.).
11. Ibid.
12. Howarth (2022).
13. Bouie (2023).
14. Liu (2022).
15. Ibid.
16. Andersen (2021).

17. Strauss and Howe (1998).
18. Howe and Strauss (2023).
19. Fukuyama (2023).
20. Rubin (2023).
21. White and Carter (2021).
22. McCrindle (2023).
23. White and Carter (2021).
24. Jamson et al. (2023).
25. White and Carter (2021).
26. Scates (2023).
27. Adamczyk (2023).
28. AP-NORC Center for Public Affairs Research (2021).
29. Rubin (2023).
30. Ellis (2011).
31. Scarpitti (2023).

Bibliography

"1 in 4 of Workers Are 'quiet Quitting,' Saying No to Hustle Culture." December 20, 2023. ResumeBuilder.com. www.resumebuilder.com/1-in-4-of-workers-quiet-quitting-saying-no-to-hustle-culture/.

"15 Ways Leaders Can More Effectively Manage Gen-z Workers." September 12, 2023. Forbes. www.forbes.com/sites/forbescoachescouncil/2023/01/17/15-ways-leaders-can-effectively-manage-gen-z-workers/?sh=26331ce94172.

"16 Gen Z Leaders Who Are Making an Impact." June 21, 2021. The Garage. https://garage.hp.com/us/en/modern-life/hp-generation-z-rising-impact.html.

"2022 Career Interest Survey." 2022. NSHSS www.nshss.org/media/35707/nshss018-report-final-v2.pdf.

"2022 Workplace Learning Report." 2022. LinkedIn Learning. https://learning.linkedin.com/content/dam/me/learning/en-us/pdfs/workplace-learning-report/LinkedIn-Learning_Workplace-Learning-Report-2022-EN.pdf?trk=bl-po&veh=LTS_Blog_Workplace_Learning_Report.

"3 in 4 Managers Find It Difficult to Work With Genz." ResumeBuilder.com. May 15, 2023. www.resumebuilder.com/3-in-4-managers-find-it-difficult-to-work-with-genz/.

"41 Percent of Gen Z-ERS Plan to Become Entrepreneurs (Infographic)." January 15, 2019. Entrepreneur. www.entrepreneur.com/leadership/41-percent-of-gen-z-ers-plan-to-become-entrepreneurs/326354#:~:text=Members%20of%20Gen%20Z%20seem,something%20that%20changes%20the%20world.

"91% of Gen X and Baby Boomers Feel Overwhelmed by Technology, Study Finds." n.d. Digital Information World. www.digitalinformationworld.com/2022/09/91-of-gen-x-and-baby-boomers-feel.html.

"About Linkedin." n.d. About LinkedIn. https://about.linkedin.com/#:~:text=About%20LinkedIn&text=950%20million%20members%20in%20more%20than%20200%20countries%20and%20territories%20worldwide (accessed October 17, 2023). "Ageism in the Workplace: Its Impact and How to Prevent IT—Indeed." n.d. Indeed. www.indeed.com/hire/c/info/ageism-in-the-workplace (accessed January 19, 2024).

"An Early Outlook of a Millennial-Led Economy in 2030." November 7, 2019. UPCEA. https://upcea.edu/an-early-outlook-of-a-millennial-led-economy-in-2030/#:~:text=Looking%20at%20the%20workforce%20in,35%20to%2049%20years%20old.

"Changing Attention Span and What It Means for Content." June 20, 2022. Ranieri & Co. www.ranieriandco.com/post/changing-attention-span-and-what-it-means-for-content-in-2021.

"Children Should Be Seen and Not Heard—Meaning." October 13, 2020. Literary Devices. https://literarydevices.net/children-should-be-seen-and-not-heard/.

"CIGNA Healthcare 360 Global Well-Being Survey." 2022. Cigna. www.cigna.com.hk/iwov-resources/docs/Cigna-Healthcare-Staying-Well-amidst-the-Cost-of-Living-Crisis-(Hong-Kong-Insights-Report-2023).PDF.

"Diversity Executive Leadership Program." n.d. ASAE. www.asaecenter.org/programs/leadership-development/diversity-executive-leadership-program (accessed February 19, 2024).

"Diversity Executive Leadership Program." n.d. ASAE. www.asaecenter.org/programs/leadership-development/diversity-executive-leadership-program (accessed February 6, 2024).

"Employers Wasting Billions on the Wrong Training." July 9, 2020 Business Wire. www.businesswire.com/news/home/20200709005535/en/Employers-Wasting-Billions-on-the-Wrong-Training.

"Generation Z: 'The Loneliest, Least Resilient Demographic Alive.'" November 17, 2023. Welcome to SHRM. www.shrm.org/topics-tools/news/inclusion-equity-diversity/the-least-resilient-demographic-alive.

"Generational Differences in the Workplace [Infographic]." n.d. Purdue Global. www.purdueglobal.edu/education-partnerships/generational-workforce-differences-infographic/ (accessed April 30, 2023).

"Hattie Effect Size List - 256 Influences Related to Achievement." 2018. VISIBLE LEARNING. https://visible-learning.org/hattie-ranking-influences-effect-sizes-learning-achievement/.

"How Do You Measure Your Personal Brand?" September 19, 2023. How to Measure Your Personal Brand Effectively. www.linkedin.com/advice/1/how-do-you-measure-your-personal-brand-skills-branding#:~:text=To%20measure%20your%20personal%20brand%3A%20Check%20online%20presence%20and%20social,Evaluate%20networking%20and%20relationships.

"How to Attract and Retain Millennial Employees." February 12, 2021. Leading Effectively. www.ccl.org/articles/leading-effectively-articles/3-ways-to-engage-attract-and-retain-millennials/.

"How to Avoid Ageism." March 30, 2019. SHRM. www.shrm.org/topics-tools/news/all-things-work/how-to-avoid-ageism.

"It's Not a Stretch: Gen Z and Millennials Want Flexibility and Balance." June 6, 2023. deloitte.com. https://action.deloitte.com/insight/3375/its-not-a-stretch-gen-z-and-millennials-want-flexibility-and-balance.

"Millennial Parents: 6 Surprising Ways They're Raising Kids Differently." n.d. KinderCare. www.kindercare.com/content-hub/articles/2016/may/millennial -moms-dads-6-ways-theyre-raising-kids-differently#:~:text=Millennial%20 Parents%20Value%20Positive%20Parenting,on%20behavior%2C% E2%80%9D%20says%20Gerson (accessed July 5, 2022).

"Millennials Want a Healthy Work-Life Balance. Here's What Bosses Can Do." July 23, 2020. Forbes. www.forbes.com/sites/ellevate/2020/07/23/millennials-want -a-healthy-work-life-balance-heres-what-bosses-can-do/?sh=7bba37917614.

"More Than 80% of Organizations Have Taken Action on DEI Initiatives in 2021." September 28, 2021. WorldatWork. https://worldatwork.org/about/ press-room/more-than-80-percent-of-organizations-have-taken-action-on-dei -initiatives-in-2021.

"MTV/AP-Norc Poll: Younger Generations Stand out on Identity, Acceptance, and Progressive Policies—AP-NORC." December 21, 2021. AP-NORC Center for Public Affairs Research. https://apnorc.org/projects/younger-generations-stand -out-on-identity-acceptance-and-progressive-policies/.

"Nearly Half (48% Each) of Gen Z and Millennials With Work Experience Have Applied to Jobs They Found via Social Media." August 23, 2022. PR Newswire: Press Release Distribution, Targeting, Monitoring and Marketing. www.prnewswire.com/news-releases/nearly-half-48-each-of-gen-z-and -millennials-with-work-experience-have-applied-to-jobs-they-found-via -social-media-301610609.html.

"OK Boomer! 28 Boomer Comments That Drive Gen Z and Millennials Crazy." June 30, 2023. A Dime Saved. https://adimesaved.com/tired-of-hearing -from-older-generations.

"Online 'Personal Brands' Are Key to Job Success for Gen Z, Says Study." March 10, 2023. Phys.org. https://phys.org/news/2023-03-online-personal-brands -key-job.html#google_vignette.

"Randstad US Survey Finds Casual Dress Is (Almost) Always in Fashion in Today's Workplace." August 27, 2019. Randstad USA. www.randstadusa. com/about/press-room/press-releases/randstad-us-survey-finds-casual-dress -almost-always-fashion-todays/#:~:text=despite%20more%20casual%20 workplaces%20overall,code%20at%20all%20(20%25).

"SHRM and Boston College Study Reveals 64 Percent of Organizations Say DE&I Is Important yet 62 Percent Have Allocated Little to No Resources to DE&I." October 25, 2022. SHRM. www.shrm.org/about-shrm/press-room/ press-releases/pages/shrm-and-boston-college-study-reveals-63-percent-of -organizations-say-dei-is-important-yet-63-percent-have-allocated-litt.aspx.

"Survey: Performance Reviews Drive One in Four Millennials to Search for a New Job or Call in Sick." October 27, 2015. TriNet. www.trinet.com/about -us/news-press/press-releases/survey-performance-reviews-drive-one-in-four -millennials-to-search-for-a-new-job-or-call-in-sick.

"The 10 Characteristics of a Good Leader." October 4, 2023. Leading Effectively. www.ccl.org/articles/leading-effectively-articles/characteristics-good-leader/.

"The Deloitte Global 2023 Gen Z and Millennial Survey." 2023. Deloitte. www.deloitte.com/global/en/issues/work/content/genzmillennialsurvey.html.

"The Lasting Impact of Covid-19 by Generation: How Employers Can Focus Their Efforts." June 2, 2022. Brown & Brown. www.bbrown.com/us/insight/the-lasting-impact-of-covid-19-by-generation-how-can-employers-focus-their-efforts/.

"The Silent Generation in the Workplace." October 31, 2022. Nativ3. www.nativ3.io/blog/silent-generation-workplace.

"Trend 2: Gen Zers and Millennials Expect More Employer Support for Mental Health." November 16, 2023. Calm Business. https://business.calm.com/resources/blog/gen-z-expects-employer-mental-health-support/#:~:text=They%20expect%20employers%20to%20help,reduce%20their%20stress%20and%20anxiousness.

"Trends in Personal Branding—BBG." November 3, 2021. Brand Builders Group. https://brandbuildersgroup.com/study/.

"Understanding Generational Communication Differences." October 3, 2023. Vervent. www.vervent.com/generational-communication-differences/.

"What Is Diversity, Equity, and Inclusion?" August 17, 2022. McKinsey & Company. www.mckinsey.com/featured-insights/mckinsey-explainers/what-is-diversity-equity-and-inclusion.

"What We Know about How Ageism Affects the Workplace, Vantage Aging." August 11, 2020. VANTAGE Aging. https://vantageaging.org/blog/how-ageism-affects-the-workplace/.

"What You Should Know When Working With the Silent Generation." August 8, 2022. Career Guide. www.indeed.com/career-advice/career-development/silent-generation.

"Work-Life Balance Overtakes Salary Post-Pandemic." August 24, 2022. Aviva. www.aviva.com/newsroom/news-releases/2022/08/work-life-balance-overtakes-salary-post-pandemic/.

Adamczyk, A. December 15, 2023. "Gen X Has the Largest Wealth Gap of Any Generation, and It Means 'the American Dream of Retirement Is Going to Be a Nightmare' for Them." Fortune. https://fortune.com/2023/12/15/gen-x-largest-wealth-gap-unprepared-for-retirement/.

Akhtar, A. June 3, 2019. "More Than Half of Baby-Boomer Job Seekers Say They've Faced Age Discrimination, and It's Costing Them Work." Business Insider. www.businessinsider.com/baby-boomer-job-seekers-experiencing-age-discrimination-2019-5.

Allison. October 3, 2023. "The Greatest Generation: Birth Years, Characteristics, and History • Familysearch." FamilySearch. www.familysearch.org/en/blog/greatest-generation-years-characteristics.

Anders, G. September 6, 2023. "Who's Most Committed to Hybrid Work? Millennials Lead the Way." LinkedIn. www.linkedin.com/pulse/whos-most -committed-hybrid-work-millennials-lead-way-george-anders/.

Andersen, K. July 30, 2021. "Part One: Underrepresentation in Congress: What Are the Consequences?" Common Cause Illinois. www.commoncause.org/ illinois/democracy-wire/part-one-underrepresentation-in-congress-what-are -the-consequences/.

Anglesey, A. April 25, 2022. "Dollar Tree Manager Who Posted a Sign Bashing Gen z's Work Ethic Loses Job." Newsweek. www.newsweek.com/dollar-tree -manager-who-posted-sign-bashing-gen-zs-work-ethic-loses-job-1700679.

Arruda, W. September 29, 2022. "Personal Branding and the New World of Work." Forbes. www.forbes.com/sites/williamarruda/2022/09/18/personal -branding-and-the-new-world-of-work/?sh=45256b4e77b4.

Autenrieth, N. April 27, 2021. "6 Signs of Ageism in the Workplace and How to Deal With It." TopResume. www.topresume.com/career-advice/signs-of- ageism-in-the-workplace.

Batchelor, M. July 3, 2023. "Shaping Millennials to Be the Leaders of Tomorrow." The CEO Magazine. www.theceomagazine.com/business/management -leadership/millennial-leaders/.

Bloznalis, S. August 23, 2022. "Workplace Culture: What Is It and Why Is It Important in 2023?" Workhuman.com. www.workhuman.com/blog/ workplace-culture/.

Bochantin, J. July 3, 2018. "Developing Your Personal Brand as a Millennial." Belk College of Business. https://belkcollege.charlotte.edu/news/2017-03 -06/developing-your-personal-brand-millennial.

Boehike, J. June 3, 2019. "How Does Exercise Improve Work Productivity?." Livestrong. www.livestrong.com/article/422836-how-does-exercise-improve -work-productivity/.

Bohanan, L, and C. J. Cohen. July 23, 2020. "Millennials and Gen Z Want Affordable Child Care: Findings From Next100 and Genforward." Next100. https://thenext100.org/millennials-and-gen-z-want-affordable-child-care/.

Bouie, J. October 24, 2023 "Millennials and Gen Z Are Tilting Left and Staying There." The New York Times. www.nytimes.com/2023/10/24/opinion/gen -z-millennials-republicans.html.

Brand, A. November 10, 2022 "Gen Z Workers Are the Happiest and Hardest- Working Generation." HRreview. .www.hrreview.co.uk/hr-news/gen-z-workers- are-the-happiest-and-hardest-working-generation/147234#:~:text=A%20new %20report%20from%20Gympass,and%20also%20the%20hardest%20 working.

Brindle, K.C. May 31, 2021 "Participation Trophies and Perfectionism." Croswaite Counseling PLLC. https://croswaitecounselingpllc.com/ blog/2021/5/3/participation-trophies-and-perfectionism.

Brower, T. August 28, 2022. "What the Generations Want From Work: New Data Offers Surprises." Forbes.www.forbes.com/sites/tracybrower/2022/08/28/what-the-generations-want-from-work-new-data-offers-surprises/?sh=93d47983f32d.

Brown, S. May 23, 2023. "Younger Workers Turn to Side Hustles to Stay Afloat." FM Magazine. www.fm-magazine.com/news/2023/may/younger-workers-turn-side-hustles-stay-afloat.html.

Bruner, R. October 29, 2021 "Why Young People Are Quitting Jobs-and Not Going Back." Time. https://time.com/6111245/young-workers-quitting/.

Brush, K. February 17, 2020. "What Is Upskilling and Why Is It Important?" WhatIs.com. www.techtarget.com/whatis/definition/upskilling.

Bump, P. November 29, 2021. "5 Things Gen Z Will Spend Money on & Why Marketers Need to Care." HubSpot Blog. https://blog.hubspot.com/marketing/what-gen-z-spends-money-on.

Burg, B. and J.D. Mann. 2007. *The Go-Giver: A Little Story About a Powerful Business Idea*. New York, NY: Portfolio.

Cain, Á. October 12, 2018. "The Progression of Office Culture From the 50s to Today." Business Insider. www.businessinsider.com/office-culture-then-and-now-2018-5#in-the-years-following-world-war-ii-friedman-wrote-that-most-offices-consisted-of-a-vast-open-space-with-rows-and-rows-of-identical-desks-crammed-tightly-together-1.

Callaham, S. March 27, 2023. "Five First Steps for Addressing Workplace Ageism." Forbes. www.forbes.com/sites/sheilacallaham/2023/03/26/five-first-steps-for-addressing-workplace-ageism/?sh=28e3e1777065.

Carlson, S. February 21, 2022 "Top Employee Benefits for Baby Boomers." BASIC. www.basiconline.com/blog/top-employee-benefits-for-baby-boomers/.

Carnegie, D. 1936. *How to win friends and influence people*. New York, NY: Simon and Schuster.

Carnegie, M. April 19, 2023. "The Fading Glamour of Hustle Culture." BBC News. www.bbc.com/worklife/article/20230417-hustle-culture-is-this-the-end-of-rise-and-grind.

Carufel, R. August 11, 2023. "Gen Z's Unfiltered Truth About AI: New Research Reveals That Teens Understand, Like, Are Empowered by-but Also Fear-the Technology." Agility PR Solutions. www.agilitypr.com/pr-news/public-relations/gen-zs-unfiltered-truth-about-ai-new-research-reveals-that-teens-understand-like-are-empowered-by-but-also-fear-the-technology/.

Chandler, C. February 24, 2023. "Why Gen Z Is 'Generation Quit.'" Unleash. www.unleash.ai/talent-management/why-gen-z-is-generation-quit/.

Chen, T.P. March 9, 2023. "More Companies Start to Offer Daycare at Work." *The Wall Street Journal*. www.wsj.com/articles/more-companies-start-to-offer-daycare-at-work-95d267bb.

Choi, A. January 22, 2024. "Record Number of Anti-LGBTQ Bills Were Introduced in 2023 | CNN Politics." CNN. www.cnn.com/politics/anti-lgbtq-plus-state-bill-rights-dg/index.html.

Choi-Allum, L. July 2022. "Older Workers Experience Age Discrimination at Work and in Hiring." AARP. www.aarp.org/research/topics/economics/info-2022/workforce-trends-older-adults-age-discrimination.html.

Chokhani, T. February 22, 2023 "A Deep Dive Into the Shrinking Attention Span." eLearning Industry. https://elearningindustry.com/a-deep-dive-into-the-shrinking-attention-span#:~:text=The%20study%20led%20by%20Microsoft,12%20seconds%20to%208%20seconds.

Christ, G. September 19, 2023 "Report: Baby Boomers Most Likely to Prefer Flexible, Remote Work." HR Dive. www.hrdive.com/news/baby-boomers-most-like-to-prefer-flexible-remote-work/693978/.

Cooks-Campbell, A. July 14, 2022. "Improving Communication in the Workplace: Tips & Techniques." BetterUp. www.betterup.com/blog/why-communication-is-key-to-workplace-and-how-to-improve-skills#:~:text=Communication%20in%20the%20workplace%20is,individuals%2C%20teams%2C%20and%20organizations.

Cornelius, E. April 26, 2023. "How to Build a Strong Personal Brand as a Gen Z Professional." LinkedIn. www.linkedin.com/pulse/how-build-strong-personal-brand-gen-z-professional-elizabeth/.

Cottrell, S. January 29, 2023. "A Year-by-Year Guide to the Different Generations." Parents. www.parents.com/parenting/better-parenting/style/generation-names-and-years-a-cheat-sheet-for-parents/#:~:text=Generation%20X%20parents%20were%20famously,children's%20social%20and%20educational%20development.

Creary, S. February 7, 2023. "How National Politics Are Impacting Dei in the Workplace." Knowledge at Wharton. https://knowledge.wharton.upenn.edu/podcast/knowledge-at-wharton-podcast/how-national-politics-are-impacting-dei-in-the-workplace/.

Currier, E. January 26, 2018. "How Generation X Could Change the American Dream." The Pew Charitable Trusts. www.pewtrusts.org/en/trend/archive/winter-2018/how-generation-x-could-change-the-american-dream.

Czerwonka, E. October 26, 2023. "How Do Companies Track Employees?" Buddy Punch. https://buddypunch.com/blog/how-do-companies-track-employees/#:~:text=Some%20just%20collect%20data%20about,was%20doing%20in%20the%20office.

Daly, C. May 27, 2022. "5 Ways to Overcome Leadership Bias." ThoughtExchange. https://thoughtexchange.com/blog/overcoming-leadership-bias/.

Daugherty, G. February 23, 2023. "What Is Quiet Quitting-and Is It a Real Trend?" Investopedia. www.investopedia.com/what-is-quiet-quitting-6743910.

Davidson, P. December 27, 2019. "Millennials, Gen Xers to Baby Boomers: Can You Retire so I Can Get a Job Promotion?" USA Today. www.usatoday.com/story/money/2019/11/07/jobs-baby-boomers-older-workers-may-block-millennials-careers/4170836002/.

Davis, M. December 5, 2022. "Survey: Side Hustlers on the Rise." LendingTree. www.lendingtree.com/debt-consolidation/side-hustlers-survey/.

De Smet, A., B. Dowling, B. Hancock, and B. Schaninger. July 13, 2022. "The Great Attrition Is Making Hiring Harder. Are You Searching the Right Talent Pools?" McKinsey & Company. www.mckinsey.com/capabilities/people-and-organizational-performance/our-insights/the-great-attrition-is-making-hiring-harder-are-you-searching-the-right-talent-pools.

Delgado, M. January 9, 2019. "How Do People Find Jobs?." Clutch. https://clutch.co/resources/how-do-people-find-jobs.

Diaz, J. May 15, 2023. "Florida Gov. Ron DeSantis Signs a Bill Banning DEI Initiatives in Public Colleges." NPR. www.npr.org/2023/05/15/1176210007/florida-ron-desantis-dei-ban-diversity.

Dill, K. November 4, 2019. "Younger Workers Report Seeing More Discrimination." *The Wall Street Journal.* www.wsj.com/articles/younger-workers-report-seeing-more-discrimination-11572793201.

DiNardi, G. April 5, 2023. "11 Employee Wellness Programs That Work." Culture Amp. www.cultureamp.com/blog/employee-wellness-programs.

Doran, S. August 23, 2023. "Boomers vs. Millennials: Do We Feud Because We're Actually a Lot Alike?" Medium. https://medium.com/crows-feet/boomers-vs-millennials-do-we-feud-because-were-actually-a-lot-alike-521d6c4d3f8b.

Dow, N. March 10, 2023. "These 20 Companies Provide Child Care—or Help Pay You for It." The Penny Hoarder. www.thepennyhoarder.com/make-money/career/companies-with-child-care/.

Dreibelbis, E. May 19, 2023. "Americans Check Their Phones an Alarming Number of Times per Day." PCMAG. www.pcmag.com/news/americans-check-their-phones-an-alarming-number-of-times-per-day.

Duckworth, A. 2016. *Grit.* New York, NY: Simon and Schuster.

Dunlop, A. and M. Pankowski. March 28, 2023. "Hey Bosses: Here's What Gen Z Actually Wants at Work." Deloitte Digital. www.deloittedigital.com/us/en/blog-list/2023/gen-z-research-report.html?id=us:2ps:3gl:hxgz23:awa:cons:041123:workforce%20trends:b:c:kwd-303606181129.

Ellis, D. October 21, 2011. "'The Arc of the Moral Universe Is Long, but It Bends Toward Justice.'" National Archives and Records Administration. https://obamawhitehouse.archives.gov/blog/2011/10/21/arc-moral-universe-long-it-bends-toward-justice#:~:text=Martin%20Luther%20King%2C%20Jr.%2C,time%2C%20but%20it%20does%20happen.

Emiliani, R. June 22, 2023. "Keeping It Real: Gen Z's Hunger for Authentic Marketing and Purpose-Driven Brands." Catalyst Marketing Agency. https://catalystmarketing.io/blog/gen-zs-hunger-for-authentic-marketing-and-purpose-driven-brands/.

Employee Well-Being Report. May 2021. www.glintinc.com/wp-content/uploads/2021/05/Glint-May-2021-Employee-Well-Being-Report.pdf.

Engstrom, E. n.d. "Hiring for Diversity: 6 Reasons Baby Boomers Are Great for Business." Trakstar Hire Blog. https://hire.trakstar.com/blog/hiring-for-diversity-baby-boomers (accessed January 17, 2024).

Epperson, S. June 4, 2014 "Step Away From the Smartphone! Companies Tell Workers to UNPLUG." TODAY.com. www.today.com/money/these-companies-tell-workers-unplug-work-life-balance-2d79753890.

Espada, M. August 23, 2022. "What Is Quiet Quitting? Why Companies Worry About New Trend." Time. https://time.com/6208115/quiet-quitting-companies-response/.

Falcone, P. June 5, 2023. "Dealing With Microaggression in the Workplace." SHRM. www.shrm.org/resourcesandtools/hr-topics/employee-relations/pages/dealing-with-microaggression-in-the-workplace.aspx#:~:text=%22Microaggressions%20can%20be%20generally%20defined,Institute%20in%20Portland%2C%20Ore.%2C.

Ferland, M. June 27, 2023. "Why Leaders Need to Listen to Gen Z—Fast Company." Fast Company.www.fastcompany.com/90914667/pov-why-leaders-need-to-listen-to-gen-z-to-build-the-workplace-of-the-future.

Focardi, R. September 23, 2021. "Gen Z: Misunderstood in Their Quest for Purpose (and Why They Need Us to Help Them Change the World)." LinkedIn. www.linkedin.com/pulse/genz-misunderstood-quest-purpose-why-need-us-help-them-focardi/.

Focht, J. October 17, 2022. "13 Questions You Should Ask to Understand If a Company Cares about Diversity, Equity, and Inclusion." Mediabistro. www.mediabistro.com/candidates/13-questions-you-should-ask-to-understand-if-a-company-cares-about-diversity-equity-and-inclusion/.

Fowell, T. July 22, 2022. "3 Types of Hybrid Work Models (and the Pros and Cons of Each)." Envoy. https://envoy.com/blog/3-types-of-hybrid-work-models/.

Fox, M. April 27, 2022. "Are You Being Paid Fairly? Young Workers Share Salary Information as Pay Transparency Gains Steam." CNBC. www.cnbc.com/2022/04/27/young-workers-share-salary-information-as-pay-transparency-gains-steam.html.

Frommer, F. n.d. "1960s Counterculture." Encyclopædia Britannica. www.britannica.com/topic/1960s-counterculture (accessed November 18, 2023).

Fuscaldo, D. October 23, 2023. "How to Manage Millennials in the

Workplace." Business News Daily. www.businessnewsdaily.com/15974-millennials-in-the-workplace.html.

Gallaga, O.L. May 29, 2023. "How to Make Meetings Shorter (for Real)." www.wired.com/story/how-to-make-meetings-shorter/.

Gauthier, M. August 12, 2019. "Gen Alpha: Littlest Travelers Have Big Impact on Family Trips." WEX Inc. www.wexinc.com/insights/blog/wex-travel/consumer/gen-alpha-littlest-travelers-have-big-impact-on-family-trips/.

Gianfagna, M. June 30, 2021 "What Is Moore's Law?: Is Moore's Law Finally Ending?" Synopsys. www.synopsys.com/glossary/what-is-moores-law.html.

Gillespie, L. April 3, 2023. "Survey: 56% of Workers Plan to Look for a Job in the next 12 Months." Bankrate. www.bankrate.com/personal-finance/job-seekers-survey/#likely-to-look.

Giridharadas, A. February 26, 2010. "Branding and the 'Me' Economy." *The New York Times*. www.nytimes.com/2010/02/27/us/27iht-currents.html.

Gitlin, S., A. Gummadi, A. Krivkovich, and K. Modi. May 9, 2022. "The Childcare Conundrum: How Can Companies Ease Working Parents' Return to the Office?" McKinsey & Company. www.mckinsey.com/featured-insights/sustainable-inclusive-growth/future-of-america/the-childcare-conundrum-how-can-companies-ease-working-parents-return-to-the-office.

Goldberg, E. November 28, 2022. "Have the Anticapitalists Reached Harvard Business School?" *The New York Times*. www.nytimes.com/2022/11/28/business/business-school-social-justice.html?searchResultPosition=1.

Goodgold, L. January 14, 2021. "Is It Branding or Bragging?" LinkedIn. www.linkedin.com/pulse/branding-bragging-liz-goodgold.

Gostick, A. November 8, 2022. "5 Ways to Combat Quiet Quitting." Forbes. www.forbes.com/sites/adriangostick/2022/08/23/5-ways-to-combat-quiet-quitting/?sh=28f96b7e4c49.

Graniello, S. September 11, 2023. "Employee Engagement." Holaspirit. www.holaspirit.com/blog/influence-company-culture-on-employee-engagement#:~:text=A%20positive%20and%20open%20culture,that%20disengaged%20employees%20are%20costly.

Gupta, S. January 27, 2023. "Study: Gen Z Does Not Feel Prepared for Success in a Digital World." FastCompany. www.fastcompany.com/90839901/dell-study-gen-z-success-in-digital-world.

Hall, I. October 13, 2022. "Difficult Conversations: Approaching Taboos With Gen Z." Voxburner. www.voxburner.com/blog/how-to-approach-taboos-with-gen-z/.

Hancock, B., C. Higgins, J. Law, S. Olson, N. Patel, and K. Van Dusen. November 15, 2022. "Taking a Skills-Based Approach to Building the Future Workforce." McKinsey & Company. www.mckinsey.com/capabilities/

people-and-organizational-performance/our-insights/taking-a-skills-based
-approach-to-building-the-future-workforce.

Hangsterfer, Y. April 15, 2020. "What You Should Know About Recruiting Gen X in 2019." Yello. https://yello.co/blog/the-generation-x-files-what-you -should-know-about-recruiting-gen-x-in-2019/.

Harter, J. November 6, 2023. "Is Quiet Quitting Real?" Gallup.com. www. gallup.com/workplace/398306/quiet-quitting-real.aspx.

Hastwell, C. June 8, 2023. "The 8 Elements of Great Company Culture." Great Place to Work. www.greatplacetowork.com/resources/blog/elements-of -great-company-culture.

Hastwell, C. November 14, 2022. "What Is Employee Experience? Definition & Proven Strategies." Great Place to Work. www.greatplacetowork.com/ resources/blog/what-is-employee-experience.

Hattie, J. "Hattie's Barometer of Influence - Infographic." January 21, 2022 VISIBLE LEARNING. https://visible-learning.org/2022/01/hatties -barometer-of-influence-infographic/.

Hawkins, E. December 17, 2022. "Dei Communications Means Different Things to Different Generations." Axios. www.axios.com/2022/12/17/dei -communications-divide-generations.

Herrity, J. March 29, 2023. "How to Create a Personal Brand (and Why It's Important)." Indeed Career Guide. www.indeed.com/career-advice/career -development/how-to-create-a-personal-brand.

Hetler, A. July 3, 2023. "The Great Resignation: Everything You Need to Know." WhatIs.com. www.techtarget.com/whatis/feature/The-Great-Resignation -Everything-you-need-to-know#:~:text=Employees%20across%20 multiple%20sectors%20came,the%20term%20the%20Great%20 Resignation.

Hoffower, H. April 26, 2022. "Meet the 'Sandwich Generation': Financially Strapped Gen Xers Helping out Both Their Parents and Their Children." Business Insider. www.businessinsider.com/meet-gen-x-sandwich-generation -tasked-with-parents-kids-care-2022-4.

Hoier, M. June 3, 2023. "Gen Z: Redefining Work-Life Balance in the Modern Workplace." LinkedIn. www.linkedin.com/pulse/gen-z-redefining-work-life -balance-modern-workplace-maria-hoier/.

Holland, J.N. January 14, 2023. "The Evolution of Performance Reviews." Medium. https://thejodyholland.medium.com/the-evolution-of-performance -reviews-eb9a44380c21#:~:text=One%20of%20the%20most%20 significant,more%20timely%20and%20actionable%20information.

Holman, J. October 1, 2023. "Gen Z Wants Feminine Care Brands to Just Say Vagina." The *New York Times*. www.nytimes.com/2023/10/01/business/ womens-vaginal-health-honey-pot.html.

Howarth, J. October 10, 2022. "25+ New Generation Z Statistics (2022)." Exploding Topics. https://explodingtopics.com/blog/gen-z-stats.

Huddleston, T. June 12, 2022. "Millennials and Gen Zers Do Want to Buy Homes-They Just Can't Afford It, Even as Adults." CNBC. www.cnbc.com/2022/06/12/millennials-and-gen-zers-want-to-buy-homes-but-they-cant-afford-it.html.

Hyatt, D. "The Great Resignation Is Officially Over." Investopedia. www.investopedia.com/the-great-resignation-is-officially-over-7963266#:~:text=Key%20Takeaways,known%20as%20The%20Great%20Resignation (accessed November 19, 2023).

Iacurci, G. February 1, 2023. "2022 Was the 'Real Year of the Great Resignation,' Says Economist." CNBC. www.cnbc.com/2023/02/01/why-2022-was-the-real-year-of-the-great-resignation.html.

Iqbal, N. July 21, 2018. "Generation Z: 'We Have More to Do Than Drink and Take Drugs.'" The Guardian. www.theguardian.com/society/2018/jul/21/generation-z-has-different-attitudes-says-a-new-report.

Italie, L. November 27, 2023. "What's Merriam-Webster's Word of the Year for 2023? Hint: Be True to Yourself." AP News. https://apnews.com/article/merriam-webster-word-of-year-2023-a9fea610cb32ed913bc15533acab71cc.

Jackson, A. July 6, 2022. "One Expert's Message to Black Women Burned out at Work: 'Workplace Dei Is a Company Issue, Not Yours.'" CNBC. www.cnbc.com/2022/07/06/expert-dei-is-a-company-issue-not-responsibility-of-black-women.html.

Jamson, P., L. Meckler, P. Gordy, and C. Alcantara. October 31, 2023. "Home Schooling's Rise from Fringe to Fastest-Growing Form of Education." The Washington Post. www.washingtonpost.com/education/interactive/2023/homeschooling-growth-data-by-district/.

Jarvis, J. August 2, 2021. "Why Millennials and Gen Z Aren't Proud to Be American." Newsweek. www.newsweek.com/patriotism-gap-millennials-gen-z-baby-boomers-gen-x-1611749.

Jenkins, R. June 25, 2019. "This Is How Generation Z Employees Want Feedback." Inc.com. www.inc.com/ryan-jenkins/this-is-how-generation-z-employees-want-feedback.html.

Jha, M. June 20, 2023. "Communicating With Generation Z in the Workplace." ContactMonkey. www.contactmonkey.com/blog/gen-z-employees.

Jones, C. and J. Munday. June 1, 2020. "How to Deliver Feedback to Employees From Different Generations." Insights From AEU LeadDefault. www.aeulead.com/main-navigation/insights/article/how-to-deliver-feedback-to-employees-from-different-generations.

Jones, J.M. June 5, 2023. "LGBT Identification in U.S. Ticks up to 7.1%." Gallup.com. https://news.gallup.com/poll/389792/lgbt-identification-ticks-up.aspx.

Kaminskaya, N. February 2, 2023. "Millennials Perspective: Trends in Personal Branding." LinkedIn. www.linkedin.com/pulse/millennials-perspective-trends-personal-branding-kaminskaya-mba/.

Kaplan, J. and R. Knight. n.d. "The Millennial Boss' Guide to Managing Gen Z, Based on 5 Stereotypes of the Younger Generation." Business Insider. www.businessinsider.com/how-to-manage-gen-z-employees-guide-for-millennial-bosses-2023-2 (accessed August 2, 2023).

Kaplan, J. February 18, 2023. "Welcome to Generation Quit." Business Insider. www.businessinsider.com/gen-z-jobs-generation-quiet-quitting-great-resignation-recession-economy-2023-2.

Kayser, A. October 3, 2023. "The State of Quiet Quitting: 5 Recent Updates." Becker's Hospital Review. www.beckershospitalreview.com/workforce/the-state-of-quiet-quitting-5-recent-updates.html#:~:text=60%25%20of%20employees%20worldwide%20are,lost%20productivity%2C%20the%20firm%20estimates.

Kelly, J. June 28, 2023. "'Loud Quitting' Is the Next Step From 'Quiet Quitting,' 'bare Minimum Mondays' and 'Acting Your Wage.'" Forbes. www.forbes.com/sites/jackkelly/2023/06/26/loud-quitting-is-the-next-step-from-quit-quitting-bare-minimum-mondays-and-acting-your-wage/.

Khan, F. July 13, 2021. "Gen Z: The Acceptable Nature of the New Generation Towards Taboos." Medium. https://fariyafatimakhan.medium.com/gen-z-the-acceptable-nature-of-the-new-generation-towards-taboos-eff9506aee00.

Kim, S. November 10, 2022. "Millennial Boss Moaning Gen Z Staff Are 'A Massive Headache' Sparks Debate." Newsweek. www.newsweek.com/generation-z-employees-work-culture-ethics-1758596.

Knights, J. December 3, 2021. "Workplace Culture: How Has It Evolved?" Vistatec. https://vistatec.com/changing-workplace-culture/.

Kodé, A. and K. Hanley. August 10, 2023. "Gen Z Can't Afford the Rent." The New York Times. www.nytimes.com/interactive/2023/08/10/realestate/gen-z-rent-homeowner.html.

Korte, M. June 2020. "The Impact of the Digital Revolution on Human Brain and Behavior: Where Do We Stand?[SEP]." Dialogues in Clinical Neuroscience. www.ncbi.nlm.nih.gov/pmc/articles/PMC7366944/#:~:text=It%20is%20hardly%20a%20stretch,processing%20in%20a%20social%20context.

Kratz, J. April 26, 2023. "How to Stop Generational Differences From Derailing Dei Initiatives." LinkedIn. www.linkedin.com/pulse/how-stop-generational-differences-from-derailing-dei-julie-kratz/.

Kuligowski, K. June 23, 2023. "How to Work With a Multigenerational Workforce." business.com. www.business.com/articles/hiring-multigenerational-workforce/.

Kumar, V.S. November 16, 2023. "Gen Z in the Workplace: How Should Companies Adapt?" Johns Hopkins University. https://imagine.jhu.edu/blog/2023/04/18/gen-z-in-the-workplace-how-should-companies-adapt/.

Larsen, T. August 23, 2023. "The Gen-X Impact on Redefining Work-Life Balance." LinkedIn. www.linkedin.com/pulse/gen-x-impact-redefining-work-life-balance-trond-larsen/.

Leonhardt, M. February 20, 2022. "Meet a Millennial Who Is Turning 40, Starting yet Another New Career and Has $47,000 in Debt. 'I've Worked Very Hard and It Didn't Pay off. It Feels Very Unfair.'" Fortune. https://fortune.com/2022/02/20/millennial-turning-40-starting-new-career-carrying-debt/#:~:text=Overall%2C%20the%20average%20millennial%20carries,debt%20averages%20%24255%2C527%20per%20person.

Levine, B. March 3, 2021. "The Business Case for Giving All Workers Paid Time off." The Workforce Institute at UKG. https://workforceinstitute.org/the-business-case-for-giving-all-workers-paid-time-off/.

Liu, J. November 9, 2022. "25-Year-Old Maxwell Frost Will Be the First Gen Z Member of Congress." CNBC. www.cnbc.com/2022/11/09/maxwell-frost-will-be-the-first-gen-z-member-of-congress.html.

Llarena, M. June 7, 2018. "How to Overcome Baby Boomers Who Are Bottlenecking Your Jobs." Melissa Llarena. www.melissallarena.com/overcome-baby-boomers-bottlenecking-jobs/.

Lobosco, M. January 18, 2022. "The Reinvention of Company Culture: Why It Should Be Your Top Priority This Year." LinkedIn. www.linkedin.com/business/talent/blog/talent-strategy/global-talent-trends-report?trk=MarkLinkedInPost-global-talent-trends-2022.

Loh, K K. and R, Kanai. September 24, 2014. "Higher Media Multi-Tasking Activity Is Associated With Smaller Gray-Matter Density in the Anterior Cingulate Cortex." *PLOS ONE*. https://journals.plos.org/plosone/article?id=10.1371%2Fjournal.pone.0106698.

Lomu, K. December 7, 2023. "What Managers Should Know About Generation Z Work Ethic." Contractbook. https://contractbook.com/blog/what-managers-should-know-about-generation-z-work-ethic.

Love, J. September 24, 2021. "15 Questions to Define Your Personal Brand." Jude Love. https://judelove.com.au/15-questions-for-defining-your-personal-brand/.

Lowrey, A. May 15, 2020. "Millennials Don't Stand a Chance." The Atlantic. www.theatlantic.com/ideas/archive/2020/04/millennials-are-new-lost-generation/609832/.

Lynch, A. July 8, 2015. "Gen Z Kids Are Like Their Great-Grandparents. Here's Why." www.generationaledge.com/blog/posts/genz-like-grandparents.

Madell, R. August 25, 2023. "What Is Loud Quitting?" U.S. News. https://money. usnews.com/money/blogs/outside-voices-careers/articles/what-is-quiet -quitting.

Manik, S. April 5, 2023. "Ways to Give Effective Feedback to Multi-Generational Workforce." SightsIn Plus. https://sightsinplus.com/practices/performance/ ways-to-give-effective-feedback-to-multi-generational-workforce/.

Martic, K. June 8, 2023. "Millennials in the Workplace: 11 Ways to Attract and Keep Them." Haiilo. https://haiilo.com/blog/millennials-in-the-workplace -11-ways-to-attract-and-keep-them/.

Marx, W. February 23, 2022. "Overcome the 5 Worst Boomer Personal Branding Mistakes." Job Hunt. www.job-hunt.org/worst-boomer-branding-mistakes/.

Mashao, T. S. September 16, 2022. "Gen Z 101: The Do's and Don'ts of Personal Branding." LinkedIn. www.linkedin.com/pulse/gen-z-101-dos-donts-personal -branding-tshegofatso-sarah-mashao/.

McCrindle, M. October 12, 2023. "Understanding Generation Alpha." McCrindle. https://mccrindle.com.au/article/topic/generation-alpha/generation -alpha-defined/.

McKenna, A. December 23, 2023. "Generation X." Encyclopædia Britannica. www.britannica.com/topic/Generation-X.

McKnight, K. December 7, 2018. "Gen Z and the Challenges of the Most Individualistic Generation yet." Illume Network. https://illumestories.com/ gen-z-and-the-challenges-of-the-most-individualistic-generation-yet/.

Meister, J. November 8, 2022. "The Great Resignation Becomes the Great Reshuffle: What Employers Can Do to Retain Workers." Forbes. www.forbes. com/sites/jeannemeister/2022/04/19/the-great-re-shuffle-of-talent-what -can-employers-do-to-retain-workers/?sh=222127aa4cf3.

Miller, M. April 13, 2019. "The Dirty Little Secret Baby Boomers Need to Know." Career Sherpa. https://careersherpa.net/the-dirty-little-secret-baby -boomers-need-to-know/.

Miller, S. April 5, 2023. "'War' on LGBTQ Existence: 8 Ways the Record Onslaught of 650 Bills Targets the Community." USA Today. www.usatoday. com/story/news/nation/2023/03/31/650-anti-lgbtq-bills-introduced -us/11552357002/.

Minkin, R. May 17, 2023. "Diversity, Equity and Inclusion in the Workplace." Pew Research Center's Social & Demographic Trends Project. www. pewresearch.org/social-trends/2023/05/17/diversity-equity-and-inclusion -in-the-workplace/.

Molla, R. April 30, 2022. "The Great Resignation Is Becoming a 'Great Midlife Crisis.'" Vox. www.vox.com/recode/23042785/the-great-resignation-older -tenured-higher-paid.

de la Mora, T. July 17, 2019. "Boomers, Gen X, Gen Y, and Gen Z Explained." LinkedIn. www.linkedin.com/pulse/boomers-gen-x-y-z-explained-delamora -y-madrigal-cfe-cams-cfci/.

Morrison, M. December 2, 2022 "History of Coaching—A True Insight Into Coaching." RapidBI. https://rapidbi.com/history-of-coaching-a-true-insight -into-coaching/.

Morrow, C. January 15, 2016. "5 Objections to Hiring Boomers (and How to Combat Them)." Next Avenue. www.nextavenue.org/the-5-unspoken -objections-to-hiring-boomers/.

Morse, M. February 18, 2020. "Generational Hiring: Wants, Needs, and Everything in Between." HR Daily Advisor. https://hrdailyadvisor.blr. com/2020/01/21/generational-hiring-wants-needs-and-everything-in -between/.

Nezich, H. May 30, 2023. "The Impact of Ageism in the Workplace." American Society of Employ. www.aseonline.org/News-Events/Articles/the-impact-of -ageism-in-the-workplace.

Nulsen, C.R. March 23, 2021. "A Look at the Different Generations and How They Parent." FamilyEducation. www.familyeducation.com/family-life/ relationships/history-genealogy/a-look-at-the-different-generations-and -how-they-parent.

Onque, R. September 23, 2022. "54% of Student Loan Borrowers Say Their Mental Health Issues Like Anxiety and Depression Are Directly Related to Their Debt." CNBC. www.cnbc.com/2022/09/21/americans-mental-health| -continue-to-struggle-amid-student-loan-debt.html.

Palmer, K. December 29, 2022. "10 Facts About Age Discrimination in the Workplace." AARP. www.aarp.org/work/age-discrimination/facts-in-the -workplace/.

Pan, J. October 3, 2023. "'Overworking Only Gets You so Far': The New Workplace Trend Called ..." Moneywise. https://moneywise.com/employment/ overworking-only-gets-you-so-far-new-workplace-trend-called-quiet -quitting.

Parker, K. and E. Patten. July 31, 2020. "The Sandwich Generation." Pew Research Center's Social & Demographic Trends Project. www.pewresearch. org/social-trends/2013/01/30/the-sandwich-generation/.

Parker, K. and J. M. Horowitz. March 10, 2022. "Majority of Workers Who Quit a Job in 2021 Cite Low Pay, No Opportunities for Advancement, Feeling Disrespected." Pew Research Center. www.pewresearch.org/fact -tank/2022/03/09/majority-of-workers-who-quit-a-job-in-2021-cite-low -pay-no-opportunities-for-advancement-feeling-disrespected/.

Pelta, R. February 14, 2023. "How to Bridge Communication Gaps Between Generations: FlexJobs." FlexJobs Job Search Tips and Blog. www.flexjobs. com/blog/post/workplace-generational-communication-gaps/.

Perlow, L.A. and J.L. Porter. August 27, 2021. "Making Time off Predictable-and Required." *Harvard Business Review*. https://hbr.org/2009/10/making-time -off-predictable-and-required.

Perry, E. August 21, 2023. "Quiet Quitting: A Warning Sign of a Real and Deeper Problem." BetterUp. www.betterup.com/blog/quiet-quitting#:~:text=A%20 lack%20of%20appreciation%20is,point%20of%20investing%20their%20 energy.

Perry, E. August 3, 2023. "5 Generations in the Workplace: Differences and How to Manage Them." BetterUp. www.betterup.com/blog/generations-in-the -workplace.

Perry, E. May 7, 2021. "Ikigai: Japanese Philosophy to Inspire Your Life & Career." BetterUp. www.betterup.com/blog/what-is-ikigai.

Peters, T. August 31, 1997 "The Brand Called You: Tom Peters." Fast Company. www.fastcompany.com/28905/brand-called-you.

Pittinger, B. February 14, 2023. "Gen Z Isn't 'Quiet Quitting'" Fast Company. www.fastcompany.com/90865021/gen-z-isnt-quiet-quitting-theyre -grappling-with-a-lack-of-interpersonal-connection.

Pollak, L. July 26, 2023. "'We Didn't Give Ourselves the Trophies'— Millennials." Lindsey Pollak. https://lindseypollak.com/are-millennials-trophy-generation/.

Polles, F. August 9, 2023 "Aging in the Workplace: How Gender and Racial Biases Impact Older Workers." CWI Labs. www.cwilabs.org/aging-in-the -workplace-how-gender-and-racial-biases-impact-older-workers/.

Prackash, P. June 24, 2023. "Gen Z Workers Came of Age Amid the Pandemic-and Now Quitting Their Job Is Always Front of Mind." Yahoo! Finance. https:// finance.yahoo.com/news/great-resignation-dead-lives-minds-110000967. html.

Rasp, S. April 11, 2020. "Join the Apple Retail Team, and Bring What You Love to What You Do." Stephan Rasp on LinkedIn. www.linkedin.com/posts/ stephan-rasp-07ba7594_join-the-apple-retail-team-and-bring-what-activity -6654793266342445056-NTyh.

Reid, A. May 20, 2022. "35 Best Job Search Engines for 2022 (Unbiased Job Board Review)." theJub. www.thejub.com/millennial-career-resources/2018/9/24/7 -best-job-search-engines-for-millennials#:~:text=Zip%20Recruiter%2C%20 LinkedIn%2C%20Google%20for,still%20establish%20a%20personal%20 preference.

Robinson, A. December 12, 2023. "Quiet Quitting: How to Prevent & Combat It at Work." teambuilding.com. https://teambuilding.com/blog/quiet -quitting#:~:text=Quiet%20quitting%20does%20not%20start,lose%20 faith%20in%20their%20leaders.

Roller, A. August 11, 2023a. "Quiet Quitting vs. Loud Quitting: A Step-by-Step Guide to Identify, Understand and Mitigate." HRMorning. www.hrmorning.com/articles/quiet-quitting-versus-loud-quitting/#:~:text=%E2%80%9CLoud%20quitting%E2%80%9D%20is%20another%20form,to%20leave%2C%E2%80%9D%20says%20McKenzie.

Roller, A. May 11, 2023b. "5 Questions for an Effective Stay Interview—and Why They Really Matter." HRMorning. www.hrmorning.com/articles/stay-interview-questions/.

Rook, D. November 7, 2019. "The Multi-Generational Definition of Work-Life Balance." JP Griffin Group. www.griffinbenefits.com/blog/changing-definition-work-life-balance.

Rubin, A. November 5, 2023. "Gen Z Shakes up Workplace Communication." Axios. www.axios.com/2023/11/05/gen-z-workplace-communication.

Rubin, A. September 14, 2023. "Gen Z's Surprise Optimism About the Future." Axios. www.axios.com/2023/09/14/gen-z-survey-future-optimism-youth-outlook.

Russell, C. January 1, 1993 "The Baby Boom Breaks the Rules." SpringerLink. https://link.springer.com/chapter/10.1007/978-1-4899-6016-0_4.

Sachs, S. January 16, 2023. "Gen Z Has 'Lowest' Patriotic Sentiment in Us, Poll Shows." WFLA. www.wfla.com/news/national/gen-z-has-lowest-patriotic-sentiment-in-us-poll-shows/#:~:text=According%20to%20the%20poll%2C%20Gen,as%20they%20have%20entered%20adulthood.

Sakpal, M. n.d. "CIOs Should Embrace Dei to Build Successful Teams." Gartner. www.gartner.com/smarterwithgartner/diversity-and-inclusion-build-high-performance-teams (accessed October 5, 2023).

Scarpitti, S. February 1, 2024. "Multi-Gen Leadership Interview With Jessica James." Other.

Scarpitti, S. July 11, 2023. "Multi-Gen Leadership Interview With Connor Inglis." Personal.

Scarpitti, S. July 24, 2023. "Multi-Gen Leadership Interview With Heath Ritter." Personal.

Scarpitti, S. July 7, 2023. "Multi-Gen Leadership Interview With anonymous Banker." Personal.Scarpitti, S. June 7, 2023. "Multi-Gen Leadership Interview With Perry Fitzgerald." Personal."

Scarpitti, S. May 17, 2023. "Mulit-Gen Leadership Interview With Bryce Ungerott." Personal.

Scarpitti, S. May 17, 2023. "Multi-Gen Leadership Interview With a Leader." Other.

Scarpitti, S. May 31, 2023. "Multi-Gen Leadership Interview With Mike Taylor." Personal.

Scarpitti, S. February 1, 204AD. "Multi-Gen Leadership Interview With Landen Stacy." Personal.

Scarpitti, S. November 28, 2023. "Multi-Gen Leadership Interview With Tara Harland. Personal."

Scates, J. May 31, 2023. "The Impact of Baby Boomers Retiring in 2023." J2Talk. www.j2t-recruiting.com/post/the-impact-of-baby-boomers-retiring-in-2023.

Scholl, S. September 22, 2023. "The Rise of Gen Z: Embrace the Digital Generation." Fast Compnay. www.fastcompany.com/90956028/the-rise-of -gen-z-embrace-the-digital-generation.

Schroeder, B. December 5, 2022. "Gen Z and Millennials Need to Cultivate This to Fuel Their Career or a Startup Company." Forbes. www.forbes. com/sites/bernhardschroeder/2022/12/03/key-insights-on-how-to -develop-your-grit-which-will-fuel-your-career-or-a-potential-startup -company/?sh=24e5c8a33c6a.

Schroeder, H. October 6, 2023. "Great Leaders Have Balance." SIGMA Assessment Systems. www.sigmaassessmentsystems.com/work-life-balance/# :~:text=A%20healthy%20work%2Flife%20balance,their%20best%20 without%20burning%20out.

Seeberger, C., M. Shepherd, G.Griffin, K. Holmes, S.J. Glynn, K. Bahn, R. Erickson, et al. November 2, 2016. "Breadwinning Mothers Continue to Be the U.S. Norm." Center for American Progress. www.americanprogress.org/ article/breadwinning-mothers-continue-u-s-norm/#:~:text=In%20most%20 families%20with%20children,unmarried%20mothers%20(73.2%20 percent).

Segal, E. September 12, 2023. "How Gen Z's Impact on the Workplace Continues to Grow." Forbes. www.forbes.com/sites/edwardsegal/2023/05/24/how-gen -zs-impact-on-the-workplace-continues-to-grow/?sh=7134a4f46a5b.

Sharma, A, V. Madaan, and F.D. Petty. 2006. "Exercise for Mental Health." *Primary Care Companion to the Journal of Clinical Psychiatry.* www. ncbi.nlm.nih.gov/pmc/articles/PMC1470658/#:~:text=Exercise%20 improves%20mental%20health%20by,self%2Desteem%20and%20 cognitive%20function.&text=Exercise%20has%20also%20been%20fo- und,self%2Desteem%20and%20social%20withdrawal.

Simmons, C. June 23, 2023. "Age Discrimination in the Workplace: Examples & How to Prevent It." RetireGuide. www.retireguide.com/retirement-life -leisure/working-after-retirement/ageism-in-the-workplace/.

Siu, D.N. February 7, 2023. "Gen Z Workers Have Fueled Job Title Inflation. It Was Perfectly Timed With the Great Resignation." Business Insider. www.businessinsider.com/inflation-gen-z-job-title-early-career-great -resignation-2023-2.

Smith, R. November 18, 2021. "Generation X: History and Characteristics." FamilySearch Blob. www.familysearch.org/en/blog/generation-x-characteristics -history.

Smith, M. January 18, 2023. "Gen Z and Millennials Are Leading 'The Big Quit' in 2023-Why Nearly 70% Plan to Leave Their Jobs." Make It. www.cnbc.com/2023/01/18/70percent-of-gen-z-and-millennials-are-considering-leaving-their-jobs-soon.html.

Smith, M. October 25, 2022. "Personal Branding: The What, Why, and How." Constant Contact. www.constantcontact.com/blog/personal-branding/.

Smith, M. and C. Kissell. July 25, 2023. "15 Essential Job Hunting Tips for Baby Boomers." FinanceBuzz. https://financebuzz.com/boomer-job-hunting-tips.

Smith, R. June 29, 2023. "Why Is the Silent Generation Called 'Silent'?" FamilySearch Blog. www.familysearch.org/en/blog/silent-generation-characteristics.

Smith, R. November 17, 2021. "The Baby Boomer Generation-Birth Years, Characteristics, and History • Familysearch." FamilySearch Blog. www.familysearch.org/en/blog/baby-boomer-generation-characteristics#:~:text=They%20were%20raised%20with%20the,hard%20work%20makes%20a%20difference.

Spector, N. November 6, 2019. "'OK Boomer' Has the Internet in a TIFF. How Did We Get Here?" NBCNews.com. www.nbcnews.com/better/lifestyle/ok-boomer-diving-generation-what-does-it-mean-ncna1077261.

Stahl, A. December 15, 2022 "3 Reasons Why Gen Z Is Job Hopping." *Forbes*. www.forbes.com/sites/ashleystahl/2022/12/13/3-reasons-why-gen-z-is-job-hopping/?sh=4b84d6267170.

Stahl, A. March 4, 2022. "Are Boomers the Answer to the Great Resignation?" *Forbes*. www.forbes.com/sites/ashleystahl/2022/03/03/are-boomers-the-answer-to-the-great-resignation/?sh=2663195b44b6.

Stanchak, J. September 15, 2022. "Quiet Quitting Is Real. Here's What You Should Do About It." Welcome to SHRM. www.shrm.org/executive-network/insights/quiet-quitting-real-heres.

Stange, J. January 14, 2021. "Coaching to Engage: 12 Rules to Effective, Ongoing Employee Coaching." Employee Success Software. www.quantumworkplace.com/future-of-work/12-rules-for-effective-employee-coaching.

Sull, C, D. Sull, and B. Zweig. January 11, 2022. "Toxic Culture Is Driving the Great Resignation." *MIT Sloan Management Review*. https://sloanreview.mit.edu/article/toxic-culture-is-driving-the-great-resignation/.

Tan, H. January 24, 2022. "Some 36% of US Millennials Say Student Loan Debt Is Stopping Them Owning Homes." Business Insider. www.businessinsider.com/us-millennials-student-loan-debt-major-barrier-to-home-ownership-2022-1#:~:text=US%20student%20loan%20debt%20averaged,an%20Experian%20consumer%20debt%20study.

Tannian, M. March 22, 2022. "7 Tips for Recruiting Millennials in Today's Job Market." NEOGOV Blog. https://blog.neogov.com/recruiting-millennials-tips.

Teo, K.X. October 2, 2023. "Gen Z Workers Don't Think Talking About Wages and Telling Managers What They're Doing Wrong Are Taboo Subjects." Business Insider. www.businessinsider.com/gen-z-manager-feedback-compensation-not-taboo-adobe-survey-2023-10#:~:text=Three%2Dquarters%20of%20Gen%20Z,changing%20long%2Dheld%20workplace%20norms.

Thebault, R. November 5, 2019. "'Ok, Boomer': 25-Year-Old Lawmaker Shuts Down Heckler During Climate ..." Washington Post. www.washingtonpost.com/climate-environment/2019/11/05/ok-boomer-year-old-lawmaker-shuts-down-heckler-during-climate-change-speech/.

Thier, J. June 22, 2022. "Gen Z Actually Doesn't Want to Work From Home." Fortune. https://fortune.com/2022/06/22/gen-z-dismisses-remote-work-sick-of-zoom/.

Toffler, A. 1970. *Future Shock*. New York, NY: Bantam Books.

Tolan, J. February 18, 2016. "6 Millennial Recruiting Techniques You Need to Know About." Human Resources Blog. https://hr.sparkhire.com/talent-acquisition-2/6-millennial-recruiting-techniques-you-need-to-know-about/.

Tong, G.C. August 31, 2022. "Is 'quiet Quitting' A Good Idea? Here's What Workplace Experts Say." CNBC. www.cnbc.com/2022/08/30/is-quiet-quitting-a-good-idea-heres-what-workplace-experts-say.html.

Torres, R. September 21, 2023. "Gen Z, Millennials Want More Tech in the Workplace." CIO Dive. www.ciodive.com/news/gen-z-millennial-technology-needs-workplace/694274/.

Turpin, M. August 21, 2023. "Most Execs Are Now Gen X. What Does That Mean?" The HT Group. www.thehtgroup.com/most-execs-are-now-gen-x-what-does-that-mean/.

Univserity of East Anglia. March 10, 2023. "Online 'Personal Brands' Are Key to Job Success for Gen Z, Says Study." Phys.org. https://phys.org/news/2023-03-online-personal-brands-key-job.html.

Urwin, M. August 24, 2022. "Ageism in the Workplace: Statistics to Know." Built In. https://builtin.com/diversity-inclusion/ageism-in-the-workplace.

Veras, E. March 24, 2023. "Prevent Quiet Quitting With These 5 Tips." business.com. www.business.com/hr/prevent-quiet-quitting/.

Walker, C. June 2, 2023. "In Months Leading to Pride, More Than 530 Anti-LGBTQ Bills Have Been Proposed Across the Country in 2023." Truthout. https://truthout.org/articles/more-than-530-anti-lgbtq-bills-have-been-proposed-across-the-country-in-2023/.

White, M.E. and D.L. Carter. 2021. *Leading Schools in Disruptive Times: How to Survive Hyper-Change*. Thousand Oaks, CA: SAGE PUBLICATIONS INC.

White, M. and S. Scarpitti. July 31, 2023. Multigen Interview With a Millennial Business Leader. Personal.

White, M, and S. Scarpitti. October 11, 2023. "Caitlin Ziegert McCombs Multi-Gen Leadership Interview." Personal.

White, M. August 4, 2023. "Multi-gen Leadership Interview with Francesco C. Leboffe. Personal."

White, M. June 23, 2022. "Multi-Gen Leadership Interview With a Boomer Business Leader." Personal.

White, M. June 7, 2023. "Interview With a Gen Z Teacher." Personal.

White, M. June 7, 2023. "Multi-Gen Leadership With a Gen X Principal in Texas." Personal.

White, M. March 22, 2023." Multi-Gen Leadership Interview With a Gen X Principal. Personal.

Wigert, B. and J. White. April 6, 2023. "The Advantages and Challenges of Hybrid Work." Gallup.com. www.gallup.com/workplace/398135/advantages-challenges-hybrid-work.aspx.

Will, M. July 19, 2023. "Here's What Teachers Say They Need Most to Manage Stress, Mental Health." Education Week. www.edweek.org/teaching-learning/heres-what-teachers-say-they-need-most-to-manage-stress-mental-health/2023/07.

Williams, S. February 25, 2020. "Evolution of Diversity in the Workplace." LinkedIn. www.linkedin.com/pulse/evolution-diversity-workplace-stacey-williams/.

Williams, T. June 13, 2023. "Gen Z Is Incredibly Ambitious. They're Just Not Interested in Climbing Your Corporate Ladder." Yahoo! Finance. https://finance.yahoo.com/news/gen-z-incredibly-ambitious-just-212027559.html.

Wilmes, M. March 9, 2023. "From Boomers to Gen Z: Understanding Generational Communication Styles." AnswerNet. https://answernet.com/blog-generations-styles-communication/.

Wolfe, P.E. September 4, 2018. "5 Tips for Building a Workplace That Includes Everyone." Indeed/Lead. www.indeed.com/lead/emotional-intelligence-in-the-workplace.

Young, H. February 15, 2023. "How to Restyle the Office Dress Code for Generation Z." Startups.co.uk. https://startups.co.uk/people/gen-z-office-dress-code/#:~:text=Even%20CEOs%20were%20dialling%20into,style%20is%20all%20they%20know.

Zelazko, A. January 4, 2024. "Millennial." Encyclopædia Britannica. www.britannica.com/topic/millennial.

Zinkula, J. September 14, 2022. "Gen Z and Millennials Aren't the Only Ones Quitting Their Jobs. Gen X Is Quietly Helping Drive the Great Resignation." Business Insider. www.businessinsider.com/gen-x-joining-great-resignation-millennials-gen-z-quitting-jobs-2022-9.

About the Authors

Mark White is an award-winning educator, leader, and author. He is the co-author of *What's in Your Space: Five Steps for Successful School Redesign* (Corwin Press 2016) and *Leading Schools in Disruptive Times: How to Survive Hyper-Change* (Corwin Press 2018), and he is the author of *5-Gen Leadership: Leading 5 Generations in Schools in the 2020's* (Corwin Press 2021). As a consultant, he has coached thousands of professionals across America. Mark is a frequent speaker at national conferences, and he is an adjunct instructor at two universities where his books are taught for graduate credit. Mark may be reached at suptmarkwhite@gmail.com.

Sami Scarpitti is a multi-generational workplace consultant and author. She has spent her career in sales, marketing, and corporate training. She has created and delivered world-class adult education for global companies and many other diverse organizations that create real change within their company culture and independent employee successes. She has consulted with numerous companies on their sales and marketing strategies and led keynotes, interactive workshops, and other employee development initiatives on topics covered in this book along with business strategy and succession planning. Sami may be reached at Sami.Scarpitti@xpgrowth.com.

Index

OTHER TITLES IN THE COLLABORATIVE INTELLIGENCE COLLECTION

Jim Spohrer and Haluk Demirkan, *Editors*

- *Lead With AI* by Amir Elkabir
- *HR Tech Strategy* by Marlene de Koning
- *Let's Meet Blockchain* by Sylvain Metz
- *The Edge Data Center* by Hugh Taylor
- *Journey to the Metaverse* by Antonio Flores-Galea
- *Doing Digital* by Ved Sen
- *Breakthrough* by Martin Fleming
- *How Organizations Can Make the Most of Online Learning* by David Guralnick
- *Teaching Higher Education to Lead* by Sam Choon-Yin
- *Business and Emerging Technologies* by George Baffour
- *How to Talk to Data Scientists* by Jeremy Elser
- *Leadership in The Digital Age* by Niklas Hageback
- *Cultural Science* by William Sims Bainbridge
- *The Future of Work* by Yassi Moghaddam, Heather Yurko, Haluk Demirkan, Nathan Tymann and Ammar Rayes
- *Advancing Talent Development* by Philip Gardner and Heather N. Maietta
- *Virtual Local Manufacturing Communities* by William Sims Bainbridge
- *T-Shaped Professionals* by Yassi Moghaddam, Haluk Demirkan and James Spohrer

Concise and Applied Business Books

The Collection listed above is one of 30 business subject collections that Business Expert Press has grown to make BEP a premiere publisher of print and digital books. Our concise and applied books are for...

- Professionals and Practitioners
- Faculty who adopt our books for courses
- Librarians who know that BEP's Digital Libraries are a unique way to offer students ebooks to download, not restricted with any digital rights management
- Executive Training Course Leaders
- Business Seminar Organizers

Business Expert Press books are for anyone who needs to dig deeper on business ideas, goals, and solutions to everyday problems. Whether one print book, one ebook, or buying a digital library of 110 ebooks, we remain the affordable and smart way to be business smart. For more information, please visit www.businessexpertpress.com, or contact sales@businessexpertpress.com.